MW01195522

A Critical Introduction to Formal Epistemology

BLOOMSBURY CRITICAL INTRODUCTIONS TO CONTEMPORARY EPISTEMOLOGY

Series Editor:

Stephen Hetherington, Professor of Philosophy, The University of New South Wales, Australia

Editorial Board:

Claudio de Almeida, Pontifical Catholic University of Rio Grande do Sul, Brazil; Richard Fumerton, The University of Iowa, USA; John Greco, Saint Louis University, USA; Jonathan Kvanvig, Baylor University, USA; Ram Neta, University of North Carolina, USA; Duncan Pritchard, The University of Edinburgh, UK

Bloomsbury Critical Introductions to Contemporary Epistemology introduces and advances the central topics within one of the most dynamic areas of contemporary philosophy.

Each critical introduction provides a comprehensive survey to an important epistemic subject, covering the historical, methodological, and practical contexts and exploring the major approaches, theories, and debates. By clearly illustrating the changes to the ways human knowledge is being studied, each volume places an emphasis on the historical background and makes important connections between contemporary issues and the wider history of modern philosophy.

Designed for use on contemporary epistemology courses, the introductions are defined by a clarity of argument and equipped with easy-to-follow chapter summaries, annotated guides to reading, and glossaries to facilitate and encourage further study. This series is ideal for upper-level undergraduates and postgraduates wishing to stay informed of the thinkers, issues, and arguments shaping twenty-first century epistemology.

Titles in this series include:

A Critical Introduction to the Epistemology of Memory, Thomas D. Senor
A Critical Introduction to the Epistemology of Perception, Ali Hasan
A Critical Introduction to Knowledge-How, J. Adam Carter and Ted Poston
A Critical Introduction to Scientific Realism, Paul Dicken
A Critical Introduction to Skepticism, Allan Hazlett
A Critical Introduction to Testimony, Axel Gelfert

A Critical Introduction to Formal Epistemology

DARREN BRADLEY

Bloomsbury Academic
An imprint of Bloomsbury Publishing Plc

B L O O M S B U R Y
LONDON • NEW DELHI • NEW YORK • SYDNEY

Bloomsbury Academic

An imprint of Bloomsbury Publishing Plc

50 Bedford Square	1385 Broadway
London	New York
WC1B 3DP	NY 10018
UK	USA

www.bloomsbury.com

BLOOMSBURY and the Diana logo are trademarks of Bloomsbury Publishing Plc

First published 2015

British Library Cataloguing-in-Publication Data
A catalogue record for this book is available from the British Library.

ISBN: PB: 978-1-78093-714-4
HB: 978-1-78093-832-5
ePDF: 978-1-78093-764-9
ePub: 978-1-78093-752-6

Library of Congress Cataloging-in-Publication Data
Bradley, Darren.
A critical introduction to formal epistemology / Darren Bradley. – 1 [edition].
pages cm. – (Bloomsbury critical introductions to contemporary epistemology)
Includes bibliographical references and index.
ISBN 978-1-78093-832-5 (hb) – ISBN 978-1-78093-714-4 (pb) –
ISBN 978-1-78093-752-6 (epub) – ISBN 978-1-78093-764-9 (epdf)
1. Knowledge, Theory of. I. Title.
BD161.B725 2015
121–dc23
2014045772

Typeset by Newgen Knowledge Works (P) Ltd., Chennai, India
Printed and bound in Great Britain

Contents

Series editor's preface

It would be an exaggeration to say that philosophy is nothing without epistemology. But this much is true: philosophy *has* long been greatly enriched and empowered by epistemology. At times, epistemology has been the lungs of philosophy. It has never been far from philosophy's elusive heart. Epistemology discusses such apparent phenomena as knowledge, evidence, reason, perception, memory, probability, testimony, fallibility, and more. It discusses methods of inquiry, too—including methods that might underlie all philosophical thoughts. Self-awareness, inference, intuition, hypothesizing, doubting, and so on: methods as fundamental as these fall within the epistemological gaze.

This is where Bloomsbury's series, *Critical Introductions to Contemporary Epistemology*, enters the philosophical ferment. The series consists of accessible introductions to aspects of how epistemology proceeds—its past, its present, perhaps its future.

Each book in this series brings to the fore some key epistemological concepts and methods, along with a sense of their history. Each book will guide readers to and through a central piece of the expanding puzzle that is epistemology. Each book will engage critically both with older and with newer epistemological ideas.

This series as a whole is unique—a compact reference library devoted to this central part of philosophy. Advanced philosophy students, graduate students, professional philosophers, and others wishing to partake of epistemology's opportunities, challenges, and skirmishes will welcome this series.

Stephen Hetherington
The University of New South Wales, Australia
Editor-in-Chief, *Bloomsbury Critical Introductions*
to Contemporary Epistemology

Acknowledgments

I am very grateful to Mike Titelbaum and Alan Hájek for detailed comments on this entire book, which led to numerous improvements. For comments on parts of this book, I am grateful to David Christensen, Roger Clarke, Dylan Dodd, Adam Elga, Peter Godfrey-Smith, Aidan Lyon, Jim Joyce, Chris Meacham, and Michael Strevens. Lots of people have helped me understand this material over the years, and with apologies to the people I have inevitably forgotten, I'd like to thank Jens Christian Bjerring, David Chalmers, Kenny Easwaran, Branden Fitelson, Hilary Greaves, Daniel Nolan, Johnathan Weisberg, Susan Vineberg, and several classes at the City College of New York. Finally, I'd like to thank Clare O'Reilly and Diana Sofronieva for proofreading this book.

Introduction

What is formal epistemology?

First, what is epistemology? The term "epistemology" is derived from the Ancient Greek for an account of knowledge (*episteme* means knowledge, *logos* means account). "Epistemology" now refers to the branch of philosophy which asks a range of questions related to the study of knowledge, such as: which conditions are necessary for knowledge? Which are sufficient? What is the relation between knowledge and truth?

In practice, the field of epistemology is just as concerned with the study of justification, where similar questions are asked: Which conditions are necessary for justification? Which are sufficient? What is the relation between justification and knowledge?

So, what is formal epistemology? It is the branch of philosophy which applies mathematical (formal) methods to epistemological questions. Most notably, it applies logic and probability to epistemological questions. So defined, formal epistemology covers a wide range of activities.

This book does not aim to cover all of them. Instead, it focuses on one of the core projects of formal epistemology – the application of probabilities to beliefs. That is, rather than just saying that someone believes something, say that they believe it with a particular *probability*. But why should we say that?

Why do we need probability?

Start with a simple view according to which people either believe something or they don't. So for each person, we could write down a list of all the things they believe, thus fully describing their belief state. What's wrong with that?

What's wrong is that we are more *confident*, more *certain*, of some beliefs than others. There are several ways to bring out how important this is.

First, there is a feeling attached to being certain, and a different one attached to being uncertain. For example, consider your belief that there is water on Earth. That's a slam-dunk. You're certain. Compare the belief that there is water at the core of Mars. You probably aren't sure. When you think about that, it feels different. The feeling of uncertainty is a lot less pleasant than the feeling of certainty. That makes it all the more important to think about uncertainty.

Secondly, your beliefs should be based on the evidence you have, and you have more evidence for some things than others. You think you see a friend in the distance. But you are far away, and can't be sure. As you walk toward them, your evidence improves, and you should come to believe that it's them for sure. This is a gradual process, and your certainty should increase as your evidence improves. We need *partial beliefs* to describe your changing situation.

Thirdly, the strength of your beliefs affects your actions. Suppose you're off to an important meeting and you see a dark cloud on the horizon. You don't believe it's going to rain, but you can't be sure that it won't and you don't want to arrive dripping wet. So you take an umbrella. Why did you take the umbrella given that you didn't believe it was gong to rain? Because you thought it might. You had a *partial belief* that it would rain, and this was enough to cause you to take the umbrella.

All these points are missed by the simple view according to which you either believe something or you don't. The examples suggest that beliefs come in degrees, and can be ordered by the strength with which they are held.

This helps motivate the use of probabilities to represent, or to *model*, beliefs. This is often called the *Bayesian* approach. But the considerations so far only show that beliefs should be *ordered*. We need to do a bit more to show that these orderings should be *probabilities*. Some further considerations will be explained in Chapter 1, where the probabilistic approach is laid out in more detail, and the main arguments will take center stage in Chapter 3. But most of the rest of this book can be considered an indirect argument; the probabilistic approach is applied to various epistemological problems, with hopefully enlightening results.

This brings us to the content of this book, and how to use it.

How to use this book

Let me start with a summary of each chapter, then say something about which ones might be skipped.

Chapter 1 explains and motivates the use of the basic concepts we will be covering, such as probability, confirmation, and conditional belief.

Chapter 2 clarifies the probabilistic framework by discussing how it interacts with the simple all-or-nothing concept of belief.

Chapter 3 discusses the main arguments for modeling beliefs with probabilities.

Chapter 4 shows how probabilists can tell a plausible story about learning.

Chapter 5 expands the discussion to a central problem of philosophy—whether there are any objective facts about what you should believe given your evidence—and introduces inductive probabilities and the problem of induction.

Chapter 6 focuses on the problem of induction.

Chapter 7 explains Goodman's new riddle of induction.

Chapter 8 explains the Paradox of the Ravens.

Chapter 9 discusses the relation between belief and chance.

Chapter 10 asks how your beliefs should relate to future beliefs and the beliefs of others.

Chapter 11 looks more closely at the concept of confirmation introduced in Chapter 1.

Chapter 12 applies our probabilistic machinery to the classic problem of the epistemic regress.

Chapter 13 applies our probabilistic machinery to the classic problem of skepticism about knowledge.

I have drawn connections between the chapters whenever I could—one of my aims in writing this book was to make explicit how the issues are related. But I've also done my best to allow each chapter to be read alone. Occasionally, comments that refer back to earlier chapters won't make sense on their own, but you should be able to keep going and pick up the thread. The only chapter I would recommend for all students is Chapter 1. Students who are interested in getting a primer in contemporary formal epistemology should read the first four chapters. Chapters 5–8 form a natural progression, all discussing the question of what the constraints on belief might be, and all are ultimately motivated by the problem of induction. Chapters 9 and 10 are also concerned with constraints on belief, and focus on the more contemporary issues of the relation of our current beliefs to those of peers, to our future beliefs, and to chance. Chapter 11 is a detailed look at the theory of confirmation given in Chapter 1. As such, it doesn't fit in any particular place chronologically. It was originally part of a long first chapter, but I thought it best to put the theory of confirmation to work before considering objections. It also has some material that depends on earlier chapters. Chapters 12 and 13 are attempts to apply the probabilistic approach to the classic problems of epistemology—skepticism about justification and knowledge. Those who are most interested in how probabilism is relevant to these classic problems could read just Chapters 1, 4, 12, and 13.

Study questions are written with undergraduates in mind. Advanced questions are written with graduate students in mind; I have used the advanced questions to point to controversial parts in the discussions.

The four appendices contain material that goes a little further than the main text, and is not needed for continuity. But all are closely connected to the main text, and are recommended for students who want to get a good grip on the material.

1

Belief and probability

1.1 Degrees of belief

Having a belief is not like being pregnant. Being pregnant is all-or-nothing. You're either pregnant or you're not. But having a belief is not all-or-nothing. There are some things you fully believe; some you believe fairly strongly; some you believe only a little; and some you don't believe at all. In slogan form: beliefs come in degrees. At one extreme are the things you fully believe—that the Earth is round, the sun hot, that doves fly and pigs don't. At the other extreme are things you fully disbelieve—that black is white, eggs are square, donkeys talk and people don't. But most beliefs fall in between these two extremes. Do you believe there is intelligent life elsewhere in the universe? It's hard to say—there simply isn't much evidence either way. So the best attitude is to neither fully believe nor fully not believe, but to take an intermediate position. Or let's take a more mundane example. Do you believe that next time you flip a fair coin it will land Heads? Surely not. And you don't disbelieve that it will land Heads either. Instead, your degree of belief is intermediate. Rather than a light switch which is either on or off, beliefs are more like a dimmer, which can be fully on or off, and can also take intermediate values in between.

To talk about such intermediate beliefs, it is useful to assign numbers to them. We could do this in various ways, but a useful convention is that the more certain the belief, the larger the number assigned to it. These numbers represent an agent's *degrees of belief*. We'll also call them *credences*.

But how high and low should those numbers be? One option is to have no limits at all, with numbers going from infinity at the top to negative infinity at the bottom. But that doesn't seem right. There is surely a limit to how certain you can be. In fact we have a word for it—certainty. Once you reach certainty, the maximal degree of belief has been reached. Similarly, there is a minimal value, when you are certain that something is *not* the case. Then you have no belief at all that it *is* the case. It is arbitrary what numbers we assign to these maximal and minimal degrees of belief, but the obvious convention is to assign 1 as the maximum and 0 as the minimum. And now it looks almost irresistible to use *probabilities* to represent these degrees of belief.

So, what are probabilities? For now, think of a probability as a number between 0 and 1. We'll look more carefully at probabilities and why we should use them to model beliefs in Chapter 3. In this chapter, I'll fill out the picture and try to give a sense of how natural and useful it is to assign probabilities to beliefs.

Let's imagine an agent, call him Stickman, at a time, say noon, and a list of every proposition he has ever considered. If Stickman, believes some proposition H with complete certainty, then it is assigned a value of 1.[1] We'll write this as: $P_{Stickman, noon}(H) = 1$. "P" stands for "credence." And if Stickman *dis*believes some other proposition, J, with complete certainty at noon, it is assigned a value of 0. We'll write this as $P_{Stickman, noon}(J) = 0$. Intermediate beliefs will have intermediate values. (Later we'll suppress reference to the time, but remember it's always there.) We can put each proposition in a column, with the most certain at the top and the least certain at the bottom. Here is a picture, with five propositions and their corresponding credences for Stickman at a time:

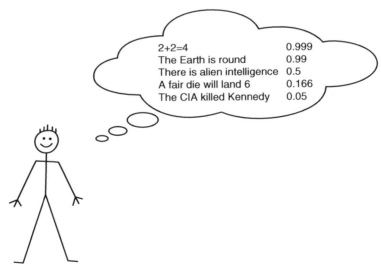

2+2=4	0.999
The Earth is round	0.99
There is alien intelligence	0.5
A fair die will land 6	0.166
The CIA killed Kennedy	0.05

Stickman and some of his beliefs.

We can represent the beliefs with a Venn diagram. The big rectangle in the following diagram contains every proposition Stickman thinks possible, and it is divided into areas that represent how *probable* each proposition is. In this diagram, two propositions, E and H are shown. As E is larger than H, Stickman thinks E is more probable than H. The region in which E and H overlap represents the possibility where both E and H are true. (If E and H don't overlap, then the agent believes they can't both be true; if they overlap completely, then the agent believes they say the same thing.)

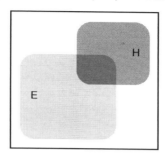

Venn diagram for H and E.

Let's make explicit the link between probability and possibility. A proposition H is impossible for Stickman when his degree of belief in H is 0. A proposition H is possible for Stickman when his degree of belief in H is greater than 0. Notice that this is perhaps an unfamiliar concept of possibility, as it is relative to an agent at a time, just like degrees of belief are. It is sometimes called *epistemic possibility*. Formally:

H is impossible for Stickman at noon if and only if $P_{Stickman, noon}(H) = 0$

H is possible for Stickman at noon if and only if $P_{Stickman, noon}(H) > 0$

And of course this doesn't only hold for Stickman; we can generalize this to any arbitrary agent, S, and time, t:

H is impossible for S at t if and only if $P_{S, t}(H) = 0$

H is possible for S at t if and only if $P_{S, t}(H) > 0$

So far we have considered beliefs about what the world is actually like. But we don't only have beliefs about what the world is actually like, we also have beliefs about what the world *would* be like given that particular things happen. We'll consider such *conditional* beliefs in the next section (1.2). Then we use conditional beliefs to introduce the concept of confirmation (1.3). Finally we consider how we might find out what other people's beliefs are (1.4) and introduce the concept of betting behavior.

1.2 Conditional probability and conditional belief

My degree of belief that there is a talking donkey is very low. But suppose the CIA have been secretly working on a program to develop intelligent donkeys with humanlike vocal chords. Given this scenario, my degree of belief that there are talking donkeys would go up. This is a *conditional* degree of belief, and contrasts with *unconditional* degrees of belief, which were discussed earlier in this chapter.

We now get to a virtue of modeling beliefs with probabilities—we can understand conditional beliefs using *conditional probabilities*. *Conditional probability* is a technical concept defined as follows:

The conditional probability of H given E is[2]

$$\frac{P(H\,\&\,E)}{P(E)}$$

We'll abbreviate this ratio as P(H|E). Intuitively, this says that to find the conditional probability of H given E, zoom in on the E possibilities and ask in what proportion of them is H also true, that is, what proportion of the E possibilities are also H possibilities?

The trick now is to use this concept of conditional *probability* to understand conditional *belief*:

S's conditional belief at t in H given E is

$$\frac{P_{s,\,t}(H\,\&\,E)}{P_{s,\,t}(E)}$$

This analysis of conditional belief allows us to derive an agent's conditional beliefs from her unconditional beliefs.

A Venn diagram shows why this is a plausible analysis of conditional belief. The analysis says that to find the credence of H given E, we zoom in on the E possibilities, and ask in what proportion of them H is true. We are comparing the area in which H and E are both true to the area in which E is true. This should seem like the right way to think about conditional belief.

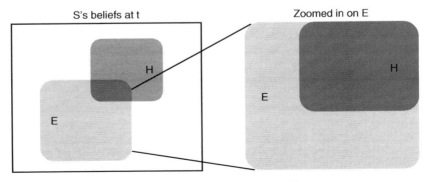

Venn diagrams zooming in on E.

Let's go through a quick example.

E = It will be sunny tomorrow

H = It will be hot tomorrow

$P_{S,t}(E) = 0.4$

$P_{S,t}(H) = 0.2$

$P_{S,t}(E\&H) = 0.1$

So in the overlapping region, it is hot and sunny; in the nonoverlapping part of E, it is sunny but not hot; and in the nonoverlapping part of H, it is hot but not sunny. These numbers allow us to calculate that the degree of belief that it will be hot given that it will be sunny is:

$P_{S,t}(H|E)$
$= P_{S,t}(H\&E)/P_{S,t}(E)$
$= 0.1/0.4$
$= 0.25$

So the degree of belief that it will be hot (H) goes up from 0.2 to 0.25 given that it will be sunny. (This is a good time to go to the exercises at the end of this chapter.)

What if we want to work out the probability of H given E, but we don't know the probability of H&E? Then we can use the following celebrated theorem:

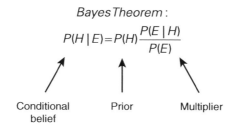

Bayes Theorem :

$$P(H \mid E) = P(H) \frac{P(E \mid H)}{P(E)}$$

Conditional belief   Prior   Multiplier

(Exercise: Derive Bayes Theorem from two applications of the definition of conditional probability.) The *prior* is a technical term for the unconditional probability of H, that is, P(H). The *multiplier* is a technical term for the ratio of P(E|H) to P(E). To calculate P(H|E) using P(H), we just multiply P(H) by the *multiplier*. If this ratio is 1, P(H|E) = P(H). If less than 1, P(H|E) < P(H). If more than 1, P(H|E) > P(H). Next we'll see how these relations between conditional and unconditional degrees of belief can be used to give an analysis of the concept of *confirmation*.

1.3 Confirmation

Confirmation is a familiar concept. The detective examining a scene is trying to *confirm* her suspicion that the butler did it. And the scientist running an experiment is trying to *confirm* a hypothesis. So what is it to confirm something? We will be using the following theory that defines confirmation in terms of degrees of belief:

Degree-of-belief-raising theory of confirmation[3]

> "E *confirms* H for S at t" means "$P_{S,t}(H|E) > P_{S,t}(H)$"
>
> "E *disconfirms* H for S at t" means "$P_{S,t}(H|E) < P_{S,t}(H)$"
>
> "E is *independent* of H for S at t" means "$P_{S,t}(H|E) = P_{S,t}(H)$"

Our main focus will be the top line, which says that "E confirms H for S at t" means "for S at t, the conditional credence of H given E is higher than the unconditional credence of H." Intuitively, this says that for E to confirm H is for E to make H more likely than H was before. By Bayes Theorem, we can put it the other way round:

> "E *confirms* H for S at t" means "$P_{S,t}(E|H) > P_{S,t}(E)$"

Intuitively, this says that for E to confirm H is for H to make E more likely than E was before. This reversal demonstrates that confirmation is symmetrical; E confirms H if and only if H confirms E.

Let's work through the earlier example . Recall the initial description told us that

$$P_{S,t}(H) = 0.2$$

and we worked out that

$$P_{S,t}(H|E) = 0.25$$

so

$$P_{S,t}(H|E) = 0.25 > P_{S,t}(H) = 0.2$$

Therefore according to the probability raising theory of confirmation, E *confirms* H for S at t.

There's a lot more to say about confirmation, and we'll look at this theory more closely in Chapter 11. For now I just want to get the degree of belief raising theory on the table and show that it's plausible, as we will be working with this theory of confirmation throughout this book. To help think about it, let's note some features of the theory, in increasing order of surprisingness.

First, E can confirm H without making H very likely at all; it just needs to make H more likely than it would otherwise be. This is true of our example. The degree of belief that it will be hot ends up at only 0.25, but is still *confirmed* according to our theory. Here our technical concept of confirmation comes apart from the ordinary language concept of confirmation.

Second, the *increase* in credence of H can be tiny. If $P_{s,t}(H|E) = 0.30001$ and $P_{s,t}(H) = 0.3$, E still confirms H. Indeed, in our example, the degree of belief that it will be hot went up by only 0.05 from 0.2 to 0.25.

Third, a piece of evidence can confirm two incompatible hypotheses. The proposition that a die lands showing an even number (E) confirms that it lands showing a 2, and also confirms that it lands showing a 4. And this is true even though it cannot be showing *both* 2 and 4.

Fourth, confirmation requires *correlation*, not causation. Two events are correlated when they tend to go together. For example, dark clouds are correlated with rain, and rain is correlated with dark clouds. It follows that dark clouds confirm rain and rain confirms dark clouds. But rain does not *cause* dark clouds.

Fifth, E can confirm H without confirming things that H entails. Here's an example:

E = Bob's pet is hairless

H = PHD = Bob's pet is a Peruvian Hairless Dog

Dog = Bob's pet is a dog

E confirms PHD, and PHD entails Dog, but E does not confirm Dog. In fact E disconfirms Dog, as you'd expect most hairless pets not to be dogs.

The diagram shows an example where the prior credences are 0.5 in Bob having a hairless pet, of which 0.1 is in PHD and 0.4 in everything else. Assume that the only hairless dogs are Peruvian Hairless Dogs. Given E, we zoom in on the top half, and credence in Dog falls dramatically, as the only dogs left are Peruvian Hairless Dogs. But credence in Peruvian Hairless Dogs goes up. So E confirms that it's a Peruvian Hairless Dog, but disconfirms that it's a Dog. (The diagram uses the standard negation symbol, where "–D" means "Bob's pet is not a Dog.")

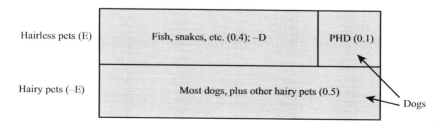

1.4 Epistemology of beliefs

Let's back up for a moment: What is a belief? Think of a belief as a concrete physical structure within the brain. The brain is an organ of the body like any other. Just as the role of the heart is to pump blood, one of the roles of the brain is to store beliefs. We can think of beliefs as our onboard maps of the world. Instead of representing the world with paper and ink, as most maps do, our onboard maps represent the world with connections between neurons.

If we were certain of everything, we would only need a single map that told us what every feature of the world was like. But, as we've noted, there are lots of things we aren't certain about. So a better model is to think of our brain as storing lots of maps, each of which is assigned a number—a probability—representing how certain we are of its accuracy.

A problem now emerges: if beliefs are stored inside people's heads, how can we know what other people believe? We cannot see inside people's heads, yet we ascribe beliefs to them. If we're only concerned with our own beliefs, we can avoid this worry—it is easy to figure out what we believe, we just have to introspect. But we're not just interested in our own beliefs—we're interested in beliefs in general, as they occur in other people, at other times, and perhaps even in other species (which is why we'll talk about agents rather than people). So, how can we know what others believe?

Let's first ask: how do we ever know about the existence of things that we cannot directly observe, such as microscopic objects? The answer is that we know about things we cannot observe due to *their effects on things we can observe*. A famous example is the observation that pollen grains placed in water move around in a seemingly random way (observed by Robert Brown in 1827 and called Brownian motion in his honor). This behavior was explained by the hypothesis that the grains were being pushed around by unseen atoms, and this helped convince scientists of the existence of atoms.

We know about others' beliefs in a similar way. Beliefs don't just represent the world, they also *cause* people to act in certain ways. Beliefs make people move around just as atoms make grains of pollen move around. Except when people move around, we describe this behavior as people doing things, making decisions, acting, speaking, and so on. (Note: Speaking is a form of behavior.)

So we know what people believe from the way they behave. If someone says it's raining, or takes an umbrella, we can conclude that they believe it's raining. Particularly useful for figuring out an agent's degree of belief is *betting behavior*.

Suppose a bookie offers a bet that pays $1 if aliens exist and nothing otherwise. The amount an agent would pay for this bet reflects their degree of belief. Let's start with the easiest cases.

Suppose Alice is completely certain that aliens exist. How much would she be prepared to pay for the bet? She considers the bet as good as a $1 bill, so she should be willing to pay anything up to $1 for the bet.

Suppose Bob is completely certain that aliens don't exist. How much would he be prepared to pay for the bet? He considers the bet to be worth nothing, so he should be willing to pay $0, and no more.

Now consider an intermediate case. Suppose Charlie believes to degree 0.8 that aliens exist. How much would he be prepared to pay for the bet? He thinks he will get the dollar with credence of 0.8, so he should be willing to pay up to 80 cents for the bet.

The pattern should be clear. The degree of belief matches the amount the agent should be willing to pay for a bet that pays $1 if the belief is true and $0 if false. Of course, the amount of $1 is arbitrary. Generally, if the degree of belief in H is p, and the bet pays V if H and 0 otherwise, then the agent should be willing to pay up to pV for the bet. We'll come back to betting in Chapters 3 and 4.

Summary

The main point of this chapter is that beliefs can be represented using probabilities. Furthermore, we used probabilities to connect unconditional with conditional beliefs. We then used probabilities to given an analysis of confirmation: the degree-of-belief-raising theory of confirmation. Finally, we saw how we could discover which beliefs an agent has by observing their behavior.

This completes the basic framework we will be using. It is often called a Bayesian framework. The term "Bayesian" has no precise meaning though, as there are numerous features that Bayesians may or may not endorse, some of which we will explore in later chapters. The core of the view however is that beliefs can be modeled with probabilities, and is also usually taken to imply a commitment to conditionalization (Chapter 4). We will be using and challenging the Bayesian framework in later chapters. But the next chapter argues that this framework has left out something important: acceptance.

Appendix: Bayes Theorem and the Base Rate Fallacy

The importance of Bayes Theorem is demonstrated by the Base Rate Fallacy. Imagine you have just been tested for some rare disease. Suppose that if you have the disease, the test correctly says you do 99 percent of the time. And if you don't have the disease, the test correctly says you don't 99 percent of the time:

Disease = You have the disease

Positive = You have a positive test result

P(Positive | −Disease) = 0.01

P(Positive | Disease) = 0.99

Now let's add the base rate—the proportion of the population who have the disease. Suppose it's only 0.0001

P(Disease) = 0.0001

So how likely are you to have the disease given a positive test result, that is, P(Disease|Positive)? The natural thought is 99 percent—but this is incorrect. We can calculate the value using Bayes Theorem:

$$P(\text{Disease}|\text{Positive}) = \frac{P(\text{Disease})P(\text{Positive}|\text{Disease})}{P(\text{Positive})}$$

The only part of the right hand side we haven't been told is P(Positive). But we have been told enough to work it out using the law of total probability:

Law of total probability

P(A) = P(A|B1)P(B1) + P(A|B2)P(B2) + ... + P(A|Bk)P(Bk), where B1, B2, ..., Bk are exclusive and exhaustive.

Applied here, the law of total probability says that

$$P(\text{Positive}) = P(\text{Positive} \mid \text{Disease})P(\text{Disease})$$
$$+ \ P(\text{Positive} \mid -\text{Disease})P(-\text{Disease})$$
$$= 0.99 \times 0.0001 + 0.01 \times 0.9999$$
$$\approx 0.01$$

Plugging in all the numbers, we get:

$$P(\text{Disease}|\text{Positive}) = \frac{P(\text{Disease})P(\text{Positive}|\text{Disease})}{P(\text{Positive})}$$
$$P(\text{Disease}|\text{Positive}) = \frac{0.0001 \times 0.99}{0.01}$$
$$\approx 0.01$$

So even after the positive test, the probability you have the disease is only about 0.01, that is, 1 percent. The test means you are about 100 times more likely to have the disease than before, so that pushes the probability from 0.0001 to 0.01.

Most people find this result very surprising. It seems odd that having the disease is still so improbable. Why do things strike us this way? One answer is that we focus on *confirmation*. That is, we compare P(Disease) with P(Disease|Positive), and find that the hypothesis that you have the disease is strongly *confirmed*. Fixating on this fact, we ignore the prior, and come to the wrong conclusion that we probably have the disease.

Something similar happens in one of the most famous examples of fallacious reasoning. Amos Tversky and Daniel Kahneman (1983) gave their subjects the following story:

> Linda is 31 years old, single, outspoken, and very bright. She majored in philosophy. As a student, she was deeply concerned with issues of discrimination and social justice, and also participated in antinuclear demonstrations.
>
> Which is more probable?
>
> H1: Linda is a bank teller.
>
> H2: Linda is a bank teller and is active in the feminist movement.

Ninety percent of subjects said that H2 was more probable. But that's impossible; there must be fewer bank tellers named Linda in the feminist movement than there are bank tellers named Linda. Generally, the probability of a conjunction, H1&H2, cannot be higher than either of the conjuncts (H1, H2).

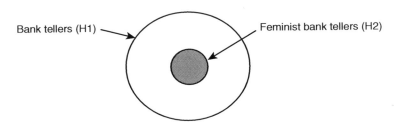

Venn diagram of the Linda story.

So why do so many people answer H2? One answer is that people focus on the probability of the story, S (that Linda is 31 years old, single, outspoken . . .) given each of H1 and H2. They compare P(S|H1) and P(S|H2). As people reasonably judge that P(S|H1) < P(S|H2), they wrongly answer that H2 is more probable. But what they mean is that H2 fits better with the story, or makes the story more likely, or is more strongly *confirmed* by the story.

Exercises[4]

1 P(H) = 0.42 and P(H&E) = 0.25. What is P(E|H)?

2 A maths teacher gave her class two tests. 42 percent of the class passed the first test and 25 percent of the class passed both tests. What percent of those who passed the first test also passed the second test?

3 A jar contains black and white marbles. Two marbles are chosen without replacement. The probability of selecting a black marble and then a white marble is 0.34, and the probability of selecting a black marble on the first draw is 0.47. What is the probability of selecting a white marble on the second draw, given that the first marble drawn was black?

4 At Kennedy Middle School, the probability that a student takes Technology and Spanish is 0.087. The probability that a student takes Technology is 0.68. What is the probability that a student takes Spanish given that the student is taking Technology?

5 P(H) = 0.2, P(E|H) = 0.6 and P(E) = 0.3. What is P(H|E)?

6 A bakery employs three bakers who all make brownies. Aunt Jemima makes 25 percent of the brownies, while Betty Crocker makes 45 percent and Timothy Leary makes 30 percent.

Everyone makes mistakes though: Aunt Jemima burns 2 percent of her brownies, while Betty and Timothy burn 4 and 5 percent of theirs, respectively. The probability that a given cookie gets burned is 3.8 percent.

6a Given that a brownie has been burned, what is the probability that it was baked by Betty Crocker?

6b Given that a brownie has been burned, what is the probability that it was baked by Timothy Leary?

Solutions

1 $P(E|H) = \dfrac{P(H\&E)}{P(H)} = \dfrac{0.25}{0.42} = 0.595$

2 H = Proportion that pass the first test; E = Proportion that pass the second test.

$P(E|H) = \dfrac{P(H\&E)}{P(H)} = \dfrac{0.25}{0.42} = 0.595$

3

$$P(White|Black) = \frac{P(Black\ and\ White)}{P(Black)} = \frac{0.34}{0.47} = 0.72$$

4

$$P(Spanish|Technology) = \frac{P(Technology\ and\ Spanish)}{P(Technology)} = \frac{0.087}{0.68} = 0.13$$

5

$$P(H|E) = \frac{P(H)\,P(E|H)}{P(E)} = \frac{0.2 \times 0.6}{0.3} = 0.4$$

6a

$$P(BC|Burnt) = \frac{P(BC)P(Burnt|BC)}{P(Burnt)} = \frac{0.45 \times 0.04}{0.038} \approx 0.47$$

6b

$$P(TL|Burnt) = \frac{P(TL)P(Burnt|TL)}{P(Burnt)} = \frac{0.3 \times 0.05}{0.038} \approx 0.39$$

Study questions

1 What does "credence" mean?

2 What does it mean to say that beliefs come in degrees? Is it true?

3 What is a conditional degree of belief? How is it calculated?

4 Explain the degree-of-belief-raising theory of confirmation.

5 What is the problem with discovering people's beliefs? How might it be solved?

Advanced questions

6 We have taken the probabilities as primitive and derived conditional probabilities. Is there a reason to do this rather than take conditional probabilities as primitive and derive probabilities? (see Hájek 2003)

7 The degree-of-belief-raising theory of confirmation says that confirmation is relative to an agent. Is it?

Further reading

Skyrms (1975) is a very user-friendly introduction to this material, as is Strevens's (ms) "Notes on Bayesian Confirmation Theory." Earman (1992) is a thorough and widely used introduction. Jeffrey (1983) gives a more advanced introduction with an emphasis on decision theory. Howson and Urbach (1996) give a more advanced introduction with an emphasis on statistics.

2

Belief and acceptance

Chapter 1 began with the claim that beliefs aren't all-or-nothing. But a lot of the time we do treat beliefs as if they were all-or-nothing. Call the concept of all-or-nothing-belief, *acceptance*. We'll use this as a technical concept, and it has two key features.

First, when it comes to acceptance, agents can only stand in one of three relations to a hypothesis H: accept H, accept not H, or withhold acceptance. We can think of acceptance as a coarse-grained version of degree of belief— whereas a degree of belief can take any value from 0 to 1, acceptance can only take three values.

Second, when an agent accepts a hypothesis, all competing hypotheses inconsistent with it are eliminated from consideration. So if an agent accepts the hypothesis that it's raining, any hypotheses that are incompatible with it raining, for example, snowing, hurricane, and so on, are not considered in deliberation.

So that's what acceptance is. In this chapter, we'll consider whether we should use the concept of acceptance. We'll start with two reasons for using the concept of acceptance (2.1) and then connect acceptance to degree of belief (2.2). This leads to the Lottery Paradox (2.3). We'll consider how the paradox might be resolved (2.4), and draw a distinction between philosophical and scientific questions (2.5).

2.1 Acceptance

First reason to use the concept of acceptance: Ordinary language

Our ordinary concept of belief in English is closer to the concept of acceptance than the concept of degree of belief. For example, suppose you are a juror listening to a witness's testimony at a trial. Your neighbor leans over and says "Do you believe him?" The natural thing to say would be either "yes," "no," or "not sure." It would be very odd to say "I believe him to degree 0.8." So when we talk about what people believe, we are normally talking about what people accept.

Second reason to use the concept of acceptance: Cognitive limits

The second reason is based on the fact that when an agent accepts a hypothesis, all competing hypotheses inconsistent with it are eliminated from consideration. And this can be very valuable for agents like us who only have a limited amount of brain power.

Think of a scientist looking through a microscope. Seeing the desired result, the scientist runs through the lab shouting "Eureka." The scientist's belief that the desired result had been achieved depended on a huge number of background assumptions, for example, that each component in the microscope was working correctly. None of these assumptions would be certain, so none would have probability 1. So the scientist who uses only degrees of belief (as opposed to acceptance) would have to do a very complex calculation, using the probabilities of all these assumptions being true, to determine whether she should believe the result of the experiment. And this would take an excessive amount of time.

So it seems she will be better off accepting that her equipment is working correctly. This frees the scientist from having to make excessively detailed and time-consuming calculations. (This is not to say that she shouldn't check her equipment if she has a reason to do so. Acceptance at one time does not entail acceptance at a later time.)

What applies to the scientist applies to people in general. Our time and brain power are limited, so it is often best to accept some things as true in order to simplify our thinking. It would be impossible to deliberate and plan if every belief were constantly being reexamined. Should you study tonight or go drinking? Well, if the Earth were destroyed tomorrow there would be no point studying. But you should probably just accept that the Earth will survive and begin your deliberations from there.

2.2 Belief and acceptance: The Threshold Theory

An obvious question now presents itself: what is the connection between degree of belief and rational acceptance? A natural suggestion is that one rationally accepts hypothesis H if and only if one has a sufficiently high degree of belief in H. Call this the Threshold Theory of Acceptance (also called The Lockean Thesis):

Threshold Theory of Acceptance

Agent A rationally accepts H if and only if A's degree of belief in H is greater than some threshold t.

For example, we might say that t = 0.95; so Agent A should accept H if and only if A's degree of belief in H is greater than 0.95. Notice that this theory connects an agent's degrees of belief with what they *rationally* accept, that is, *should* accept. (I'll use "should" and "rationally" interchangeably, and say more about these concepts at the beginning of the next chapter.) This theory looks very plausible, but it faces a serious challenge: the Lottery Paradox.

2.3 Argument against the Threshold Theory of Acceptance: The Lottery Paradox

Henry Kyburg (1961) introduced the following paradox. We first need to defend a principle called *Acceptance Closure*:[1]

Acceptance Closure

If A rationally accepts H1 and A rationally accepts H2 then A should accept H1&H2.

Acceptance Closure should seem very plausible. For example, if you rationally accept that it is warm and you rationally accept that it is sunny then you should accept that it is warm and sunny. It would be odd to say "I accept that it is warm and I accept that it is sunny, but I don't want to commit myself on whether it's warm and sunny—let's wait till the meteorologist gets back to us." So let's grant *Acceptance Closure*.

Now for the paradox. Suppose there is a lottery with 100 tickets, numbered 1 to 100. Exactly 1 ticket will win and 99 will lose. Knowing all this (we'll assume throughout that you know the setup of all the examples), you believe each ticket will lose to degree 0.99. That is, you believe to degree 0.99 that ticket 1 will lose, the same for ticket 2, and so on for all the other tickets. Let's say that the threshold for acceptance (t) is 0.95. It follows that you should *accept* that ticket 1 will lose (because 0.99 is greater than 0.95). The same applies to all the other tickets. By Acceptance Closure, you should conjoin these beliefs and accept that all the tickets will lose. But you clearly should not accept that all the tickets will lose—you know exactly one ticket will win! Paradox.

Let's examine the problem more carefully. Your degree of belief in each of the following hypotheses is 0.99:

Ticket 1 will lose

Ticket 2 will lose

⋮

Ticket 100 will lose

By the Threshold Theory of Acceptance with t = 0.95, you should accept all of those hypotheses.

By repeated applications of Acceptance Closure, you should accept the conjunction of those hypotheses, which we will call C:

C: Ticket 1 will lose and ticket 2 will lose and . . . and ticket 100 will lose

But surely you shouldn't accept C. C says that every ticket will lose; and that can't be right as you know that one ticket will win. This is bad enough, but things get even worse. Given the description of the lottery, you know exactly one ticket will win, so you should accept the negation of C:

Not C: It is not the case that [ticket 1 will lose and ticket 2 will lose and . . . and ticket 100 will lose]

So we have the conclusion that you should accept C and that you should accept Not C. And things get even worse. We can again apply Acceptance Closure (to your rational acceptance of C and your rational acceptance of Not C) and conclude that you should accept:

C and Not C

So we have reached the conclusion that you should accept a contradiction! And this can't be right.

2.4 Responses to the Lottery Paradox

First response to the Lottery Paradox: Increasing t

One thought for avoiding the Lottery Paradox is to increase the threshold t. If we increase t from 0.95 to 0.999, then you should no longer accept that each ticket will lose.

But this doesn't solve the problem for long. We can imagine a lottery with a million tickets. Now the probability that each ticket will lose, 0.999999, is greater than t, which is 0.999, so you should accept that each ticket will lose. And then we can run the same argument as earlier. And no matter how high t goes, as long as it is less than 1, there will be a large enough lottery that produces the same problem.

Fiddling with the numbers in this way won't help because the root of the problem is the mismatch between probabilistic degrees of belief (credence) and Acceptance Closure. The credence of each of two hypotheses separately is usually greater than the probability of their conjunction, that is, P(H1) > P(H1&H2); also P(H2) > P(H1&H2). (For example, the probability of being dealt an Ace in a game of poker is greater than the probability of being dealt an Ace and then being dealt another.) To generate the Lottery Paradox, we need to find two hypotheses such that each individually has credence just above t, while the conjunction has credence just below t. The Threshold Theory of Acceptance says that you should accept each of the two hypotheses individually, but not the conjunction of both of them. But Acceptance Closure says that if you accept each of the two hypotheses, you should always accept the conjunction. So these two principles tend to conflict. Can we accept both of them?

Second response to the Lottery Paradox: Certainty theory of acceptance

Here's a suggestion—perhaps increasing t is the right idea, we just need to increase t all the way to 1. This is a specific version of the Threshold Theory—it is the version where t = 1. Call this version the Certainty Theory of Acceptance.

Certainty Theory of Acceptance $A \Rightarrow (H) \wedge P(H) = 1$

Agent A rationally accepts H if and only if A's degree of belief in H is 1.

This says that mere high probability is not sufficient to accept anything; you should withhold acceptance until you are certain. There is no longer a tension with Acceptance Closure because if P(H1) = 1 and P(H2) = 1 then P(H1&H2) = 1. There is no danger that the individual beliefs will have a higher probability than the conjunction—they all have the same probability, namely 1.

This theory solves the problems we've seen, but it has problems of its own. Let's consider two arguments against the Certainty Theory of Acceptance.

First argument against the certainty theory of acceptance

According to the Certainty Theory of Acceptance, we have the same degree of belief in everything we accept. But surely we can have differing degrees of belief in hypotheses we accept. For example,

A. Millard Fillmore was the President of the United States.

B. Millard Fillmore either was or was not the President of the United States.

I accept both A and B, but I am more certain of B than of A (because B is a truth of logic, while I only have vague memories of hearing about Millard Fillmore). So it seems we don't have the same degree of belief in everything we accept, contra the Certainty Theory of Acceptance.

Second argument against the certainty theory of acceptance

It seems we might be wrong about hypotheses we accept. For example, although I believe A, it is possible I'm wrong. I could easily imagine that Millard Fillmore was never officially sworn in. Or maybe he was just invented as a hoax and never even existed. The same goes for most of the things we accept. Take your acceptance of the hypothesis that the current US president is . . . whoever you think it is. Isn't it possible that he/she has just resigned in a shock scandal? Of course. So you aren't completely certain who the President is. In fact, it is hard to think of anything you're completely certain of. You know your name? Maybe your parents lied to you. You know you're human? Maybe you're an advanced android. Think you're reading a book? Maybe you're in a computer simulation being deceived into thinking you're reading a book. So your degree of belief in all these hypotheses is less than 1. (Here we made use of the principle that "H is possible" means "$P(H) > 0$," from Chapter 1.)

But then according to the Certainty Theory of Acceptance, you should not accept any of these hypotheses. It follows that there is almost nothing you should accept. If so, the concept of acceptance isn't useful, as it will simply fail to apply to any interesting hypotheses.

2.5 Actual and ideal agents

Some probabilists have concluded that the concept of acceptance is not useful for philosophers, and should be replaced by better concepts like *degree of belief* and the other concepts of Chapter 1. Whether this is correct depends on what exactly it is that we are trying to do. Two tasks can be distinguished:

i Modeling how we humans behave

ii Modeling how ideally rational agents behave

Roughly speaking, (i) is a question in the domain of science (psychology, sociology, economics, anthropology) and (ii) is a question in the domain of philosophy. As such, our focus will be on (ii).

With this clarification made, the concept of acceptance becomes less important for us. We can see that both of the arguments in favor of using the concept of acceptance lose their force. Starting with the argument from cognitive limits—that it is less time consuming to accept hypotheses—this argument will not apply to an ideally rational agent. Such agents have unlimited resources for calculations, so even the most complex calculations can be performed instantaneously.

The argument from ordinary language—that we usually say that we either believe, disbelieve, or neither—can also be answered. Our language has evolved to serve us as limited beings, so we should not take it as a guide to what ideally rational agents do. Indeed, it seems that even we limited beings would be better off sharpening the way we speak and stating the degree to which we believe something, rather than just saying yes or no. In fact we do this to some extent with phrases like "I doubt it," "I *think* so," or most obviously "probably." So we will set aside the concept of acceptance for the rest of this book, and focus on the probabilistic concepts of Chapter 1.

Summary

This chapter discussed how full belief and partial belief are connected. We considered the Threshold Theory, which says that A rationally accepts H if and only if A's degree of belief in H is greater than some threshold t. The main objection is that someone might have a very high degree of belief that her ticket will lose without rationally accepting it. One response requires that the threshold is 1, but this has implausible consequences. Finally, we considered an argument that the concept of full belief is of limited importance to philosophical questions. This type of argument motivates the focus on probabilistic concepts of this book.

So the next question is: are those probabilistic concepts useful? They will be useful if ideally rational agents can be described using those concepts. The next two chapters assess arguments that rational agents can be described using probabilistic concepts.

Study questions

1   What is acceptance? How does it differ from degree of belief?

2   What is the Threshold Theory of Acceptance?

3   Explain acceptance closure.

4   Explain the Lottery Paradox.

5   What do you think is the best answer to the Lottery Paradox?

Advanced questions

6   We defined acceptance partly in terms of the elimination of alternative hypotheses from consideration. What other definitions might we have used?

7   What arguments could be given against acceptance closure?

8   Could the concept of acceptance be useful even if we are modeling ideally rational agents?

Further reading

For a defense of extra conditions on rational acceptance, above and beyond high degree of belief, see Pollock's (1995) *Cognitive Carpentry: A Blueprint for How to Build a Person*. For a denial of acceptance closure, see Richard Foley's (2009) "Beliefs, degrees of belief, and the Lockean thesis." Richard Jeffrey is the leading exponent of replacing acceptance with credences; see his "Dracula Meets Wolfman: Acceptance vs. Partial Belief" (1970). David Christensen defends both acceptance and credence in "Putting Logic in Its Place" (2004).

It is important to remember that acceptance is a technical concept that is often defined in different ways. For an influential discussion emphasizing that scientists can choose what to accept, an idea not discussed in this chapter, see van Fraassen's *The Scientific Image* (1980).

A useful bibliography can be found here: http://natureofrepresentation. wordpress.com/2013/09/27/bibliography-on-belief-and-degrees-of-belief/

3

Rationality constraints I: Probabilism

What rules should an agent's degrees of belief satisfy? In this chapter, we'll consider the suggestion that an agent's degrees of belief should satisfy the rules of probability.

There is a scene in the movie Erik the Viking (1989) in which the island of Hy-Brasil sinks into the sea. However, the King of Hy-Brasil denies that the island can sink and continues denying it as the island and the King himself sink into the water, with his final words turning into a gurgle of bubbles.[1]

There is *something wrong* with the King. But in what sense is something wrong with him? Consider two possibilities. The first is that he is undergoing some sort of mechanical failure, similar to being color blind, or having a blood clot. But this doesn't seem like the right way to describe the case. The second possibility is that the King is in such a mess that it is incorrect to even describe him as having beliefs. But this also doesn't seem like the right way to describe the case. So what is the right way?

Let's describe the King as *irrational*. He is not believing as he *ought* to. He doesn't have the beliefs he *should*. These are different ways of saying the same thing. Notice that we are not making a moral judgment; we're not saying he's a bad person. But we are holding him to a standard—that of a rational agent—and saying that he fails to live up to this standard. To be specific, the King is not correctly fitting his beliefs to the evidence; call this *epistemic irrationality* (I will mostly leave "epistemic" implicit). This is the sense of rationality that we will use in this chapter and beyond.

Call the rules that agents should rationally satisfy, *rationality constraints*. A central theme of epistemology is the question of what these rationality constraints are. We start, in this chapter, with a basic and widely accepted rationality constraint: *probabilism* (3.1). We'll evaluate three arguments for probabilism—the Dutch Book Argument (3.2), the Accuracy Argument (3.3), and the Representation Theorem Argument (3.4).

3.1 Probabilism

Define probabilism as follows:

Probabilism An agent's degrees of belief should be probabilities

What does it mean for degrees of belief to be probabilities? To answer this, we need to introduce the concept of a *tautology*. Think of a tautology as a sentence which is true whatever the world is like. So for example, "grass is green or grass is not green" is a tautology because whatever happens, either grass is green or grass is not green will be true, so the sentence "grass is green or grass is not green" will be true. Putting it in terms of possibilities, a tautology expresses all the possibilities, that is, there are no possibilities that are outside the possibilities expressed by a tautology. So "grass is green or grass is not green" is a tautology because there are no possibilities outside those expressed by "grass is green or grass is not green"—there are no possibilities in which "grass is green or grass is not green" is false.

Now we can say what it is for degrees of belief to be probabilities:

Degrees of belief are probabilities if and only if they satisfy the following three rules, where X & Y represent propositions and B represents the set of beliefs of the agent:

1 *Nonnegativity*: $P(X) \geq 0$ for all X in B.

2 *Normalization*: $P(T) = 1$ for any tautology T in B.

3 *Finite additivity*: $P(X \text{ or } Y) = P(X) + P(Y)$ for all X & Y in B such that X is incompatible with Y.

So probabilism amounts to the thesis that our degrees of belief should satisfy these rules. Let's go through them.

1. *Nonnegativity* says that all beliefs must have credence greater than or equal to 0. This should seem obvious—it's hard to even make sense of a credence less than 0 (although we'll try to make sense of it shortly).

2. *Normalization* says that beliefs in tautologies should have credence of 1. So I should be 100 percent sure that either it's raining or it's not raining. This rule is more controversial than it looks because it says that *all* tautologies should have credence 1, not just all *known* tautologies. These come apart if there are unknown tautologies. Take some complicated mathematical theorem, like Fermat's Last Theorem, which was proved in 1994. Like all mathematical truths, it is a tautology—it is true in all possibilities. So the normalization bit of probabilism says that all agents should have a degree of belief of 1 in Fermat's Last Theorem, even those who haven't heard about the proof! This seems wrong, so some philosophers have objected

that normalization, and therefore probabilism, should be rejected. This is called the *logical omniscience* objection to probabilism, as it is based on the fact that *probabilism* entails that rational agents should be certain of all mathematical and logical truths.

One probabilistic response is to point out that probabilism is only intended to be a constraint on fully rational agents. So it doesn't matter that we flawed humans aren't certain that Fermat's Last Theorem is true. All probabilism requires is that fully rational agents are.

But this seems to require too much of rationality. Is someone who doesn't know all mathematical truths thereby *irrational*? Surely not.

Perhaps the best probabilistic response is to say that we should assume normalization because of its simplifying power. The assumption allows us to use probability theory to model agents. If we didn't assume normalization, we would have to use some more complicated theory that might be more accurate but would be very difficult to use.[2] Let's move on to the third rule.

3. *Finite additivity* is the rule that gives probability theory its power, as it connects degrees of belief to each other and therefore imposes a structure on the beliefs. It says that if the agent believes that X and Y cannot both be true, then her degree of belief in either X or Y being true is equal to the sum of her probability that X is true and her probability that Y is true. So if it can't be sunny and cloudy, and you believe each to degree 0.4, then your degree of belief that it will be either sunny or cloudy is 0.4 + 0.4 = 0.8. This is intuitive, and if you remember one rule about probability from school, it's probably this one.

So, probabilism says that agent's degrees of belief should obey these rules. We'll look at three arguments for probabilism—the Dutch Book Argument, the Representation Theorem Argument, and the Accuracy Argument.

3.2 Dutch Book Argument

The historically most influential argument for probabilism is the *Dutch Book Argument*, which says that anyone who violates probabilism is susceptible to a sure monetary loss.

A *Dutch Book* is a series of bets that result in the bettor losing money, however the world turns out. That is, the bettor is guaranteed to lose money, and might as well have simply thrown the money in the bin. Such a fate awaits those whose credences violate the rules of probability, or so the Dutch Book Argument claims. At the core of the Dutch Book Argument is the *Dutch Book Theorem*. (You might be wondering why it's called a "Dutch Book." Good question. No-one knows.)

3.2.1 Dutch Book Theorem

We first need the concept of a *betting price*. Recall from Chapter 1 that there is a close connection between credence and betting behavior. We saw that if an agent's credence in some proposition, H, is 0.8, they should be willing to pay up to 80c for a ticket that pays $1 if H. Call this 80c the *betting price*. More generally, the *betting price* is the largest amount the agent is willing to pay for a ticket that pays $1 if H is true (and $0 if false). It is also the smallest amount for which the agent is willing to *sell* a ticket which pays out $1 if H (and $0 if false). That is, suppose you have signed a ticket that promises to pay the bearer $1 if H. If your credence in H is 0.8, then you will need at least 80c to sell it. For simplicity, we will assume the buying and selling prices are equal;[3] this is the betting price. Each agent will have a betting price for each proposition; together these constitute a set of betting prices.

Now we can state the Dutch Book Theorem:

Dutch Book Theorem If a set of betting prices violates the rules of probability, then there is a Dutch Book consisting of bets at those prices.

That is, if your betting prices violate the rules of probability, you are susceptible to a guaranteed loss. Applied to betting prices, the rules of probability look like this, where bp represents the betting price on arbitrary propositions, X & Y, in set of beliefs B:

Nonnegativity: $bp(X) \geq 0$ for all X in B.

Normalization: $bp(T) = \$1$ for any tautology T in B, for a bet that pays $1.

Finite additivity: $bp(X \text{ or } Y) = bp(X) + bp(Y)$ for all X & Y in B such that X is incompatible with Y.

Let's go through each of the rules and show how violating each of them leaves one Dutch-bookable.

1 *Nonnegativity* Suppose an agent's betting prices violate Nonnegativity, which means they have a negative betting price in some hypothesis H. A negative price means you are willing to pay someone to take it away. This makes sense for things you don't want, for example, a headache, garbage, but it doesn't make sense for a ticket that win $1. Such an agent is willing to stop a stranger in the street and pay them to take a ticket that turns into a further $1 if H. Such an agent is guaranteed to lose money, and so is Dutch-bookable.

2 *Normalization* Something similar happens to an agent whose betting prices violate normalization, which says that betting prices

in tautologies should match the payout, which we assume is 1. First suppose your betting price in a tautology, T, is greater than 1. Then you are willing to pay more than $1 for a bet that pays $1 if T. As you have paid more than $1 and can win only $1, you are guaranteed a loss. Alternatively, suppose your betting price on a tautology is less than 1. Then you are willing to bet on not T. As T is certain to happen, you are guaranteed a loss.

3 *Finite additivity* Finite additivity is the least crazy and therefore the most interesting case. Suppose that your betting prices on X and Y are 0.4 each but your betting price on [X or Y] is 0.6, that is, less than 0.4 + 0.4. You are effectively assigning each individual possibility too high a betting price, so you are prepared to bet too heavily in favor of each of them happening individually. Let's construct the Dutch Book, which consists of three bets.

Bet 1 is for a ticket that pays $1 if and only if X; Bet 2 is for a ticket that pays $1 if and only if Y. As you assign each a probability of 0.4, you are willing to pay $0.4 for each, and so $0.8 for both. For bet 3, you sell the bookie a ticket that pays $1 if and only if either X or Y is true. You sell this ticket for your betting price of $0.6. This means you get $0.6 and give the bookie a ticket that promises the bearer $1 if X or Y. After these bets are made, you are out of pocket $0.8 − $0.6 = $0.2, and there is no way you can make the money back. There are three possibilities for what happens next:

If X is true you win $1 on bet 1 but lose $1 on bet 3.

If Y is true you win $1 on bet 2 but lose $1 on bet 3.

If neither are true, no further money changes hands.

Whatever happens, you lose $0.2.

That was all put in terms of gross payouts. It is also useful to put it in terms of net results, where we can lay things out in the following table. The columns represent the three ways things could go, and the rows keep track of net gains and losses, with the total result on the bottom. (Remember X and Y cannot both be true.)

	X, Not Y	Y, Not X	Not X & Not Y
Bet 1	+$0.6	−$0.4	−$0.4
Bet 2	−$0.4	+$0.6	−$0.4
Bet 3	−$0.4	−$0.4	+$0.6
Total	−$0.2	−$0.2	−$0.2

Bet 1 results in net $0.6 if X ($1 winnings minus the $0.4 for the ticket) and −$0.4 if not X (the cost of the ticket). Bet 2 results in net $0.6 if Y and net −$0.4 if not Y. Bet 3 results in net $0.6 only if neither X nor Y, otherwise it loses net $0.4. Whatever happens, you lose $0.2.

This is just an example, but it generalizes—whenever Finite Additivity is violated, a Dutch Book can be made.[4] For example, what if your betting prices of X and Y individually are too low instead of too high? Then the bookie reverses the direction of the bets, so bets that he bought are now sold, and those he sold are now bought. So we conclude that the Dutch Book Theorem is true:

Dutch Book Theorem If a set of betting prices violates the rules of probability, then there is a Dutch Book consisting of bets at those prices.

3.2.2 *Dutch Book Argument*

We can now use the Dutch Book Theorem to argue for probabilism. I'll state the argument now, then give a brief explanation of the other premises, then consider objections.

P1. Your degrees of belief should be matched by your betting prices.

Dutch Book Theorem: If your betting prices violate the rules of probability, then there is a Dutch Book consisting of bets at your betting prices.

P2. If there is a Dutch Book consisting of bets at your betting prices, then you are susceptible to a guaranteed loss.

P3. If you are susceptible to a guaranteed loss, then you are irrational.

C. Therefore, if your degrees of belief violate the rules of probability then you are irrational.

First consider P1. Suppose an agent's degree of belief in H is 0.8. P1 says that the maximum price the agent should pay for a ticket that pays $1 if H is $0.8; and the minimum price she should take to sell a bet that pays $1 if H is $0.8. P1 is based on the theory of belief introduced in Chapter 1. We saw there that we know about people's beliefs from their behavior, and specifically their betting behavior. P1 adds that your betting prices *should* match your degrees of belief. This looks reasonable. While it is possible that someone buys a ticket for more than the betting price, she would be making a mistake. So P1 allows us to identify degrees of belief with betting prices in rational agents.

P2 connects the Dutch-bookable betting prices to being susceptible to a guaranteed loss, and P3 connects the guaranteed loss to being irrational. Both should seem plausible. C puts these steps together, linking the degrees of belief mentioned in P1 with the irrationality we arrive at in P3. The argument is valid. Let's evaluate the premises.

Objections to the Dutch Book Argument

Objection to P1

P1 says your degrees of belief should be matched by your betting prices. But there are cases where your degrees of belief should not be matched by your betting prices. Suppose a bus ticket home costs $1 but you have only 60c. Someone offers you a bet that pays $1 if and only if a fair coin lands Heads, and charges you 60c. If you really want to ride home, you may rationally choose to take the bet. Your degree of belief that that coin lands Heads is 0.5, but your betting price is 0.6. These come apart because you will be so much *happier* with $1 than you will be with 99c.

The technical term for such happiness is *utility*. Think of utility as expressing a psychological property of the agent. Just as shoe size represents a physical property of the agent, utility expresses a psychological property—how happy she is with the overall situation. (It is the same concept as used in Economics. I'll say more about this in 3.4.) The bets an agent makes depend on the interaction of their degrees of belief with their utilities.

The problem for P1 is that utility is not *proportional* to money. You have much more utility with $1 than with 99c; there is only the tiniest difference in money, but $1 is enough for the bus ride. So you are happy to pay over the odds for a bet that has a chance of winning you $1. So P1 is false.

(The fact that utility is not proportional to wealth explains many features of human behavior. For example, this is partly why the insurance industry exists. People take out insurance against large losses because they have such a disproportionate effect on our well-being, e.g. losing $10,000 is more than 10,000 times worse than losing $1.)

Responses to Objection to P1

One response is to reformulate the Dutch Book Argument, putting everything in terms of utility rather than money. But this response faces criticism on the grounds that utility is a mysterious concept, and also because putting things in terms of utility complicates the argument.

A simpler response is to stipulate that the argument only applies to agents whose utility is proportional to their money. Call them *simple* agents. For simple agents, monetary payoffs function as utilities. This ensures the truth of P1. We'll come back to simple agents shortly.

Objection to P2

P2 says that if there is a Dutch Book consisting of bets at your betting prices, then you are susceptible to a guaranteed loss. But there are ways to block this inference. For example, you are not susceptible to a guaranteed loss if you don't bet. Perhaps you foresee that you are susceptible to a Dutch Book and so refuse to make any bets at all. Or perhaps you are a puritan who disapproves of gambling. In such cases, there is a Dutch Book consisting of bets at your betting prices, but you are not susceptible to a guaranteed loss. We'll consider a response after looking at P3.

Objection to P3

P3 says that if you are susceptible to a sure loss then you are irrational. This is the premise that connects bad things happening to rationality. A denial of this premise would say that you can be susceptible to a sure loss and rational. Distinguish two ways to defend this denial. First, one could argue that all agents are susceptible to a sure loss or, second, one could argue that there is an upside to being susceptible to a sure loss. Let's take these in turn.

First, perhaps all agents are susceptible to a sure loss, whatever their beliefs. Then one cannot be accused of irrationality for being susceptible to a sure loss. Compare: If your degrees of belief violate the rules of probability, then you will eventually die. We cannot infer that your degrees of belief should satisfy the rules of probability.

But it turns out that *not* all agents are susceptible to a sure loss. In fact, probabilistic agents are never susceptible to a sure loss! That is, if your betting prices satisfy the rules of probability, you will never make a series of bets that guarantee a loss. This result was proved in 1955[5] and is known as the Converse Dutch Book Theorem.

> *Converse Dutch Book Theorem*: If your betting prices satisfy the probability calculus, then there does *not* exist a Dutch Book consisting of bets at your prices.

We will omit the proof, which is difficult, and the Converse Dutch Book Argument is left to the reader. The point is that a loss can be avoided by probabilistic agents, which makes P3 more plausible.

Let's move on to the second way to deny P3, which leads to a serious problem with the Dutch Book Argument. One could defend the possibility of being susceptible-to-a-sure-loss-and-rational by showing that there is an upside to being susceptible to a sure loss. Being susceptible to something bad might mean being susceptible to something good. Being on a roller-coaster means you are susceptible to being injured, but it also means you are susceptible to having fun. So perhaps having degrees of belief that violate the rules of probability opens up possibilities for gains that would otherwise be closed off.

A natural thought is that the nonprobabilistic agent can benefit from sets of bets that guarantee a gain, whereas the probabilistic agent will miss the opportunity. But in fact the probabilistic agent will *not* miss the opportunity—if there is a set of bets that guarantee a gain, the probabilistic agent will take it. No-one will say no to free money.

Instead, we need a more imaginative example. Suppose an eccentric billionaire gives $1m to anyone who violates the rules of probability. Now the nonprobabilistic agent can gain money that the probabilistic agent can't. Overall, the nonprobabilistic agent is susceptible to a sure loss from a Dutch bookie yet also to a sure gain from the eccentric billionaire. Why think the nonprobabilistic agent is worse off? Why think her irrational? No obvious reason!

This example brings out a general worry about Dutch Book Arguments: being susceptible to a sure loss seems to be the wrong kind of thing to show that someone is epistemically irrational. The Dutch Book Argument is a *pragmatic* (usefulness-based) argument whereas what is needed is an *epistemic* (belief/truth/evidence-based) argument.

All the objections above to P1, P2, and P3 are due to the same underlying problem—the Dutch Book Argument tells us about agents that lose money, but what we're really interested in is beliefs, and losing money is only indirectly related to beliefs. To avoid all these objections and give a more direct argument for probabilism, we want a related argument that focuses on beliefs. Call these *de-pragmatized Dutch Book Arguments.*

3.2.3 De-pragmatized Dutch Book Arguments

We'll briefly consider two attempts to use Dutch Books to construct arguments for probabilism that focus on beliefs, and which avoid making reference to practical issues like losing money.

Christensen's argument

The following argument is based on Christensen (2001). To understand it, we need two new concepts.

First, we'll put aside agents whose utilities are not proportional to their wealth, and work with agents who care only about money, *simple agents*. This rules out cases such as needing $1 for a bus ticket, raised as an objection to P1.

Second, we need the concept of *sanctioning as fair* a set of betting prices. Christensen (2001) gives us the following explanation of the concept:

> Sanctioning as fair is an informal, intuitive normative connection between an agent's beliefs and her preferences concerning possible bets. An agent's degree of belief in a certain proposition sanctions possible bets as fair if and only if it provides justification for evaluating those bets as fair, i.e. for being indifferent to taking either side of those bets. (p. 370)

We can then give the following argument:

> P1'. A simple agent sanctions as fair, betting prices matching his degrees of belief.
>
> *Dutch Book Theorem* If a set of betting prices violates the rules of probability, then there is a set of bets which will inflict on the agent a sure loss.
>
> P2'. If a simple agent sanctions as fair a set of bets that inflict a sure loss, then the agent's degrees of belief are irrational.
>
> C'. If a simple agent's degrees of belief violate the rules of probability, then they are irrational.

The argument is valid. Suppose a simple agent has beliefs that violate the rules of probability. Then by P1' the agent sanctions as fair, betting prices that violate the rules of probability. The Dutch Book Theorem shows that these betting prices inflict a sure loss, meaning the agent sanctions as fair a set of bets that inflict a sure loss, which by P2' means the beliefs are irrational.

This avoids the earlier problems, but one might object that Christensen's argument is not purely epistemic, for what an agent sanctions as fair will depend on her preferences as well as the prices.

Let's now move on to a different attempt to de-pragmatize the Dutch Book Argument.

The Dutch Book Argument as revealing inconsistency

Consider again *finite additivity*:

> *Finite Additivity*: bp(X or Y) = bp(X) + bp(Y) for all X, Y in B such that X is incompatible with Y.

If someone violates Finite Additivity, then their betting price that X-or-Y differs from their betting price for X plus their betting price for Y, for all incompatible X and Y. This means they would pay different amounts for a bet that X-or-Y than they would in total for a bet that X plus a bet that Y. But these are just two different ways of making the same bet, so the agent would pay different amounts for the same thing, depending on how it was offered. And it is *inconsistent* to value the same thing at different prices. So perhaps the point of the Dutch Book Argument isn't to show that the agent will lose money, but to reveal an *inconsistency* in the beliefs of the agent, an inconsistency which is obviously irrational.

This understanding of Dutch Books can be found in the paper that introduced them:[6]

> Any definite set of degrees of belief which broke [the laws of probability] would be inconsistent in the sense that it violated the laws of preference between options . . . If anyone's mental condition violated these laws, his choice would depend on the precise form in which the options were offered him, which would be absurd. (Ramsey 1926, p. 41)

A couple of worries might be raised here. First, this kind of inconsistency only applies to agents who violate Finite Additivity. There is no obviously analogous argument for agents who violate Nonnegativity or Nonnormalization. Second, as the inconsistency revealed is in *preferences*, it is still not a purely epistemic defect, as preferences depend on desires as well as on beliefs. We want an argument that shows that nonprobabilistic beliefs are irrational, purely as beliefs.

So let's move on to an argument that is concerned only with beliefs and their accuracy.

3.3 Joyce's Accuracy Argument for probabilism

Jim Joyce (1998) has opened up a lively area of research by giving an argument for probabilism using purely epistemic goals. When it comes to our epistemic goals, we want our beliefs to be as accurate as possible. We can make this more precise by adopting a measure of accuracy. Let's assign a value of 1 to each true proposition and 0 to each false proposition. (Careful: Previously, such numbers represented degrees of belief, but here they represent the truth-value of the proposition.) We can now measure the accuracy of a belief by the distance between the degree of belief and the truth-value of the proposition. For example, if someone believes that grass is green to degree 0.9, this belief gets an accuracy score of 0.1, that is, the distance between 1 and 0.9. Whereas if someone believes that grass is red with degree of belief 0.3, this belief gets an accuracy score of 0.3, that is, the distance between 0 and 0.3. The lower the score, the greater the accuracy. (To get a usable score we actually need to do a bit of work, such as squaring the distance between the degree of belief and the truth-value, but we won't worry about that.)

Let's now say that a set of beliefs is *dominated* if and only if there is some other set of beliefs that has a higher score whatever the world is like:

Set of beliefs B1 *dominates* set of beliefs B2 if and only if B1 is more accurate than B2 in every possibility.

We can use this to defend probabilism if we can show that beliefs that violate the rules of probability are dominated while those that don't are not:

Accuracy Theorem. If a set of beliefs violates the rules of probability then it is dominated by one that doesn't.

P1. If you hold a dominated set of beliefs then you are irrational.

C. Therefore, if your degrees of belief violate the rules of probability then you are irrational.

Let's first give an argument for the Accuracy Theorem. Take the simplest case where there is just one proposition, H, and consider a possibility where H is true and a possibility where H is false. The x and y axes in the diagram represent the agent's credence in H and not H, respectively. Point A represents a 100 percent belief that H, and point B represents a 100 percent belief that not H. By the rules of probability P(H) + P(not H) =1, so the dotted line between A and B on which P(H) + P(not H) =1 represents probabilistic beliefs; any points off the line represent nonprobabilistic beliefs. Consider point C, which is below the line. This means that the beliefs at C are nonprobabilistic; the sum of P(H) and P(not H) is less than 1. Curve 1 represents the places that are exactly as far from point A as C is. So all the points bounded by curve 1 are closer to A than C is, meaning that if H is true, all such points are more accurate than C. Curve 2 represents the places that are exactly as far from point B as C is. So all the points bounded by curve 2 are closer to B than C is, meaning that if not H, all such points are more accurate than C.

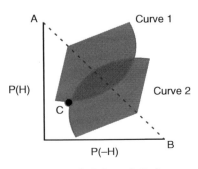

Nonprobabilistic beliefs.

Now consider the area where the curves overlap. All the points in this area are more accurate *whether H or not H is true*. Whatever possibility is actual, accuracy is increased by moving from C toward the dotted line, which means that all these points dominate C. And these points include the straight line representing probabilistic beliefs, meaning that there is a probabilistic set of beliefs that dominate C. And the same applies for any point that is not on the dotted/probabilistic line. For any nonprobabilistic beliefs, there is a set of probabilistic beliefs that dominate it. Thus, the Accuracy Theorem is true.

What about P1, which says that holding dominated beliefs is irrational? As with the Dutch Book Argument, P1 is undermined if holding dominated beliefs is unavoidable. So we need a converse theorem:

Converse Accuracy Theorem If a set of beliefs satisfies the rules of probability then it is not dominated by one that doesn't.

It is easy to see that this is true. Consider a point, D, representing a probabilistic set of beliefs, on the straight line. The curves representing equal distance from H and not H intersect at D, so there is no alternative set of beliefs that is more accurate whatever the world is like. Any move toward H is a move away from not H. So there is no set of beliefs that dominates D. Thus, the Converse Accuracy Theorem is true.

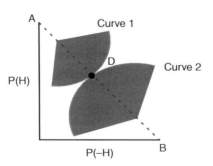

Probabilistic beliefs.

P1, which says that it is irrational to hold dominated beliefs, now looks compelling. If you can change your beliefs in a way that guarantees they become more accurate, then surely you are rationally obliged to do so. Or are you?[7]

Objection to Accuracy Argument: It is rational to hold dominated beliefs

Suppose you find yourself at point C, which, let's say, assigns credence of 0.2 to H. The earlier argument says that you should move toward the dotted line, thus increasing your credence in H. But Fitelson and Easwaran (2015) point out that you might have good reasons not to do this. For example, suppose you have *evidence* which implies that your credence in H should be no more than 0.2. Then they argue that you shouldn't move toward the dotted line, you should stay at the nonprobabilistic position of 0.2 credence in H.

Joyce (ms) disagrees. He points out that evidence that your credence in H should be no more than 0.2 is evidence that your credence in not H should be at least 0.8. So the evidence does justify you moving toward the dotted line after all—you should just move horizontally (to the right) rather than vertically.

3.4 Representation Theorem Argument

Now we move on to the third and final argument for probabilism. Let's start by clarifying the concept of *preferences*, which were in the background in 3.2.2. The preferences of an agent determine what options they would *choose*. If you would choose a banana over an apricot, then say you *prefer* a banana to an apricot. This preference results from how much you would enjoy a banana compared to an apricot. That is, it depends on the *utility* they produce, where the utility is a measure of how happy you are. If you prefer a banana to an apricot, then your utility given a banana is greater than your utility given an apricot.

Preferences also depend on beliefs. For example, the strength of your preference for a lottery ticket depends on your degree of belief that it will win. We'll assume your preferences depend on just those two things—your utilities given the outcomes, and your degrees of belief that each outcome will occur.

This allows us to argue backward—from one's preferences to what one's beliefs and utilities must be. This is how the *Representation Theorem* Argument works. Representation theorems say that if an agent's preferences satisfy reasonable constraints, then they can be represented as resulting from beliefs that satisfy the rules of probability. (I'll suppress reference to utilities as we are interested in what the representation theorem says about beliefs.)

What are these constraints? Von Neumann and Morgenstern (1944) use the following four (we won't go through the proof):

Completeness For any choice between a and b, the agent prefers a to b, or prefers b to a, or is indifferent i.e. the agent never says "I'm simply unable to compare these options."

Transitivity If a is preferred to b, and b is preferred to c, then a is preferred to c

e.g. if apricot is preferred to banana, and banana is preferred to chocolate, then apricot is preferred to chocolate.

Continuity If a is preferred to b, and b is preferred to c then there is some gamble between a and c such that the agent is indifferent between the gamble and b.

Independence An agent's choice between two options should not be affected by an outcome that is independent of the choice

e.g. if apricot is preferred to banana when they are the only options, apricot should be preferred to banana when there is a chocolate option too.

Calling these constraints C, we can give the following argument for probabilism:

Preference Consistency If an agent is rational, then their preferences satisfy constraints C.

Representation Theorem If an agent's preferences satisfy constraints C, then they can be represented as having degrees of belief, B, that satisfy the rules of probability.

Representation Accuracy If an agent can be represented as having degrees of belief, B, that satisfy the rules of probability, then the agent's actual degrees of belief are B.

Probabilism Therefore, if an agent is rational then their degrees of belief satisfy the rules of probability.

The Representation Theorem is above reproach and the other two premises look plausible. But both can be challenged.

Objection 1: Reject preference consistency

One way to reject the Representation Theorem Argument is to reject *Preference Consistency* by rejecting one or more of constraints C. The most controversial of them is *Independence*.

Allais's Paradox shows that *actual* agents violate *Independence* (which says that your choice between two options should not be affected by an outcome that is independent of the choice.) Here is a simplified version of the original paradox.[8] Which would you choose in the following two problems?

Choice 1: 60% chance of $500,000 OR 58% chance of $520,000

Choice 2: 100% chance of $500,000 OR 98% chance of $520,000

Imagine Choice 1 as a choice between two urns containing 100 balls. The first urn has 60 winning balls worth $500,000 and the second urn has 58 winning balls worth $520,000. Most people choose the second urn; it has slightly fewer winning balls, but they win more money. For Choice 2, for each urn, we replace 40 losing balls with winning balls. Both urns have improved, but the second urn has improved more, as a winning ball in the second urn is worth an extra $20,000. Nevertheless, many people switch to the first urn. This switch violates *Independence*, which says that the improvement of the 40 percent chance of winning across both urns should be independent of which urn you choose.

Choice 1				Choice 2		
Urn1	Urn2			Urn1	Urn2	
$500,000	$0	2%		$500,000	$0	
$0	$0	40%		$500,000	$520,000	
$500,000	$520,000	58%		$500,000	$520,000	

Allais's paradox.

One explanation is that people see the guaranteed $500,000 in Choice 2 and consider anything less as a *loss*. Losses are especially painful, so people choose the $500,000. But as nothing is guaranteed in Choice 1 there is no loss to be avoided. If this is rational, then *Independence* is false.

Objection 2: Reject representation accuracy

Recall *Representation Accuracy* says that if an agent's preferences can be represented as resulting from degrees of belief, B, then the agent's actual degrees of belief are B. But just because an agent can be represented as having beliefs B, it doesn't mean they really have beliefs B. It's one thing to act *as if* something is true, quite another for it to be true. Hájek (2008b) develops the problem:

> To make this concern vivid, suppose that I represent your preferences with Voodooism. My voodoo theory says that there are warring voodoo spirits inside you. When you prefer A to B, then there are more A-favouring spirits inside you than B-favouring spirits. I interpret all of the usual rationality axioms in voodoo terms. Transitivity: if you have more A-favouring spirits than B-favouring spirits, and more B-favouring spirits than C-favouring spirits, then you have more A-favouring spirits than C-favouring spirits . . . I then "prove" Voodooism: if your preferences obey the usual rationality axioms, then there exists a Voodoo representation of you. That is, you act as if there are warring voodoo spirits inside you in conformity with Voodooism. Conclusion: rationality requires you to have warring Voodoo spirits in you. Not a happy result. (p. 804)

So *Representation Accuracy* is a particularly dubious premise. It is plausible if you think that there is nothing more to having a belief than behaving as if you have that belief. Such a view might be endorsed by *instrumentalists* or *behaviorists*. *Instrumentalists* think that beliefs are not real entities, but are useful fictions that we create to tell a story about human behavior. *Behaviorists* think that beliefs are identical to behavior. These views were influential for much of the twentieth century, but most contemporary philosophers adopt a realist theory of belief, as we did in Chapter 1, and so reject *Representation Accuracy*.

Summary

To sum up, we've considered three arguments for probabilism—based on the Dutch Book, Accuracy, and Representation Theorems. The Dutch Book Argument faces the problem of being a pragmatic argument, and we are really after an epistemic argument. The Representation argument faces the problem that the constraints may not be rationally required, and that acting as if you have a belief isn't the same as having a belief. The Accuracy Argument is more promising and has generated considerable recent interest; it is perhaps too early for a consensus to have emerged about whether it succeeds.

As well as these direct arguments, we can also indirectly support the probabilistic approach by showing how useful it is. And in the following chapters, we will assume the truth of probabilism and put the theory to work. To set up the next chapter, notice that probabilism is a very weak constraint on rationality. It would be satisfied by an agent who thought that the probability that his navel rules the universe is 1, as long as he also thinks that the probability that his navel doesn't rule the universe is 0. Probabilism would also be satisfied by that agent if for no reason he suddenly changed his mind and decided that he didn't have a navel. In the next chapter, we consider a constraint on how we should change our beliefs in the light of new evidence.

Appendix: Sharp vs. unsharp values

So far we have assumed that degrees of belief take sharp values, for example, 0, 0.4, 0.5, 1, and so on. But some philosophers argue that beliefs should take intervals as values. For example, an agent's degree of belief in H might be between 0.4 and 0.6, where this doesn't mean that the degree of belief is a sharp value between 0.4 and 0.6, but means that the degree of belief is itself the *interval*. We could also say that the degree of belief is *fuzzy* or *vague* or *indeterminate* or *unsharp*. We'll use "unsharp." In this appendix, we'll consider an argument that agents should have sharp degrees of belief.

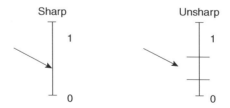

Sharp and unsharp beliefs.

Argument for unsharp values

The main argument for unsharp values is that there are cases in which your evidence does not justify a sharp degree of belief. Specifically, if your evidence is sparse and nonspecific, it seems you should not hold beliefs with precise probabilities. Adam Elga gives the following example (though he ends up arguing for sharp values):

A stranger approaches you on the street and starts pulling out objects from a bag. The first three objects he pulls out are a regular-sized tube of toothpaste, a live jellyfish, and a travel-sized tube of toothpaste. To what degree should you believe that the next object he pulls out will be another tube of toothpaste?

The answer is not clear. The contents of the bag are clearly bizarre. You have no theory of "what insane people on the street are likely to carry in their bags," nor have you encountered any particularly relevant statistics about this. (Elga 2010a, p. 1)

It seems that in such a case you ought not to have a sharp degree of belief. The evidence does not justify such a specific opinion. Suppose that someone did believe that the probability that the next object he pulls out will be another tube of toothpaste to degree 0.35. Such a degree of belief would surely be arbitrary. Why 0.35 as opposed to 0.34? There doesn't seem to be an answer, so it looks like we should have unsharp beliefs in such a case. More realistic examples are given in this influential passage of John Maynard Keynes (who uses "uncertain" where we will use "unsharp"):

The sense in which I am using the term ["uncertain"] is that in which the prospect of a European war is uncertain, or the price of copper and the rate of interest twenty years hence, or the obsolescence of a new invention, or the position of private wealthowners in the social system in 1970. (Keynes 1937, pp. 213–4)

Finally, unsharp degrees of belief are often motivated by cases where you are told that the proportion of black balls in an urn is, say, between 20 and 80 percent. If that's all you know, it seems reasonable that your degree of belief that a randomly selected ball will be black should be the interval between 0.2 and 0.8.

Elga's argument for sharp degrees of belief

Elga (2010a) argues that one's degrees of belief should always be sharp. He offers a Dutch Book Argument against an agent with unsharp values. Let H be any hypothesis, such as the hypothesis that it will rain tomorrow. Consider the following attractive series of bets:

	H	Not H
Bet A	+$20	−$10
Bet B	−$10	+$20
Net	+$10	+$10

Bet A costs $10 and pays back $20 if H; bet B costs $10 and pays back $20 if not H. Bet B is offered immediately after Bet A, so your opinions don't change in between.

These bets are attractive because you can accept both bets and therefore guarantee a net gain of $10 whatever happens. It isn't rationally required that you accept *both* bets—you might be certain H is true, and so take only Bet A. But it is rationally required that you take *at least one*. If instead you take neither, you are giving up free money, which is clearly crazy. But if you have unsharp degrees of belief, we'll see you might take neither. Thus, Elga argues, unsharp degrees of belief are irrational.

So, how would unsharp degrees of belief lead to taking neither bet? Well, what should an agent with unsharp degrees of belief do when offered a bet? Suppose your degree of belief in H has an upper bound of 0.9 and a lower bound of 0.1. Clearly a bet that pays $1 if H (and $0 if not H) should be accepted if offered at less than $0.1. But what if the bet was offered at $0.5, that is between the lower and upper bound?

The natural thing to say is that it is permissible to either accept or refuse the bet. But this means that it is permissible to refuse both Bets A and B. And this is tantamount to giving up free money. Elga concludes that, as unsharp degrees of belief allow this crazy result, it is irrational to have unsharp degrees of belief; so degrees of belief should be sharp.

There are various ways to respond to this argument, but Elga argues that none of them work. We'll just consider one line of response and Elga's reply.

Objection to Elga's argument for sharp degrees of belief

One response to Elga's argument that we'll call *Sequence* runs as follows:

Sequence: Just as individual actions can be assessed for rationality, so too can sequences of actions. And it can happen that a sequence of actions is irrational even if each of its elements is rational. In particular, suppose that an agent has rejected both bets in the Bet A/Bet B situation. Then her first action—rejecting Bet A—was rationally permissible. And her second action—rejecting Bet B—was also rationally permissible. But her performing the sequence of actions "reject-Bet-A-then-reject-Bet-B" was rationally impermissible. (Elga 2010a, p. 9)

Elga's reply

Elga replies that *Sequence* has implausible implications. These can be brought out by comparing two situations in which you are considering Bet B. In the first situation, you have previously rejected Bet A. In the second, you were never offered Bet A at all. Everything else is alike, so the consequences of accepting Bet B are identical.

Nevertheless, *Sequence* entails that in the first situation it is permissible to reject Bet B, but in the second situation it is not. For in the second situation, rejecting Bet B would complete the irrational sequence of actions "reject-Bet-A-then-reject-Bet-B," whereas rejecting Bet B in the first situation would not complete any irrational sequences. So according to *Sequence*, rejecting Bet B is rational in the first situation, but not in the second. But that can't be right, as the consequences of accepting Bet B are identical. Here is how Elga sums it up:

> Bottom line: sequence entails that rationality imposes different requirements on [the agent] in the two situations. But [the agent] can see that her choices in the two situations are alike. . . . So it must be that rationality imposes on her the same constraints in the two situations. So *Sequence* is incorrect. (Elga 2010a, p. 10)

Study questions

1   What is probabilism?

2   What is a Dutch Book?

3   Explain the Dutch Book/Accuracy/Representation Theorem Argument for probabilism.

Advanced questions

4   Is logical omniscience a plausible assumption? How important is it to hold this assumption?

5   Is the Dutch Book Argument pragmatic, rather than epistemic? Can an epistemic Dutch Book Argument, for example Christensen's, work?

6   Could Joyce respond to Fitelson and Easwaran's objection by restricting his argument to apply to *a priori* credence functions (i.e. those which have no evidence)?

7 Is it rational to violate *Independence*?

8 Could one respond to Hájek's objection by taking an instrumentalist view of beliefs?

Further reading

The classic source of the Dutch Book is Ramsey (1926). De Finetti (1937) is less accessible but very influential. For contemporary introductions, see Hájek (2008b) and Vineberg (2011). For an accessible introduction to representation theorems, see Resnik (1987). Joyce has developed his Accuracy Argument in his (1998) and (2009).

Hájek (2008a) has a helpful critical discussion dealing with many of the issues in this chapter.

4

Rationality constraints II: Conditionalization

So far we have only talked about an agent's beliefs at a single time. But when we learn things, our beliefs change. So how should we update our beliefs when we learn something new? There is a standard answer—*conditionalization*. This chapter explains conditionalization (4.1), then explains a Dutch Book in its favor (4.2), considers objections to the Dutch Book (4.3), and finally explains a purported counter-example to conditionalization (4.4).

4.1 Conditionalization

How should you update your beliefs when you learn something new? One of the selling points of probabilism is that it offers a simple and elegant answer: you should *conditionalize*.

Conditionalization says that an agent's beliefs after learning E should equal her earlier beliefs *conditional* on E. Where H is an arbitrary belief, and P_E expresses her beliefs at a later time after learning E and nothing else, we can express conditionalization as:

Conditionalization

If you are rational then $P_E(H) = P(H|E)$

This tells us what rational agents do and what all agents *ought* to do (it doesn't tell us what agents *actually* do). Call the degree of belief at the earlier time, $P(H|E)$, the *prior*, and the degree of belief at the later time, $P_E(H)$, the *posterior*. (Notice the prior expresses a conditional credence.[1])

Let's go through an example. Suppose that initially Bob's conditional probability of *Two* given *Even* is 1/3. If he then learns *Even*, his new probability in *Two* should be 1/3. That's it.

Conditionalization.

How does this look on the Venn diagram? In Chapter 1, when thinking about the conditional probability of H given E, we put it like this:

> To find the credence of H given E, we zoom in on the E possibilities, and ask in what proportion of them H is true.

When E is learnt, we don't just zoom in on E to examine it more closely, we *eliminate* every not E possibility. We start with this:

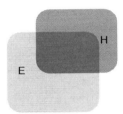

Original beliefs.

Then when E is learnt, we zoom in and eliminate the not E possibilities.

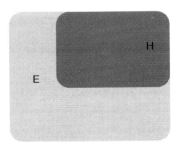

Beliefs after learning E.

Three features of conditionalization are worth commenting on. First, there is no shift in credences *within* the E possibilities—the not E possibilities are eliminated, and credence among the E possibilities remains in the same proportion.

Second, the initial distribution of priors fully determines what happens in the future when some evidence E is learnt. So given an agent's priors, we can fully predict what they will believe after learning a particular E (and so can the agent). It follows that if two conditionalizers have the same evidence but different posteriors, then they must have started out with different priors.

Third, what's the probability of E, after learning E, according to conditionalization? As H expresses any arbitrary belief, it can express E as well, so conditionalization says $P_E(E) = P(E|E)$. A simple theorem of probability theory is that the probability of any proposition conditional on itself is 1, so conditionalization says that $P_E(E) = 1$. (Exercise: Prove the theorem.)

Some object to conditionalization on the grounds that there are few things that we should be completely certain of, so few things we should have credence of 1 in. Yet conditionalization says that we should have credence of 1 in everything we learn.

Can we generalize conditionalization so it doesn't commit us to everything we learn having a probability of 1? Yes. We can suppose that the learning experience doesn't push the probability of E all the way to 1, it just changes it to a new value. *Jeffrey Conditionalization* tells us what to do when the probability of E after the learning experience is P(E):

Jeffrey Conditionalization

$P_E(H) = P(H| E)P(E) + P(H|-E)P(-E)$

When $P(E) = 1$, this reduces to conditionalization.

Despite its advantages, Jeffrey conditionalization raises problems that conditionalization doesn't, and is much more difficult to work with, so we will set it aside. Future uses of "conditionalization" can be understood as "conditionalization or Jeffrey conditionalization."

According to orthodox Bayesians, conditionalization is the *only* way beliefs should change over time. There aren't various updating rules that can be applied in different situations. There is only one way beliefs should change, and any other change is irrational. (Notice that if you forget something, you lose a belief you had earlier, so your beliefs have changed in a way that differs from conditionalization; see 10.1.) But why should beliefs change only in this way?

4.2 Diachronic Dutch Book Argument for conditionalization

The main argument is a Dutch Book Argument attributed to David Lewis in Teller (1973). It turns out that if your credence in H after learning E doesn't match your earlier conditional credence in H given E, you are Dutch-Bookable. The Dutch Book consists of three bets. The first is on E, the second is a conditional bet that is cancelled if not E, and the third is made at a later time after E is learnt. Let's go through an example.[2]

First, you make a bet that E occurs. This is needed because the fun only starts if E happens, so we need to ensure you lose money if E doesn't happen. Let's suppose that your degree of belief in E is 0.5 so you take a bet that wins $1 if E and loses $1 if not E.

The next two bets depend on whether $P_E(H)$ is more or less than $P(H|E)$. Let's suppose that $P_E(H)$ is less than $P(H|E)$; specifically,

$P(H|E) = 0.6$

$P_E(H) = 0.5$

Then Bet 2 is a bet *on* H conditional on E. A bet *conditional on E* means that if not E, the bet is called off and everyone gets their stake back. As $P(H|E) = 0.6$, you'll accept a bet that wins $8 if H and loses $12 if Tails (i.e. you'll pay $12 for a ticket that turns into $20 if H).

Bet 3 is made after E is learnt; the bet is never made if not E. As $P_E(H)$ is only 0.5, you're willing to bet against H with a bet that wins $10 if not H and loses $10 if H (i.e. you'll pay $10 for a ticket that turns into $20 if not H). These three bets constitute a Dutch Book. Here are the three possible outcomes:

Whatever happens, you are guaranteed a loss of $1.

	E&H	E&–H	–E
Bet 1	+$1	+$1	–$1
Bet 2	+$8	–$12	–
Bet 3	–$10	+$10	–
Net	–$1	–$1	–$1

This Dutch Book is based on the mismatch between your earlier conditional degree of belief in H given E and your later degree of belief in H after learning E. Here is an intuitive way of thinking about what happens: After learning E, you think H is less likely than you thought it was *given* E (0.5 instead of 0.6) so you regret making Bet 2 on H given E at such long odds. To minimize your losses, you make Bet 3 against H; so instead of being down $11 (i.e. +$1–$12) if not H, you would only be down $1. The overall result is a guaranteed loss, a Dutch Book. But this is worthwhile from your perspective at the time of Bet 3, because you get a small guaranteed loss instead of a significant chance of a large loss.

(If instead, $P_E(H)$ is greater than P(H|E), you are especially willing to bet on H after learning E. So Bet 2 will be against H and Bet 3 will be on H, with the payouts adjusted to match your degrees of belief.)

As this Dutch Book Argument involves bets made at different times, it is called a *Diachronic Dutch Book Argument*. All the objections to Dutch Book Arguments for epistemic conclusions that we saw in Chapter 3 will apply here. But let's put these aside and ask if there are any special problems that are faced by *Diachronic* Dutch Book Arguments.

Let's consider three.

4.3 Objections to Diachronic Dutch Books

First objection to Diachronic Dutch Books: Don't bet

Maher (1992) points out that the agent will be able to see the sure loss coming. Seeing it coming, the agent can simply refuse to bet with the bookie—loss avoided, argument defused. To fill this out, the agent can decide to only bet with bookies who disclose their strategies in advance. On examination of this bookies strategy, the agent sees that she can end up Dutch-booked, and avoids betting with the bookie.

But this refusal to make a Dutch Book does not solve the agent's problem. To see why not, we need to think about the disagreement between the agent at the time before E is discovered vs. after E is discovered. Before E is discovered, the agent believes H with 60 percent certainty given E. And she knows that if she later learns E, her credence in H will be only 50 percent. By her current prelearning lights, this will be too low. She considers her future-self-mistaken, and is worried that she will make a mistake by taking Bet 3 on not H at 50/50 odds. (And she *will* take the bet because it will seem fair at the time, and won't expose her to a Dutch Book.) She expects this later bet to lose money. How can she reduce her expected losses? By betting on H given E. And the bookie is offering this bet, as Bet 2. So the agent ensures a guaranteed small loss, but this is worthwhile from the agent's perspective, because it avoids the chance of a large loss.[3]

Second objection to Diachronic Dutch Books: Posting odds

Van Fraassen (1984) points out that if a bookie is going to make these bets, he must know in advance whether $P_E(H)$ is more or less than $P(H|E)$. If $P_E(H) > P(H|E)$, as in the table, Bet 2 is on H. If instead, $P_E(H) < P(H|E)$ then Bet 2 would be on not H.

So it isn't quite right to say that you only avoid Dutch Books by updating by conditionalization. What's more accurate is that if you are going to publicly post your update strategy, the only strategy you should post is conditionalization. But this leaves open a more liberal alternative. Van Fraassen suggests that you shouldn't post any strategy at all. For maybe some evidence will arrive that will shake up the way you look at the world, and you should leave open the possibility that you will not update as you now expect. One way of putting this is that we might get evidence that makes us realize that our distribution of priors was mistaken. When we adjust to take into account the priors we should have had, we end up changing our beliefs in a way that violates conditionalization.

One might respond that even if van Fraassen is right about us as flawed humans, the objection doesn't apply to rational agents. Rational agents never get their view of the world shaken up, nor do they make mistakes about the distribution of priors. So if our question is how rational agents update their beliefs, van Fraassen's objection can be avoided.

Third objection to Diachronic Dutch Books

Christensen (1991) thinks that being susceptible to a Diachronic Dutch Book is not a sign of irrationality. He presents a set of considerations designed to show that we shouldn't worry about diachronic Dutch Books. His strategy is to examine some specific cases in which Dutch Books can be made and show that they are not a sign of irrationality.

One example is a husband and wife who have a difference of opinion about some matter. By offering bets to each of them, a bookie can ensure a loss for the couple. This applies generally. Whenever there are two probability functions that differ in any way, an agent can exploit this difference and construct a Dutch Book against them. To see how, notice that any two people who disagree will be happy to bet against each other. (Arguments can be ended with the words "Wanna bet?") Now imagine that the bookie facilitates the bet and takes a small cut of the winnings for his trouble. He has effectively made two bets that guarantee his gain—the dreaded Dutch Book has been made. Is this Dutch Book a symptom of irrationality of the people who made the bets? No. There is nothing irrational about a couple disagreeing about some issue, even though it guarantees them a collective loss.

Now consider the same agent at two points in time. If there is any difference between the credences of the agent at the two points in time, then a bookie can construct a Dutch Book. The bookie needs to be able to predict how the agent's beliefs will evolve over time. But supposing he can do this, is there anything irrational about the agent changing his mind about something and opening himself up to a Dutch Book too? Surely not. As Keynes is supposed to have said, "When the facts change, I change my mind. What do you do sir?"

The upshot of these considerations is that Diachronic Dutch Books aren't a sign of irrationality unless we think the relevant belief functions *should* cohere. We don't expect a couple's belief functions to cohere, so there is nothing wrong with there being a Dutch Book against them. Similarly, Christensen claims, there is nothing wrong with someone's belief function at one time not cohering with their belief function at another time. So there is nothing wrong with there being a diachronic Dutch Book against them. The point is supposed to apply generally. As Christensen (1991) puts it,

> Without some independent reason for thinking that an agent's present beliefs must cohere with her future beliefs, her potential vulnerability to the Dutch strategy provides no support at all for . . . [conditionalization]. (p. 246)

As there is no reason for an agent's present beliefs to cohere with her future beliefs, the potential to be subject to a guaranteed betting loss is not a sign of irrationality.

But Briggs (2009) disagrees:

> [Beliefs] held at different times are indeed the sorts of things that should be coherent. As a logic, Bayesian decision theory ought to be useful for inference and planning. But some sort of intrapersonal coherence is necessary for inference and planning; an agent who conducts his or her epistemic life correctly will have earlier and later selves that cohere better than a pair of strangers [or husband and wife]. The sort of diachronic coherence in question should not be so strong as to demand that agents never change their beliefs. But it should be strong enough to bar agents from adopting belief revision policies which lead to changes that are senseless or insupportable by their current lights. (p. 67)

That seems right to me, but diachronic Dutch Books are widely considered to be less persuasive than synchronic Dutch Books.

Still, even if the Dutch Book Argument is unpersuasive, conditionalization is still a plausible principle. So are there any arguments *against* conditionalization?

4.4 Counter-example to conditionalization: Waiting for a train

Recall conditionalization says that the only rational way to change your degrees of belief is by adopting the conditional credence, P(H|E), as your new credence for H, after learning E and nothing else.

Frank Arntzenius (2003) offers an ingenious counter-example.[4] It's 11 a.m. and you're not quite sure if a train will arrive. But you know that if it does arrive, it will arrive in exactly 1 hour, at 12 p.m. There is no clock in sight, so as you sit there waiting you lose track of the exact time. Fast forward to 11:55 a.m. You now think it may be past 12 p.m., in which case the train isn't coming. So your credence that the train isn't coming is *higher* than it was before. That is, your credences have changed, and, it seems, in a rational manner. But Arntzenius now argues that this change is not due to conditionalization. Conditionalization can only generate a change when some new evidence, E, is learnt. But in this example you haven't learnt anything new. You knew at 11 a.m. that by 11:55 a.m. you would be more confident than you are now (11 a.m.) that the train would not come. So there is no new proposition, E, which you have learnt, and on which you could have conditionalized. So your beliefs can't have changed by conditionalization. Thus, *conditionalization is not the only rational rule of belief change.*

Objection to waiting for a train

Bradley (2011) argues that you have learnt something new. Let's think about why your credence that the train isn't coming goes up by 11:55 a.m. It's because for all you know it might be after noon and the train still isn't here. This is the new proposition you've learnt. To make it more concrete, let's suppose that at 11:55 a.m. your credence that it's after noon is 30 percent. Then at 11:55 a.m. you have discovered:

> *New Proposition* The train has still not arrived by the time my credence that it is after noon has gone up to 30%.

You did not believe this proposition at 11 a.m. For all you knew then, the train might have arrived before your credence that it was after noon had gone up to 30 percent. This is the new proposition learnt, which you can conditionalize on, to generate a shift in credences. Let's go through how.

In order for a new proposition, E, to generate a shift in credences via conditionalization, the following inequality must hold: $P(H|E) \neq P(H)$. By Bayes Theorem, this is equivalent to $P(E|H) \neq P(E)$. And in this case, $P(E|H) > P(E)$, where H = The train is *not* coming:

$P_{11\,a.m.}$ (The train has still not arrived by the time my credence that it is after noon has gone up to 30% | The train is *not* coming) $= 1 >$

$P_{11\,a.m.}$ (The train has still not arrived by the time my credence that it is after noon has gone up to 30%)

Thus when you conditionalize on this New Proposition, your credence that the train isn't coming increases, and there is no counter-example to conditionalization.

Summary

In this chapter, we looked at the Bayesian answer to how you should update your beliefs when you acquire a piece of evidence, E, namely that you should conditionalize: $P_E(H) = P(H|E)$. We looked at the diachronic Dutch Book Argument for conditionalization, and three objections it faces. Finally, we considered a purported counter-example to conditionalization, Waiting for a Train, and a response.

So far we have considered rationality constraints that are fairly undemanding: probabilism and conditionalization. They are the twin pillars of Bayesianism. Those who think that probabilism and conditionalization are the only rationality constraints are called *subjective Bayesians*. *Objective Bayesians* hold that there are further constraints. This debate will occupy the next three chapters.

Study questions

1 What is conditionalization?

2 Explain an argument for/against conditionalization.

3 What is a diachronic Dutch Book?

4 Explain an argument against diachronic Dutch Books.

Advanced questions

5   Give a Dutch Book Argument for Jeffrey conditionalization.

6   Are diachronic Dutch Books less persuasive than synchronic Dutch Books?

7   Is Briggs right that agents should be diachronically coherent?

8   Is Bradley right that waiting for a train fails to refute conditionalization?

9   Are there other counter-examples to conditionalization?

Further reading

The further reading here overlaps with that for Chapter 1, especially Strevens (ms) and Howson and Urbach (1996). For an alternative justification of conditionalization based on Joyce's Accuracy Argument (Chapter 3), see Greaves and Wallace (2006), though this is an advanced paper.

5

Rationality constraints III: Subjective and inductive probability

Recall the King of Hy-Brasil (p. 27), who continued to believe that his island could not sink even as it started crumbling. His belief remained firm even as he was pulled under the sea by the sinking island. And let's suppose that as this happened, his beliefs remained perfectly probabilistic. In fact at no point did he violate any of the rationality constraints we've looked at so far. Was he therefore rational?

Some people say yes; call them *subjectivists* (they are often called *subjective Bayesians*). Others say no; call them *inductivists* (they are often called *objective Bayesians*). This chapter explains inductivism (5.1), then gives an argument in its favor (5.2) followed by three connected arguments against (5.3–5.5).

5.1 Inductive probabilities

Start with subjectivists. Subjectivists hold that although agents' degrees of belief should be probabilities (and should be updated by conditionalization), there are no *further* rationality constraints on what those probabilities should be. So you are free to believe anything you like, as long as your degrees of belief remain probabilistic (and update by conditionalization). You can believe your navel is the embattled leader of the free world with credence of 0.9 as long as you believe it is not with credence of 0.1. And the King of

Hy-Brasil is making no rational error in taking the crumbling of the island to be independent of whether it will sink.

Subjectivism There are no constraints on rationality other than probabilism and conditionalization.

Inductivists, and common sense, disagree. Inductivists think that the King *ought* to believe that Hy-Brasil will sink and is irrational if he does not; his evidence *justifies* a high credence that Hy-Brasil will sink. Put another way, there is a relation of justification between the King's evidence and the proposition that Hy-Brasil will sink. As this relation doesn't vary from one person to another, the relation is objective. These objective relations are expressed by *inductive probabilities*. These are probabilities which agents' degrees of belief *ought* to match. So, for example, if an agent's total evidence is E, and the inductive probability of H given E is 0.8, then they should have credence of 0.8 in H. And if they have no evidence, and the inductive probability of H given no evidence is 0.5, then they should have credence of 0.5 in H.

Inductivism There are constraints on rationality other than probabilism and conditionalization.

It is useful to compare inductive probabilities to credences:

	Credences	Inductive Probability
What are they?	Degrees of belief	Objective relations of justification between propositions
Values are relative to	Agents at times	Evidence
Normative/Descriptive?	Descriptive	Normative
Source of our knowledge of them	Behavior, e.g. betting	The same source as the source of our deductive principles, whatever that is

Don't think of this as a choice between *either* credences *or* inductive probabilities. We are taking for granted that there are credences. The question is whether there are *also* inductive probabilities.

Let me expand on the normative/descriptive divide first. Descriptive statements simply state what the world is like; normative statements describe what the world *ought* to be like. Descriptive statements use terms like "is," "are," "will be"; normative statements use terms like "ought," "justifies," "good," "bad." Scientists use descriptive terms; philosophers, ethicists, and judges use normative terms. Subjectivists hold that when it comes to beliefs, there is only a place for descriptive talk (except for probabilism and conditionalization). We can describe what someone believes, but it doesn't make sense to talk about whether they *ought* to believe it given their evidence. By contrast, inductivists hold that there is a fact of the matter about what someone *ought* to believe given their evidence. Specifically, they ought to have credences that match the inductive probabilities.

The trick to getting your head around inductive probabilities is to start with deductive arguments:

> Deductive argument = An argument in which it is not possible that the premises are true and the conclusion false. In other words, the premises *entail* the conclusion.

Consider the following *deductive* argument:

P1. Socrates is human

P2. All humans are mortal

C. Socrates is mortal

Notice four features:

D.i) P1 and P2 entail C

D.ii) If someone believes P1 and P2 then they should believe C[1]

D.iii) ii is true because of i

D.iv) ii is true for any agent, because D.i expresses an objective relation

Now compare inductive arguments, defined as follows.

> Inductive argument = An argument in which it is possible that the premises are true and the conclusion false, but the premises justify the conclusion to at least some degree.

Consider the following *inductive* argument:[2]

P1. Socrates is human

P3. *Most* humans are mortal

C. Socrates is mortal

The conclusion is not made *certain* by the truth of the premises; the conclusion is made more *probable* than it was before. Nevertheless, the following four features apply:

I.i)   P1 and P3 *justify* C

I.ii)   If someone believes P1 and P3 then they have some reason to believe C

I.iii) ii is true because of i

I.iv)   ii is true for any agent, because i expresses an objective relation

There is a slight change in (i) and (ii). The change between D.i and I.i is that "entails" has changed to "justifies." Think of "justifies" as a weakening of "entails." If P *entails* C, then C must be true if P is; if P *justifies* C, then C is more *probable* given P than given not P. So inductive probabilities express objective relations of justification between propositions.

These objective relations expressed in (i) have consequences for the beliefs expressed in (ii): If P *entails* C, then a believer in P has a conclusive reason to believe C; if P *justifies* C, then a believer in P has *some* reason to believe C (but not a conclusive reason). (iii) and (iv) remain unchanged.

A useful way to talk about inductive probabilties is to talk about the credence that an ideally rational agent would have, which we can abbreviate as P_R. By definition, P_R always matches the inductive probabilities.

We can now define "justifies" in terms of what a rational agent believes, given their background beliefs, B:

Inductive probability-raising theory of justification

"E *justifies* H relative to B" means "$P_R(H|E\&B) > P_R(H\&B)$"

Intuitively, E justifies H if and only if E makes H more (inductively) probable than it was before. This concept of justification will play an important role in the rest of this book.

Justification is very similar to the subjectivist's concept of confirmation from Chapter 1:

Degree-of-belief-raising theory of confirmation

E *confirms* H for S at t" means "$P_{S,t}(H|E) > P_{S,t}(H)$

There are two changes. First, a rational agent, R, has replaced a particular agent, S. This is because the inductivist holds that there are objective relations between propositions—inductive probabilities—that don't vary from one agent to another. Our concept of justification makes essential use of these inductive probabilities. Second, the time has been replaced by background beliefs. The background beliefs always mattered, but subjectivists tend to add them implicitly by specifying the agent and the time of the subject. The background beliefs are whatever the agent happens to believe. Inductivists are dealing with an arbitrary rational agent, so must add the background beliefs explicitly.

But are there really objective relations of justification between propositions? That is, do inductive probabilities really exist? I think the best arguments for the existence of inductive probabilities are cases like the Hy-Brasil example given earlier. It seems the King is being *irrational*, and only the inductivist can give this verdict. Call that the *first* argument for inductive probabilities, and we'll discuss what is basically the same argument in-depth in the next two chapters on the problem of induction.

But consider a subjectivist who replies as follows:

> I maintain that the King of Hy-Brasil is making no error. Perhaps this seems odd, but we should not be unduly concerned by such cases. You and I would not share the beliefs of the King of Hy-Brasil, nor would anyone else I know. So we can set aside such bizarre cases and focus on studying the actual beliefs of actual agents.

In the face of this response, the inductivist can press the point in a slightly different way—they can argue that there is something unacceptably *arbitrary* about those actual beliefs.

5.2 Second argument for inductive probabilities: Arbitrariness

Imagine you are on a jury and have to determine whether the defendant, Smith, is guilty. Prior to hearing any evidence, you do not have any opinion about whether he is guilty. Given the evidence, you have high credence that Smith is guilty. This means that your credences are such that $P(Guilty|E) > P(Guilty)$.

But if you're a subjectivist you think that you could have had different credences without being mistaken in any way, so you could have rationally believed $P(Guilty|E) < P(Guilty)$. And relative to such beliefs, the evidence *dis*confirms Guilty, and you would now believe Smith was innocent. As a subjectivist, you think it perfectly rational to hear the evidence and come to the verdict that Smith is not guilty—the evidence itself doesn't support one verdict or the other.[3]

If so, then surely you cannot reasonably maintain the belief that Smith is guilty. The problem stems from the *arbitrary* nature of the degrees of belief—the fact that the subjectivist offers no reasons for why they should have one value rather than another.

There is something absurd about forming an arbitrary belief. To bring this out, imagine you are given a choice of two pills. One says "guilty" and will cause you to believe Smith is guilty; the other says "not guilty" and will cause you to believe Smith is not guilty. Try to imagine taking the "guilty" pill. The story says that you now believe that Smith is guilty. But assuming you were fully aware of what was going on, you should discount your own belief, as you are aware that you could have easily believed Smith was not guilty. There seems to be something unstable about a belief that is known to be arbitrary.

Yet subjectivists are in the same position. If they believe Smith is guilty, they also believe that they could, without error, have believed he is not guilty, and vice versa. So it seems subjectivists should discount their own beliefs, as they recognize that there is no objective reason that they have their actual beliefs rather than some others. But subjectivists do not discount their beliefs in this way. They maintain their beliefs, even while agreeing that there is no reason why they don't have other beliefs. This looks like an untenable position.

Despite these arguments for inductive probability, they have been unpopular since the late twentieth century. So for the rest of this chapter we'll follow one line of argument against inductive probability. The argument is driven by a skepticism about the source of our knowledge of inductive probabilities (see the table on p. 62).

5.3 First objection to inductive probabilities: Evidence and regress

What could be the source of our knowledge of inductive probabilities? The source of most of our knowledge is our evidence. But this cannot give us knowledge of inductive probabilities, for we need prior knowledge of inductive probabilities to know what our evidence supports. Let me explain.

Take a statement of inductive probability:

E justifies H.

How could we know this? One suggestion is that we know it because it is justified by our other evidence "E*." This amounts to:

"E*" justifies "E justifies H."

But this is itself an expression of inductive probability. How are we to know it? We would need further evidence. We are launched on a regress. And it is a vicious regress that will never allow evidence to confirm a statement of inductive probability. As inductive probabilities tell us which evidence supports which hypotheses, we need prior knowledge of inductive probabilities in order for any hypothesis to be supported by any evidence. Bottom line: Our knowledge of the values of inductive probabilities cannot be based on evidence.

Inductivist Response to the Evidence and Regress Objection: The A Priori and the Good Company Defense

So what other source of knowledge of inductive probabilities could there be? Call knowledge that need not be based on evidence *a priori* knowledge:

A Priori knowledge = Knowledge that need not be based on evidence.

The question of how we might have such knowledge will be central to the next chapter (6.5), but for now the inductivist can side-step it by pointing out that we must have *a priori* knowledge somehow—for our knowledge of *deductive* logic must be *a priori*. How do we know that ["Socrates is human" and "All humans are mortal" entails "Socrates is mortal"]? How do we know that the propositions expressed bear the relation of entailment? It cannot be due to evidence, for we would face the same regress we just saw above: to know that a piece of evidence supports the claim that one proposition entails another, we'd have to know that such evidence bears the relation of support (justification or entailment) to the proposition that one proposition entails another.

Yet we surely know deductive logic somehow. And recall that inductive probabilities are a weakening of deductive entailments. So perhaps the inductivist can answer: *we know of inductive probabilities the same way we know of deductive entailments*. This can be thought of as a "Good Company" defense. The idea is that the inductivist has no problems that are worse than everyone else's—and everyone (we can assume) accepts deductive logic—so there is no reason to reject inductive probabilities.

But this response requires that there are no relevant differences between inductive and deductive arguments. And it is on this point that the criticism of inductive probabilities continues.

5.4 Second objection to inductive probabilities: Disagreement about values

Everyone agrees on which deductive arguments are good, but there is not the same level of agreement about which inductive arguments are good. Here's Frank Ramsey:

> But let us now return to a more fundamental criticism of Mr. Keynes' [inductivist] views, which is the obvious one that there really do not seem to be any such things as the probability relations he describes. He supposes

that, at any rate in certain cases, they can be perceived; but speaking for myself I feel confident that this is not true. I do not perceive them, and if I am to be persuaded that they exist it must be by argument; moreover, I shrewdly suspect that others do not perceive them either, because they are able to come to so very little agreement as to which of them relates any two given propositions. (1926, p. 27)

We can put Ramsey's argument as follows (it is an instance of denying the consequent):

P1. People are able to come to very little agreement about the values of inductive probabilities.

P2. If inductive probabilities existed, people would be able to come to agreement about their values.

C. Inductive probabilities do not exist.

Why think P1 is true? Ramsey offers the following argument:

If . . . we take the simplest possible pairs of propositions such as "This is red" and "That is blue" or "This is red" and "That is red," whose . . . [inductive] relations should surely be easiest to see, no one, I think, pretends to be sure what is the probability relation which connects them. (p. 28)

Inductivist response to the disagreement about values objection

Maher (2006) denies P1 and argues that people are able to come to agreement about inductive probabilities. Starting with Ramsey's example, Maher points out that as nobody is sure about the numerical values, this is a case of *agreement*—everyone agrees that there are no clear inductive probabilities in this case. What the example really shows is that inductive probabilities can be imprecise, but this is no objection to their existence.

Maher also denies that this is a case where the inductive relations are easiest to see, and gives the following example instead:

Inductive argument
(P3) A ball is either black or white
With probability 1/2, (C1) the ball is white

Maher argues that practically everyone accepts this argument, and therefore people can come to agreement about inductive probabilities, so P1 is false.

One might also deny P2. If there is disagreement about inductive probabilities, it may be because some people are mistaken. The discussion here will depend on the source of *a priori* knowledge, which we leave for the next chapter.

Nevertheless, to make a convincing case for inductive probabilities it would be helpful if there were a systematic approach whereby agreement about inductive probabilities could be reached. The third objection is that such approaches have failed.

·5.5 Third objection to inductive probabilities: Failure of principles of indifference

To understand this objection, we first need to introduce Principles of Indifference and argue that inductivists need them. Then the objection to inductivism is that Principles of Indifference cannot be justified.

Principles of Indifference

Recall Maher's example:

(P1) A ball is either black or white

With probability 1/2, (C1) the ball is white

Where did this probability of 1/2 come from? The natural answer is that there are two possibilities, and no reason to favor one over the other, so each possibility gets the same probability: 1/2. Let's generalize this rule as follows:

Principle of Indifference If there is no reason to assign one of the *n* possibilities a higher probability than any of the other possibilities, then each possibility should be assigned a probability equal to $1/n$.

This is the most plausible candidate for a systematic approach, and there are plenty of cases where it gives the correct verdict. To what degree should you believe that a coin will land Heads, when it is not specified whether the coin is fair or biased? 1/2. To what degree should you believe a 6 will be rolled on a die when it is not specified whether it is fair or biased? 1/6.

A related argument for the Principle of Indifference is that any answer that rejects the Principle of Indifference is *arbitrary*. For example, suppose someone believed to degree 1/5 that a 6 would be rolled on a fair die. The natural response would be to ask why they favor 6? Why think a 6 is more likely than, say, a 1? It seems that no answer to this question could be given. So it looks like they just *arbitrarily* favor 6 rather than 1, and are irrational for doing so.

Early writers on probability (e.g. Bernoulli, Laplace, Leibniz) assumed that the Principle of Indifference must be true (Leibniz called it the Principle of Sufficient Reason). And in the twentieth century there was an ambitious project, led by Carnap (1950, 1971), to construct a general system of inductive probabilities based on the Principle of Indifference. But that project is widely regarded to have failed, due to the following problems for the Principle of Indifference.

Objections to the Principle of Indifference

Just as there are examples favoring the Principle of Indifference, there are counterexamples that seem to refute it. The root of these counterexamples is that there is more than one way to divide up the possibilities. We assumed in the earlier examples that the possibilities are divided up in a particular way, for example, the possibilities which all get equal probability for the die are

[1, 2, 3, 4, 5, 6].

But there are other ways of dividing up the same possibilities, for example:

[6, not 6].

If we assign equal probabilities to these possibilities, then each will get a probability of 1/2. So

P(6) = P(not 6) = 1/2.

And this way of dividing possibilities is incompatible with the first way; the latter says that P(6) = 1/2 whereas the former said P(6) = 1/6. Contradiction.

What's needed to remove the contradictions is a *privileged* way of dividing possibilities. In this example, it looks like there is a privileged way. Surely the correct way is to assign 1/6 to each number. But there are other examples where there does not seem to be a privileged way of dividing possibilities.

The problems are most acute in cases where the possible values are *continuous* rather than *discrete*. A discrete variable can take only particular values; the number a die shows is a discrete variable, as it can only show numbers 1 to 6. A continuous variable can take any value between a maximum and a minimum; lengths, heights, ages, and weights are usually continuous variables. We defined the Principle of Indifference above to be applicable only to discrete variables, as the principle makes reference to *n* possibilities. But for many purposes we need a version of the Principle of Indifference that's applicable to continuous variables, and here we run into problems. We'll look at one famous example.

Suppose a factory produces squares with edge length of between 1 and 2 cm. It therefore produces squares with area between 1 and 4 cm².

Question-length: What is the probability that a square has length less than 1.5 cm given that it was produced by that factory?

If we apply the Principle of Indifference to the *length*, the answer is 1/2, as 1.5 cm is the half-way point between 1 and 2 cm. Now let's ask the *same* question in different words:

Question-area: What is the probability that a square has *area* smaller than 2.25 cm² given that it was produced by that factory?

It's the same question because a square with length less than 1.5 cm has area less than 2.25 cm². So it should have the same answer of 1/2.
But:
If we apply the Principle of Indifference to the *area* then there will be a 50 percent probability that the square has area less than 2.5 cm², because the half-way point between 1 and 4 cm² is 2.5 cm². So the probability that the square has area less than 2.25 cm² is less than 1/2. And this contradicts the answer we got when applying the Principle of Indifference to the length. So we get contradictory answers depending on whether we apply the Principle of Indifference to the length or the area.[4]

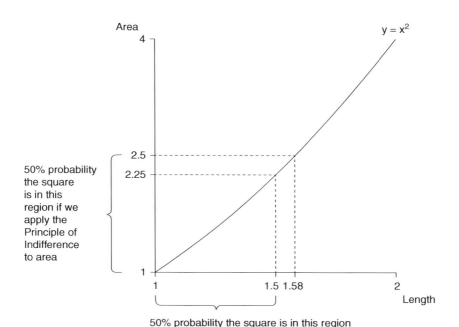

50% probability the square is in this region
if we apply the Principle of Indifference to length

There are lots of similar cases. The problem arises whenever there are two or more continuous variables that are not directly proportional to each other and no privileged way to divide up the possibilities.

Inductivist responses

The defender of inductive probabilities can respond that they do not require the formulation of Principles of Indifference, and for a couple of reasons. First, they can argue that Principles of Indifference exist, even if we haven't yet figured out what they are. As Maher puts it:

> Of course, once we have acquired the concept of inductive probability, we can then attempt to form general hypotheses about it, but the failure to find a correct general hypothesis of a certain kind cannot show that the things we are hypothesizing about do not exist. For example, failure to formulate a correct general theory of English grammar is no reason to doubt that some sentences are grammatical and some are not. Thus the difficulties with the Principle of Indifference are not a reason to doubt the existence of inductive probabilities. (2006, p. 199)

A second inductivist response allows that a range of credences are permissible; perhaps, it is reasonable to apply the Principle of Indifference to *either* length or area in the earlier example. This falls short of the subjectivist position that anything goes. We assumed earlier that either (a) your beliefs are totally constrained, so there is only one reasonable credence function you can have or (b) anything goes. But why shouldn't rationality constraints allow a little leeway? (This was actually Carnap's view; see his (1980, p. 119).)

Reply and re-cap

But even if there is no reason here to reject the existence of inductive probabilities, the difficulties with the Principle of Indifference remove a *possible defense* of inductive probabilities. Recall the subjectivist initially objected that there is no plausible source of knowledge of inductive probabilities. The inductivist responded that the source is the same as the source of our knowledge of deductive entailments, whatever that is. The subjectivist complained that we agree about deductive entailments, but disagree about inductive probabilities. In response, inductivists tried to find Principles of Indifference that would be applied only to privileged properties, and thereby command agreement. But there has been no agreement on what these privileged properties are.

Summary

This chapter introduced the concept of inductive probabilities—degrees of belief that agents ought to have. Inductive probabilities can be thought of as objective relations between propositions. These relations are relations of support, analogous to, but weaker than deductive relations. Such relations would vindicate the thought that it is irrational to hold beliefs that do not fit the evidence, and remove the arbitrariness that otherwise infects degrees of belief. The main objection is the problem of how we might have access to these relations; we cannot have access to them using evidence, as this would be circular. One reply is that we have access to them the same way we have access to deductive logic, which is presumably *a priori*. The objection is pressed that we agree about substantive principles of deductive logic, but do not agree about analogous principles of indifference, leading us to doubt the existence of substantive principles, and the usefulness of any that might exist.

But I think the best arguments for inductive probabilities are still ahead of us—inductive probabilities would solve one of the central problems of philosophy, the problem of induction.

Study questions

1   What are inductive probabilities? What is their connection to rational belief?

2   What do you think are the best arguments for and against inductive probabilities?

3   Explain the three arguments against inductive probabilities and how they are connected.

4   What is the relation between inductive probabilities and deductive entailments?

Advanced questions

5   Are arguments that we have *a priori* access to inductive probabilities any worse than arguments that we have *a priori* access to deductive probabilities?

6   Is Maher right that the "difficulties with the Principle of Indifference are not a reason to doubt the existence of inductive probabilities"?

7   Under what conditions should you believe C, given you believe that E and that E entails C? (see Harman 2008; Steinberger ms)

Further reading

The debate between subjectivists and objectivists can be traced to a debate between two of the greatest minds of the twentieth century, John Maynard Keynes and Frank Ramsey, and the best place to start remains Keynes (1921, chapter 1) and Ramsey (1926). Close behind is Carnap (1950, chapter 2). For more recent overviews, see Howson and Urbach (1996, chapter 15) for subjectivism and Maher (2006) for inductivism.

6

The problem of induction

The Securities and Exchange Commission gives a warning to anyone investing in the stock market: "Past performance is not an indication of future returns." This is a surprisingly strong claim—is past performance really no indication *at all* of future returns? Shouldn't it be some kind of indicator, albeit a fallible one? According to David Hume, the SEC is exactly right—the past is no guide at all to the future. For Hume, this wasn't a lesson limited to the stock market; the lesson is a general one, and threatens our reasons to believe anything we don't directly perceive.

I'll first explain the basic argument (6.1), then extend the problem to show its full skeptical implications (6.2). Then we'll consider proposed solutions based on our evidence (6.3 and 6.4) and those not based on evidence (6.5). Finally, we'll consider what can be said if the problem of induction cannot be solved (6.6).

6.1 Beliefs about the future

Let's start with a belief that only a philosopher would doubt. Do you believe the sun will rise tomorrow? I'm going to assume you do. But is this belief justified? Suppose you met someone who had the same evidence as you, but didn't believe the sun was going to rise tomorrow. Call her a *skeptic*. Common sense says that the skeptic is mistaken; common sense says that given our evidence, we ought to expect that the sun will rise tomorrow; common sense says that the belief that the sun will rise is justified. But what justifies it? The *problem of induction* is the problem of justifying such beliefs. More generally, the problem of induction is the problem of *justifying any belief that is not guaranteed to be true by our evidence*. The force of the problem is best understood by seeing how obvious answers fail.

One obvious answer is that our belief that the sun will rise tomorrow is justified by the belief that it has risen in the past. Written out as an argument, we have:

Premise: The sun rose yesterday

justifies

Conclusion: The sun will rise tomorrow

But why does the belief that the sun rose yesterday justify the belief that it will rise tomorrow? The natural answer is that the inference is justified by a belief in the laws of nature. For example, the laws of classical mechanics say that a rotating body will continue to rotate unless acted upon by an outside force. (We'll leave implicit the other assumptions needed.) Adding this as a premise, we have a good argument:

Premise: The sun rose yesterday

Premise: (Classical mechanics) A rotating body will continue to rotate unless acted upon by an outside force

justifies

Conclusion: The sun will rise tomorrow

But this belief in classical mechanics faces the same challenge—it held yesterday, but why should you believe it will hold tomorrow? We now want a justification for the following inference:

Premise: The laws of classical mechanics held yesterday

justifies

Conclusion: The laws of classical mechanics will hold tomorrow

This argument has the same structure as the original argument that the sun will rise tomorrow. It is an inference from something happening yesterday to the same thing happening tomorrow. So the appeal to laws of nature hasn't helped.

What we need in both cases is a *Principle of Uniformity*:

Principle of Uniformity: The future will resemble the past[1]

But why should we believe that the future will resemble the past? There is a natural but hopeless answer:

We should believe the future will resemble the past because it always has before. Think back to 2012. The post-2012 world resembled the pre-2012 world. So on that occasion the future resembled the past. And think back to 2011. The post-2011 world resembled the pre-2011 world. So also on that occasion the future resembled the past. So we should infer that in the future, the future will resemble the past.

Put succinctly, we have the following hopeless argument for the Principle of Uniformity:

1 In the past, the future resembled the past

2 *Principle of Uniformity*: The future will resemble the past
justifies

Conclusion: In the future, the future will resemble the past (Principle of Uniformity[2]).

Clearly this argument fails because it assumes what it is supposed to show, namely, the Principle of Uniformity. The Principle of Uniformity appears as a premise, so the argument is circular. So the original inference, from "the sun rose yesterday" to "the sun will rise tomorrow," is left unjustified. The problem of induction remains. The problem is simple, but easy to misunderstand, so here are some clarifications about skepticism (that also apply in Chapters 12 and 13).

Clarifications: (i) We're not trying to *fully* justify a belief, or find conclusive reasons to believe. We're not being that ambitious. The question is whether we have *any reason at all* to have any beliefs about the future, that is, whether there is justification to any degree at all. This is what I will mean when I talk about having justification.

(ii) We can grant that the belief that the sun rose yesterday *causes* the belief that the sun will rise tomorrow. We are not concerned with the cause of beliefs; we are concerned with their justification. It's not whether someone has a belief, but whether they ought to.

(iii) It is tempting to reply to a skeptic: "You claim to *know* that we have no knowledge. So you contradict yourself." But a skeptic need not claim this. A skeptic can reply: "I do not claim to *know* we don't know anything. I *assert* we don't know anything, I *believe* we don't know anything, I *justifiably believe* we don't know anything. (Perhaps you think I should only assert what I know; obviously I disagree.)"

(iv) But even the skeptic just quoted says more than she needs to. One could challenge that skeptic to justify her belief that the sun will not rise tomorrow. But the skeptic need not believe that the sun will not rise tomorrow. She merely claims we don't *know* it will. In fact, the skeptic need not be understood as making any kind of positive suggestion. She is merely challenging us. She is our own unquiet conscience.

(v) How does this map onto the subjectivist vs. inductivist debate of Chapter 4? The skeptic is a subjectivist; the defender of induction an inductivist. Recall the subjectivist says that there are no rationality constraints on belief (other than probabilism and conditionalization). So the subjectivist says that if someone takes the sun rising yesterday to confirm that the sun will rise tomorrow, that is up to her; she is equally entitled to take the sun rising yesterday to confirm that tomorrow it will put its feet up and have a day off. The subjectivist rejects the concept of justification as an objective relation between beliefs.

The inductivist holds that there is a fact of the matter about what an agent *should* believe given her evidence; there are objective justificatory relations between beliefs—inductive probabilities. The nonskeptic is an inductivist, arguing that such justification relations exist. This is common sense, and the question is whether it stands up to scrutiny.

Main points

Deduction: The process of inferring from premises to a conclusion entailed by those premises.

Induction: The process of inferring from premises to a conclusion not entailed by those premises.

The Problem of Induction: The problem of justifying induction.

6.2 Extending the problem

Our examples were about what we should believe about the future. But the problem of induction applies to any nondeductive inference. That is, the problem of induction applies to any argument where the truth of the premises do not guarantee the truth of the conclusion. A few more examples will bring out the importance of the problem. First, we can extend the argument from beliefs about the future to beliefs about the past: why do you believe that the law of gravity held in the distant past?

It is tempting to think that the past had to be a particular way in order to get to where we are now. But it didn't. The world could have popped into existence 5 minutes ago, with all the memories and dinosaur fossils included. Why do you think this didn't happen?

It is tempting to answer that you *remember* 10 minutes ago, so the world must be more than 5 minutes old. Well you *think* you remember 10 minutes ago. But those "memories" consist of structures in your brain which could have been made 5 minutes ago. Why do you think this didn't happen?

Furthermore, we can extend the argument from beliefs about other times to beliefs about other places. For example, the law of gravity holds around here. Why should we believe that it holds in remote parts of the universe?

We would need to assume that far away regions of space resemble nearby regions of space. Why should we believe this?

There is an underlying pattern in these worries. We want to make an inference from what we *are observing* to what we *are not observing*. What we are observing is described in our evidence. The problem is whether the evidence justifies claims not described in our evidence. Put in this way, we can see that the problem extends to sampling inferences, and these will play an important role in the next chapter. Here's a quick preview.

Suppose you have a sample of objects of some type F, of which a certain proportion have some property, say, being green. It is natural to take this as evidence that the whole population of Fs has the same proportion of green objects.

1. x% of observed Fs are green

justifies

Conclusion: x% of unobserved Fs are green

But why should we believe that the proportion of green objects in the sample is probably the same as the proportion of green objects in the rest of population? We would need a Principle of Uniformity taking us from the sample to the rest of the population (where G = green):

1. x% of observed Fs are green

2. *Principle of Uniformity-Sampling*: Samples resemble the rest of the population

justifies

Conclusion: x% of unobserved Fs are green

But once again, this principle of uniformity is in need of justification.

And things get even worse (here we preview Chapter 12). Consider that we directly experience only our sensations, and use them to infer the existence of objects. Then our belief in such objects is based on an inference from what is experienced to what is unexperienced:

1. I am having a red experience

justifies

Conclusion: There is a red object in front of me

To defend this inference, we need something like:

1. I am having a red experience

2. *Principle of Accuracy*: Experiences resemble reality[3]

justifies

Conclusion: There is a red object in front of me

And it is unclear how the Principle of Accuracy can be justified. Without it, it seems we can have no justification to believe any hypothesis that goes beyond our immediate experience. So you may have justification to believe you are having a white experience, or are feeling cold, but that is as far as it goes. The King of Hy-Brasil was justified in believing that his ankles were wet and cold, but not that his island was sinking. You have no justification to believe that you are not the only agent in the world, or hallucinating, or that you are a butterfly dreaming that you are a human. As Russell put it:

> It is therefore important to discover whether there is any answer to Hume [i.e. the sceptic] . . . If not, there is no intellectual difference between sanity and insanity. The lunatic who believes that he is a poached egg is to be condemned solely on the ground that he is in a minority. (Russell 1946, p. 646)

What would an answer to Hume look like? What's needed is a justification for the Principles of Uniformity. Answers can be divided into those which offer a justification based on our evidence (6.3 and 6.4), and those which offer a justification that is independent of our evidence (6.5). It might be useful to connect this with Bayes Theorem:

$$P(H|E) = P(H)\frac{P(E|H)}{P(E)}$$

Justifications based on our evidence will focus on $P(E|H)$, and justifications independent of our evidence will focus on $P(H)$.[4]

6.3 Circularity

Could evidence justify our belief that nature is uniform? We saw in 5.3, and in a different way in 6.1, that there is a problem with any argument that starts with our evidence and concludes that nature is uniform. The evidence used would be about the observed; the conclusion that nature is uniform is partly about the unobserved. So such an argument would go from (observed) evidence to a conclusion about the unobserved. So it would need to assume that nature is uniform. And for this reason the argument would fail. We are trying to *show* that what is observed can give us justification about the unobserved. So it is circular to *assume* that what is observed can give us evidence about the unobserved.

Nevertheless, some philosophers have argued that the circularity needed is acceptable. I will sketch an argument associated with Max Black (1954).[5] Recall an argument from earlier:

Premise-Circular Argument

1. In the past, the future resembled the past

2. *Principle of Uniformity*: The future will resemble the past

justifies

Conclusion: In the future, the future will resemble the past (Principle of Uniformity).

Call this type of argument *premise-circular* because the conclusion appears as a premise. Black offers an alternative argument that is not premise-circular. The key is to understand the Principle of Uniformity, not as a premise, but as a rule of inference.

First, we need to introduce the concept of a *rule of inference*. A rule of inference is a rule that tells us when we should make an inference from premises to conclusion. For example, the deductive rule of affirming the antecedent (*modus ponens*) licenses the following inference:

1. A

2. A → B

Conclusion: B

We might express the rule itself as:

Affirming the antecedent Infer from "A" and "A → B" to "B"

Notice that the rule itself is not a premise of the argument. Instead, it licenses the inference from premises to conclusion.

Now consider the following inductive rule of inference, which we'll call R:

R Infer from "in the past, X" to "in the future, X" (where X is a type of event)

This is the Principle of Uniformity reformulated as a rule of inference. It is sufficient to justify the kind of inferences we want, for example, where X = Sunrise:

Premise: In the past, the sun has risen

justifies

Conclusion: In the future, the sun will rise

The obvious worry is whether we are justified in using R. At this point, Black argues that R can be justified by using R:

> *Rule-Circular Argument*
>
> Premise: In the past, R has been successful
>
> justifies
>
> Conclusion: In the future, R will be successful

In case you've forgotten what R is, let's make it explicit:

> *Rule-Circular Argument*
>
> Premise: In the past, inferring from "in the past, X" to "in the future, X" has been successful
>
> justifies
>
> Conclusion: In the future, inferring from "in the past, X" to "in the future, X" will be successful

This argument is rule-circular, that is, the argument uses a rule, R, whose correctness is asserted by the conclusion.[6] (Well not quite. The conclusion only talks about the future. But that's the bit we're interested in. We already know R was successful in the past.) R supports itself. And Black claims that rule-circularity is acceptable.

Objection to rule-circular arguments

But why think rule-circularity is acceptable? Why think that any rule that can be used to support itself is acceptable? No reason has been given. And there are rules which support themselves that do not seem acceptable, for example:

> *Anti-R* Infer from "in the past, *not* X" to "in the future, X"

This licenses the following inference:

> Premise: In the past, Anti-R has *not* been successful
>
> justifies
>
> Conclusion: In the future, Anti-R will be successful

Anti-R supports itself in the same way that R does, so the fact that a rule supports itself does not seem to give us any reason to think it's a good rule.

And we can also give the following parody, introducing a new rule, T:

T Tea-leaf reading is reliable

This licenses the following inference:

Premise: The tea leaves say that tea-leaf reading is reliable.

justifies

Conclusion: *T* Tea-leaf reading is reliable.

In both cases, the crazy rule allows the inference from the premise to the conclusion, and the conclusion says that the rule is a good one. These parodies arise because Black's reasoning seems to allow us to infer that a rule is reliable just by using it, without antecedent justification for it. The same problem comes up for foundationalism in Chapter 12 where it is called "bootstrapping," and where we'll look at it more carefully.

This section argued that understanding the Principle of Uniformity as a rule of inference rather than a premise doesn't by itself justify the Principle's use. Still, the defender of induction might well argue that one *part* of a defense of induction it to insist that the Principle of Uniformity is only used as a rule of inference, not as a premise. I will remain neutral on this issue from now on. So although I will sometimes state the Principle of Uniformity in a way that makes it look like a premise, feel free to understand it as a rule of inference. I'll express the Principle in whichever way is clearer at the time, and will freely go back and forth between rules and premises.

6.4 Sampling

Let's now consider David Stove's (1986) attempt to justify induction. His argument has been somewhat neglected, but is interesting for testing our understanding of the problem, and provides a useful connection with the next chapter.

Recall that one version of the problem of induction is that we can't make an inference from a sample to the population; we would need, and don't have, justification to believe:

Principle of Uniformity-Sampling: Samples resemble the rest of the population.

But Stove offers a statistical argument that a population probably resembles a random sample taken from it. If correct, we can rationally infer from a sample to the population, which would solve the problem of induction.

Here is what I take to be the essence of Stove's argument. Suppose there is a population of two emeralds that are either green or white, generating three hypotheses:

Green = Both emeralds are green

Mixed = One emerald sampled is green and the other is white

White = Both emeralds are white

Now we need the concept of a random sample:

Random sample = A sample such that each member of the population has an equal probability of being in it.

Now suppose the evidence is that a green emerald has been sampled at random:

E = One emerald has been sampled at random and is green

These conditional beliefs follow:

$P(E|Green) = 1$

$P(E|Mixed) = 1/2$

$P(E|White) = 0$

And, crucially,

$P(E|Green) = 1 > P(E)$

Applying the probability raising theory of justification, which says that E justifies H if and only if $P(E|H) > P(E)$, E justifies Green. Therefore, the evidence justifies the hypothesis that all emeralds are green. And this solves the problem of induction.

Objections to Stove

There are two ways to object to Stove's argument—one might deny that our sample is random, and one might deny that the desired conclusion follows even if it is.

First, Stove's argument assumes that our sample is selected at random. But why should we think that our samples are selected at random? Why should we think that each member of the population has an equal probability of being in it? This assumption would require a Principle of Indifference (5.5), which would itself be in need of justification.[7] (This is yet another appearance of the argument at the beginning of 6.3.)

But let's grant that our samples are randomly selected. Now *some* inductive inferences are justified, but we have to take care about exactly which ones.[8] The evidence justifies that *all* emeralds are green, but still does not justify the hypothesis that the *next* emerald is green. We can see this by being more specific about the hypotheses. If we take into account the order in which the emeralds are observed, there are not three hypotheses, but four:

GG = Both emeralds are green

GW = The first emerald sampled is green and the other is white

WG = The first emerald sampled is white and the other is green

WW = Both emeralds are white

$P(E|GG) = 1$

$P(E|GW) = 1$

$P(E|WG) = 0$

$P(E|WW) = 0$

E justifies that the *next* emerald is green if and only if $P(E|GG \text{ or } WG) > P(E)$. But we've been given no reason to think this inequality holds. Indeed the evidence refutes WG, and it justifies GW just as strongly as it justifies GG, as $P(E|GG) = P(E|GW) = 1$, and GW says that the next emerald is white!

This can be seen with a picture. The probability that the next emerald is green is represented by the size of the top left and bottom right boxes, GG and WG. E eliminates the bottom row. GG and GW both increase in probability, and remain in the same proportions. Intuitively, why shouldn't we think that the observed emeralds are one color (green) and the unobserved emeralds another (white)?

Venn diagram of green and white emeralds.

Stove might reply that in the long run, a random sample of green emeralds is more likely to come from a population of green emeralds than non-green emeralds. This is true but irrelevant. It isn't relevant to appeal to the long run because at any given time we only have a finite number of observed emeralds in our sample. However many green emeralds are in our sample, we are interested in whether the unobserved emeralds are green. And the following hypotheses will be equally supported by the evidence:

(a) There are many green emeralds in my sample, and the rest are green.

(b) There are many green emeralds in my sample, and the rest are white.

So we may have reason to believe:

Principle of Uniformity-Sampling: Samples resemble the (whole) population.

But this falls short of what we need:

Principle of Uniformity-Sampling: Samples resemble the rest of the population.

The moral is that even if we assume we have random selection, and fix the values of $P(E|H)$, this isn't enough to justify reasonable beliefs about the unobserved—they also depend on the initial value of $P(H)$.

6.5 Semantic justification

An argument that $P(H)$ should have a particular initial value would require an *a priori* argument, that is, an argument that is independent of any evidence. Specifically, we need a reasonably high *a priori* probability that the future will resemble the past. Could there be an *a priori* argument that nature is uniform? (Here we return to the question we set aside in 5.3.)

There are two main candidate sources of *a priori* justification. The first is that we have some faculty that allows us to "see" (metaphorically) that some sentences are probably true. This view is associated with Immanuel Kant, who argued that we have intuitions that allow us *a priori* justification of various areas, notably mathematics and geometry. For example, Kant (1786/2004) argued that we have *a priori* justification to believe Newton's theories.[9] This is a remarkable claim—it says that we can acquire justification for beliefs about the world just by reflection, with no need for observation. Thus, it denies *empiricism*, which says that experience is the only source of justification (about the relevant subject).

Kant's theory was challenged by Einstein's theory of relativity, which showed that Newton's theories are false. Far from it being possible to deduce

Newton's theories *a priori*, they turned out to be not even true, and faculties of intuition have never really recovered from this blow.[10]

The second source of *a priori* justification is that some sentences can be justified in virtue of understanding the meanings of the words they contain. Call these sentences *analytic*.

Analytic sentence = A sentence which can be justified in virtue of understanding the meanings of the words it contains.

We now look at Peter Strawson's (1952) application of this second source to the problem of induction.

6.5.1 Semantic solution

Let's first consider some examples of sentences that can be justified in virtue of understanding the meanings of the words they contain. The easiest cases are when we invent words that are defined in terms of other words. Suppose my nephew invents a new word, "yego," which means "yellow piece of lego." Then it is *a priori* that if something is yego then it is yellow. And there are plenty of terms in English that function in a similar way. For example, "vixen" means "female fox," so it is *a priori* that if something is a vixen then it is a fox. And it is plausible that understanding meanings is sufficient for justifying belief even in cases of non-made-up words, for example, if something is red, then it is colored.

Now let's apply this to induction. The idea is that the Principle of Uniformity can be justified *a priori*, in virtue of its meaning. An example might be: "if someone believes the sun rose yesterday then they have justification to believe it will rise tomorrow." Could that sentence be analytic?

Strawson (1952, pp. 256–7) argues that it is. Strawson thought that part of the meaning of "the sun rose yesterday" is "there is justification to believe that the sun will rise tomorrow." Think about this strange claim before reading on. As it stands it doesn't look very plausible, but Strawson gives an ingenious argument.

He first claims that it is analytic that if you have observed instances of the sun rising, then you have evidence that the sun will rise tomorrow. He then claims that it is analytic that if you have evidence that the sun will rise tomorrow, you have justification to believe the sun will rise tomorrow. Thus the argument runs:

1   S has observed instances of the sun rising

2   S has evidence that the sun will rise tomorrow

3   Therefore S has justification to believe that the sun will rise tomorrow.

Each step is supposed to follow analytically from the last. Schematically, where X is a type of event, the argument has the form:

1   S has observed instances of X

2   S has evidence that X will occur in the future

3   Therefore S has justification to believe X will occur in the future.

We can put the argument in terms of which inferences are licensed. For example, the meaning of "vixen" licenses the inference:

"Foxy is a vixen" → "Foxy is a female fox"

Similarly, Strawson is arguing that the meaning of "evidence" licenses both of the following inferences:

"Past instances of X" → "Evidence for future X" → "Justification to believe in future X"

If Strawson is right, we have *a priori* justification for the inductive principles we need to solve the problem of induction.

6.5.2 First objection to the semantic solution: Implausibility

The first objection returns to the initial implausibility of the position. Surely "the sun rose yesterday" is only about what the sun did yesterday. But according to Strawson, it is also partly about what the sun will do tomorrow! Strawson's theory says that part of the *meaning* of "the sun rose yesterday" is that the sun will probably rise tomorrow. So according to Strawson, words have meanings we didn't expect. And one might object that our words simply do not mean what Strawson's theory says they mean.

6.5.3 Second objection to the semantic solution: Ambiguity

BonJour (1998, p. 198) argues that 1–3 are ambiguous. There is one sense of "evidence for future X" which means "there are past instances of X" and another which means "there is justification to believe in future X." The inference from 1 to 2 is correct given the first meaning; the inference from 2 to 3 is correct given the second meaning; but the inference from 1 to 3 is fallacious.

6.5.4 Carnapian rejoinder

But neither of those objections really settles the matter. Even if the objectors are right about the actual meaning of "evidence," we could easily have spoken a slightly different language containing a word that has the meaning Strawson suggests. So why wait for natural language to supply us with such a word? We can just use the word "evidence" to express Strawson's meaning, that is, to allow the inference:

"Past instances of X" → "Evidence for future X" → "Justification to believe in future X"

After all, we are free to use language however we like—it is our tool, not our master. And it seems that if we use the word "evidence" in this way, we have *a priori* justification for induction.

6.5.5 Third objection to the semantic solution: Defective concepts

This rejoinder is problematic. For we have an independent grip on the concepts of *evidence about the past* and on *justification about the future*, and we need an argument that they can be connected in the way Strawson suggests. An example will bring out the problem.

Dummett (1981) points out that someone might use "boche" in such a way that "if S is German then S is boche" and "if S is boche then S is cruel" are both analytic. This seems to allow them to infer, on meeting George the German, that George is cruel:

"George is German" → "George is Boche" → "George is cruel"

But this would be a mistake. Instead, we should look at the world, notice that not all Germans are cruel, and reject "boche" as a *defective* concept. It is defective because it licenses inferences from true sentences to false ones. Similarly, Strawson's concept expressed by "evidence" plays an analogous role to that expressed by "boche":

"Past instances of X" → "Evidence for future X" → "Justification to believe in future X"

"Evidence" may be defective for the same reason as "boche." Certainly we have no *a priori* reason to think it is *not* defective, so Strawson has failed to give an *a priori* argument for Principle of Uniformity.

I've focused on Strawson, but similar objections apply to any semantic solution to the problem of induction. Whereas Strawson tried to solve the problem of induction by analyzing *natural* language, Carnap (1950) tried to solve the problem by inventing *artificial* languages (this is why I called the previous section a "Carnapian Rejoinder"). But the same problems apply. Inventing the term "evidence" may be no better than inventing the term "boche"; they both might be defective concepts. *An analysis of language alone cannot tell us anything about what the world is like.*

Let's now consider two influential but less ambitious responses to Hume. Both agree with Hume's skepticism to a large extent, but hold out hope that all is not lost.

6.6 Skeptical responses

6.6.1 Pragmatic vindication of induction

Hans Reichenbach (1949) suggested that we should use induction because if anything works, induction works. The possibilities can be laid out as follows. Our options are down the left and the possible states of the world are along the top. The four possibilities show whether predictions we make will be successful, that is, true.

	Nature is uniform	Nature is not uniform
Use induction	Success	Failure
Don't use induction, e.g. use crystal ball	Success or failure	Failure

If nature is not uniform then nature is random and unpredictable, so any method we use for prediction will fail. We only have a chance of success if nature is uniform. And if nature is uniform then we will make successful predictions by using induction. Admittedly we might also make successful predictions by using other methods for predicting the future, such as crystal-ball gazing. But if so, some inductive inferences will be correct—specifically the inductive inference from the success of crystal-ball gazing in the past to the success of crystal-ball gazing in the future.

Reichenbach (1949) offers the following analogy:

A blind man who has lost his way in the mountains feels a trail with his stick. He does not know where the path will lead him, or whether it may take him so close to the edge of a precipice that he will be plunged into the abyss. Yet he follows the path, groping his way step by step; for if there is any possibility of getting out of the wilderness, it is by feeling his way along the path. As blind men we face the future; but we feel a path. And we know: if we can find a way through the future it is by feeling our way along this path. (p. 482)

Objection to the pragmatic vindication of induction

Suppose I offer to give you £100 if you believe the moon is made of cheese. Do you have justification to believe the moon is made of cheese? There is a sense in which you do—you will be paid and you like being paid. We can say that you have a *pragmatic* (usefulness) justification to believe that the moon is made of cheese. But you don't have justification to think the belief is *true*—you don't have an *epistemic* reason (compare the opening of Chapter 3). If you're only interested in the *truth* of the statement that the moon is made of cheese, then my offer of payment is irrelevant.

The same applies to the pragmatic vindication of induction. You have been given a type of justification to believe that the future will resemble the past—it is the best strategy for acquiring true beliefs about the future. But that doesn't mean it is a good strategy, just the best of a bad bunch. And Reichenbach has not provided any justification to believe that this strategy will generate true rather than false beliefs.

BonJour (1998) responds to Reichenbach's analogy as follows:

We can all agree that the blind man should follow the path and that he is, in an appropriate sense, acting in a justified or rational manner in doing so. But is there any plausibility at all to the suggestion that when we reason inductively, or accept the myriad scientific and commonsensical results that ultimately depend on such inference, we have no more justification for thinking that our beliefs are likely to be true than the blind man has for thinking that he has found the way out of the wilderness? (pp. 195–6)

6.6.2 Popper's falsificationism

Karl Popper (1959b) accepted Hume's skeptical conclusion—evidence never justifies hypotheses. But Popper claimed this wasn't a problem as scientists don't try to justify theories! Popper thought that although we can't have induction, we shouldn't worry because we never needed it anyway.

If scientists can't justify theories, what should they do? According to Popper, they should try to *falsify* theories. Scientists are best off trying to falsify theories, rather than establish them, due to the following asymmetry between establishing a law and falsifying it. Establishing a law, such as "All objects attract," requires observing *every* object in the universe and checking that it attracts. Falsifying a law only requires a *single* counterexample—one object that doesn't attract. So scientists should devise experiments that try to falsify promising theories. When a theory has survived such an experiment, Popper says it has been *corroborated*. But being corroborated doesn't mean we have justification to believe the theory is true; it just means it has survived an attempt to falsify it. (Be careful not to attach mysterious properties to the name and then wonder what the mysterious properties are. "Corroborated" just means "has survived possible refutation." It's an abbreviation, as is all technical terminology.) So the practice of science requires only deductive logic; inductive logic must be rejected, and is not needed anyway.

Let's work through the example we used in the discussion of Stove. Suppose there are four hypotheses, and a random sample of 1:

GG = Both emeralds are green

GW = The first emerald sampled is green and the other is white

WG = The first emerald sampled is white and the other is green

WW = Both emeralds are white

E = 1 emerald has been sampled at random and is green

$P(E|GG) = 1$
$P(E|GW) = 1$
$P(E|WG) = 0$
$P(E|WW) = 0$

WG and WW are falsified—they can be eliminated by deductive logic alone. GG and GW survive falsification and so are corroborated. For Popper, that's as much as can be said—the evidence does not give us any justification to believe GG or GW.

Objections to Popper

The first thing to say is that Popper accepts Hume's skeptical conclusion that we have no justification to believe the sun will rise tomorrow.

And Popper's positive attempt to describe how science could function without induction can be criticized. For deductive logic alone is never enough to refute theories. In the face of an observation that seems to refute a theory, we can always keep the theory and give up something else instead. For example, we might give up the assumption that our equipment is working properly.

This may allow us to keep our main hypothesis, even in the face of seemingly incompatible evidence. (This is called the *Duhem-Quine* problem.)

However, there is a surprising similarity between Popper's views and the inductivists (surprising because they are traditionally cast as mortal enemies, not least by Popper himself). According to inductivists, the only way to update your beliefs is by conditionalization (Chapter 4). And we saw that what happens when we conditionalize is that we eliminate hypotheses. "Elimination" means the same as "falsification." The only disagreement between Popper and inductivists is over the starting point—inductivists think that each hypothesis begins with some prior probability, whereas Popper rejects the concept of prior probability as applicable to science. After that disagreement, both agree that science proceeds by the elimination of hypotheses.

Summary

In this chapter, we looked at the problem of induction—why should we have any particular beliefs about the unobserved based on what we've observed? Black's circular argument ran into theoretical problems about where the justification came from, and the practical problem of parodies that seem to support unacceptable inferences. Stove's sampling argument assumed a random selection procedure, and also failed to justify specific plausible hypotheses about the unobserved. The semantic arguments of Strawson and Carnap face the problem that we seem to need antecedent justification to think that their concepts aren't defective. Finally we considered the less ambitious responses of Reichenbach and Popper, but saw that these are far from satisfying. Not for nothing has induction been called the glory of science and the scandal of philosophy. And the next chapter shows that the problem is even more difficult than we have seen so far.

Study questions

1 Explain the problem of induction.

2 Explain the argument that we have circular justification to believe in induction. Does it succeed?

3 Explain Strawson's argument that we have *a priori* justification to believe in induction. Does it succeed?

4 Which of the two skeptical responses is best? Is it a satisfactory response?

Advanced questions

5 Is the problem of deduction any easier to solve than the problem of induction? If not, does this reflect well on induction or poorly on deduction? (see Haack 1976)

6 The text says that an analysis of language alone cannot tell us anything about what the world is like. What exactly does this mean? Is it true?

7 What assumptions must be added to Stove's argument to get the result that E confirms that the next emerald is green?

8 Is the pragmatic vindication of induction any better or worse than Dutch Book arguments?

9 Is Popper really as close to Bayesians as the text suggests?

10 Is the distinction between *a priori* and *a posteriori* solutions helpful?

11 "That which is used to prove everything else . . . cannot itself be proved" Bentham (1789/1961, p. 19). Discuss.

Further reading

The classic source for the problem of induction is Hume (1739/1987, Book 1, Part iii, section 6) and his discussion remains one of the finest expositions of any problem in philosophy.

For a contemporary critical discussion that closely engages with Hume's argument, see Lange (2011). For a detailed critical overview of several responses, see Salmon (1979, chapter 1) and Vickers (2014).

7

Grue: The new problem of induction

In this chapter, we grant all the Principles of Uniformity of Chapter 6. You might think this solves the problem of induction and allows us to make inductive inferences. Sadly, you would be wrong. For there is a closely related but even more devilish problem, called the *new problem of induction*. The root of the problem is that there are many different ways in which the world could be uniform, so we need justification to believe that the world is uniform in one way rather than another.

I explain the problem with some intuitive examples first (7.1) then we work toward the influential example of Nelson Goodman (7.2 and 7.3). We consider the response that a special class of properties is *projectible* (7.4), then an alternative response that good inferences depend on the way in which our evidence has been selected for observation (7.5).

7.1 Bad inferences

Let's start by assuming that we have justification for believing the following principle:

Principle of Uniformity-Sampling Samples probably resemble the rest of the population.[1]

This licences the following plausible inferences:

All observed emeralds are green

justifies

All unobserved emeralds are green

All observed ravens are black

justifies

All unobserved ravens are black

In general, we have:

All observed Fs are G

justifies

All unobserved Fs are G.

So far so good. But not all instances of this pattern are acceptable. Here are three examples where we end up with clearly unjustified conclusions:

Imagine a food critic, who has only seen chickens which were on his dinner plate, making the following argument:

All observed chickens have been dead

justifies

All unobserved chickens are dead

Suppose I ask someone in the audience at a lecture how many siblings he has, he replies that he has one, and I offer the following argument:

All audience members I've asked have one sibling

justifies

All audience members I haven't asked have one sibling

All observed emeralds have been observed

justifies

All unobserved emeralds have been observed.

This last argument really nails the problem—it has exactly the same structure as the others, making an inference from observed objects having a particular property to unobserved objects having that property. But when the property we're talking about is *having been observed*, the mistake is obvious.

It seems that in some cases we can infer that observed patterns continue into the unobserved, but in other cases we can't. The question of this chapter is—what distinguishes the cases? Why can we make such an inference in some cases but not in others?

The most discussed example where the inference goes wrong was introduced to philosophy by Nelson Goodman (1955) who used a made up word: grue. Goodman's example is a bit complicated, so if you don't like it you should just skip to 7.4 and think about the examples earlier—it's exactly the same point being made. But for better or worse, the philosophical literature tends to use Goodman's example.

7.2 Warm-up: Greenblue

Goodman's example is so difficult that we'll start with a warm-up. Suppose there is an urn that you know has 100 objects in it, you've just drawn 99 objects from the urn and they have all been green. Assume H1 and H2 are the only possibilities:

E = The first 99 objects are green

H1 = All 100 objects are green

H2 = The first 99 objects are green and the 100th is blue

Assuming the Principle of Uniformity, does E support H1, H2, or neither? The natural answer is that E supports H1. Why? Because the observed objects have been green, so the Principle of Uniformity says the unobserved objects are probably green. To put it another way, if the objects resemble each other then they are all green (H1).

But this inductive argument has made an implicit assumption. It assumed being green was the only way objects could resemble each other. There are other ways, and they will lead to conflicting conclusions.

To see how, let's introduce a new way in which objects can resemble each other—a way that only a philosopher would dream up. Consider the property of being either one-of-the-first-99-and-green or the-100th-and-blue. There is no word in English for this property, so let's call it "greenblue."

Greenblue = Being either one-of-the-first-99-and-green or the-100th-and-blue

A couple of points that might help you get to grips with this definition. First, one thing that's confusing about this definition is that it's disjunctive, that is, it has "or" in the middle. This means it applies to things that we don't normally group together. It's like making up a new word, "frall," for things that are tall or fragile. "Frall" applies to a weird array of objects. It applies to the Empire State building (tall), and also to a raw egg (fragile). Similarly, "greenblue" applies to one of the first 99 things if green and also to the hundredth thing if blue.

Also, notice the presence of "and" in the last two sentences. Although the definition is disjunctive, we naturally refer to the *objects* that have the property with "and." Just remember we're not talking about the property of being tall-and-fragile; we're talking about the property of being tall-or-fragile, and this applies to tall things *and* to fragile things. (We might say the property is disjunctive and the set of objects that have it is conjunctive.)

It follows from this definition of "greenblue" that we can re-state H2 as:

H2 = All 100 objects are greenblue

Let's add some pictures. The budget did not stretch to coloured pictures, so you'll have to use your imagination. Suppose the following picture shows a green emerald:

And the following picture shows a blue sapphire:

Here are pictures of what the last four objects to be drawn from the urn might look like if each hypothesis is true:

H1 = All 100 objects are green

H2 = All 100 objects are greenblue

Earlier we assumed that if the objects resemble each other then they are all green. But they can also resemble each other by all being greenblue. If they resemble each other in this way, then H2 is supported by the evidence and Principle of Uniformity.

How? Let's go through the inductive argument earlier, but this time applying it to the property of being greenblue. We just re-state the evidence as "the first 99 objects are greenblue."

E = The first 99 objects are greenblue

H1 = All 100 objects are green

H2 = All 100 objects are greenblue

Assuming the Principle of Uniformity, does E support H1, H2, or neither? The *new* answer is that E supports H2:

All observed emeralds have been greenblue

justifies

All unobserved emeralds are greenblue.

So our evidence justifies the hypothesis that the hundredth object is greenblue. So our evidence justifies the hypothesis that the hundredth object is *blue*! But this is crazy.

And we can come up with more conflicting hypotheses that seem to be justified by the evidence. For example, let "greenwhite" be short for "being either one-of-the-first-99-and-green or the-100th-and-*white*." By parallel reasoning, it seems that our evidence justifies the hypothesis that the next emerald is white. And why stop there? Let "greenelephant" be short for "being either one-of-the-first-99-and-green or the-100th-and-*an-elephant*." We seem to have evidence that the next emerald is an elephant.

With this toy example in hand, let's now get to Goodman's example.[2]

7.3 Grue

Let's invent the following word:

Grue = Green-and-first-observed-before-the-year-2100 or blue-and-first-observed-after-the-year-2100

"Grue," like greenblue, is disjunctive. It applies to green things first-observed-before-2100 and also to blue things not observed until after 2100. So consider a green emerald on the Queen's crown. It is observed before 2100 and green, so it is grue. Now consider a blue sapphire deep underground that will be unearthed after 2100. It is first-observed-after-2100 and blue, so it is also grue. We would naturally say that the Queen's emerald and the underground sapphire are different colors. But they are both colored grue.

Now consider a green emerald that will be not be observed until after 2100. Is this grue? No. It is neither green-and-first-observed-before-2100 (because it is not first-observed-before-2100) nor is it blue-and-first-observed-after-2100 (because it is green). And consider a blue sapphire on the Queen's crown. Is it grue? No. It is neither green-and-first-observed-before-2100 (because it is blue) nor is it blue-and-first-observed-after-2100 (because it is first-observed-before-2100).

The following diagram shows some objects that are grue. It is a weird collection—the emeralds over ground and the sapphires underground.

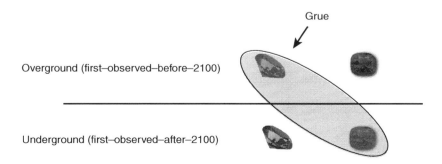

Grue

Overground (first–observed–before–2100)

Underground (first–observed–after–2100)

Now let's apply the Principle of Uniformity—let's suppose that if some objects have a property, then this gives us justification to believe that other objects have the property. Specifically, let's apply this to grue emeralds. Our evidence is that many emeralds are grue, that is, green and first-observed-before 2100. Applying the Principle of Uniformity, we should infer that emeralds first-observed-after-year 2100 will be grue.

All observed emeralds have been grue

justifies

All unobserved emeralds are grue.

But emeralds first-observed-after-2100 are grue only if they are blue! (Just check the diagram.) So our observations of grue emeralds give us justification to believe that emeralds first-observed-after-2100 will be blue. And that's crazy.

What these examples of greenblue and grue show is that we cannot apply an unrestricted version of the Principle of Uniformity. If we apply it to green we get reasonable beliefs, but if we apply it to greenblue or grue, we get crazy beliefs. This is a serious challenge to the Principle of Uniformity. If we can't restrict it to the cases where it gives reasonable beliefs, it will have to be abandoned, and all the work that went into solving (we're assuming) the old problem of induction will have been in vain.

There are two main types of responses to the grue problem. The first (7.4) is to find a principled way to rule out properties like grue and rule in properties like green for use in a Principle of Uniformity. The second (7.5) is to argue that whether we should apply a Principle of Uniformity depends on our background beliefs. Let's take these in turn.

7.4 First response: Projectible properties

It seems that applying the Principle of Uniformity to some properties—green, blue, white—gives reasonable beliefs, but applying the Principle of Uniformity to other properties—greenblue, greenelephant, grue—does not. Let's name the first set of properties *projectible* and the second set *unprojectible*.

Projectible = A property such that observed Fs having it justifies that unobserved Fs have it.[3]

The suggestion is that if we are to apply a Principle of Uniformity, we must restrict its use to projectible properties. So whereas the old unadorned Principle said (in rule form):

Principle of Uniformity-Sampling

All observed Fs are G

justifies

All unobserved Fs are G.

The suggestion now is that we should use the following restricted Principle:

Principle of Uniformity-Sampling, Projectible

All observed Fs are G

and G is projectible

justifies

All unobserved Fs are G.

But "projectible" is just a name, not a solution. (It's surprisingly easy to confuse naming a problem with solving it.) What we need to solve the new problem of induction is a general formulation of the distinction between projectible and the unprojectible properties.

Many suggestions were made in response to Goodman (1955), but none found much acceptance. Let's see why not.

(i) Goodman's own response was that projectible properties are those that have already been used with some success by scientists. (Goodman called these properties *entrenched*.) This correctly allows familiar properties like being green, or being an electron, and rules out properties like being grue.

But this implies that new properties that scientists come up with are not projectible. If scientists weren't allowed to come up with new properties and project, then scientific progress would grind to a halt.

(ii) A related view is that the problem with "grue" is that the word is made up. Perhaps, the projectible properties are those that are referred to with noninvented terms.

But scientists regularly invent new terms. Terms like "spin" and "charm" were made up by scientists relatively recently, and they are projectible.

(iii) Perhaps we need to appeal to *lawlike* properties, which are properties that are of the right kind to appear in laws of nature. Properties like greenness are lawlike, whereas properties like grueness are not. So perhaps the projectible properties are the lawlike properties.[4]

There are two problems here. First, we now need criteria for being a lawlike property, and there is little agreement on how this can be done. So if the fraught concept of projectibility depends on the fraught concept of a lawlike property, then we haven't made much progress.

Second, there seem to be projectible properties that are not lawlike. If all the coins in my left pocket are Euros, this justifies that all the coins in my right pocket are Euros; but the property of being a Euro is not lawlike.

(iv) The new terms were always introduced with complicated definitions involving "or." So perhaps all terms based on such definitions refer to unprojectible properties.

But we need not use complicated definitions to refer to grueness. We could instead take "grue" as a primitive term, and define "green" in terms of "grue." Goodman's explanation of this ingenious maneuver is largely responsible for the lasting importance of his discussion. Imagine an alien race that speaks a language similar to English, except they use the word "grue" in the way described here. They also use the word "bleen" to refer to objects that are blue-and-first-observed-before-2100 or green-and-first-observed-after-2100.

Grue   Bleen

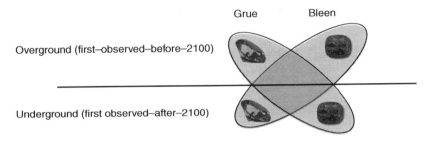

Overground (first–observed–before–2100)

Underground (first observed–after–2100)

The alien thinks that our terms "green" and "blue" are disjunctive terms. When a visiting alien anthropologist figures out our language, it will write something like:

Green = Grue-and-first-observed-before-2100 or bleen-and-first-observed-after 2100

Blue = Grue-and-first-observed-after-2100 or bleen-and-first-observed-before 2011

It will then have to go home and explain to its species that humans have these weird disjunctive terms instead of plain old "grue" and "bleen." There is a symmetry between the speaker of the green-language and the speaker of the grue-language. So why should the grue-language be shamed with the tag of being unprojectible?

(v) Perhaps green is more simple than grue, and only simple properties are projectible.

The alien example earlier suggests that this is not true. The alien finds "grue" simple and "green" complicated. We would need some independent account of which properties are simple, and none have been convincing. The same applies to other derogatory names that "grue" gets called, like "gerrymandered," or "artificial."

(vi) Carnap (1971, pp. 73–5) claimed that properties that describe the intrinsic nature of an object are projectible, but properties that locate an object in time or space are not intrinsic. "Grue" makes reference to the time, so it is unprojectible.

An objection is that some projectible properties make reference to the time. For example, scientists think there was a period of inflation shortly after the big bang, in which the universe expanded at an exponential rate. This means there were uniformities during this period of time that do not extend to other periods of time, for example, all objects moved away from each other at an exponential rate.

Carnap would respond that he is only talking about the properties designated by our *primitive* concepts. For Carnap, languages have a number of primitive concepts, plus complex concepts constructed from them. Projectibility is defined in the first instance over primitive concepts, and then derivatively over nonprimitive concepts. Carnap's claim is only that projectible primitive concepts do not locate the object in time or space. This allows that a complex concept like "shortly after the big bang all objects moved away from each other at an exponential rate" is projectible.

Despite Carnap's best efforts, this response never really took hold. Interest in defining projectibility has waned in recent years, partly due to the influence of Frank Jackson, who argued that any attempts are doomed to fail.

Objection to projectible properties

Frank Jackson (1975) argued that the attempt to make a principled distinction between projectible and unprojectible properties was misguided. He thought it all depended on the context—that in some contexts even grue is projectible!

To see how grue might be projectible, suppose we know that there is a species of shy chameleon that is blue when unobserved and turns green with embarrassment when observed. Observing such green chameleons does not allow us to infer that unobserved chameleons are green. Instead, we should infer that the unobserved chameleons are blue, that is, all chameleons are grue![5] In this case, grue is projectible and green is unprojectible. There are other more realistic examples—observed blood is red, and unobserved blood in veins is blue, as blood turns red when it absorbs oxygen. The moral is that it is a mistake to think that some properties are projectible and others unprojectible; instead, Jackson argued, it depends on *counterfactuals*.

7.5 Second response: Sampling

7.5.1 Jackson's counterfactual condition

What's gone wrong in the examples of the previous paragraph? The problem regarding the chameleons is that observation *makes* the chameleons green. The chameleons would not have been green if they had not been observed; the Fs are G, but *would not have been if they had not been observed*. That's why the inference is bad. To ensure a justified inference, we have to believe that the property does not vary with whether the object is observed. So Jackson argued that we need to add to the Principle of Uniformity the following counterfactual:

> *Counterfactual*: If the Fs had not been observed then they would still have been G.

This is called a *counterfactual* because it tells us what the world would have been like if things had gone differently. And it says that whether the observed objects have G does not depend on whether they were observed. The result is the following strengthened Principle of Uniformity:

> *Principle of Uniformity-Sampling-Counterfactual*
>
> All observed Fs are G and
>
> if they had not been observed, they would still have been G
>
> justifies
>
> All unobserved Fs are G.

The counterfactual holds for familiar properties, for example, G = Being green

> *Principle of Uniformity-Sampling-Counterfactual*
>
> All observed emeralds are green and
>
> if they had not been observed, they would still have been green
>
> justifies
>
> All unobserved emeralds are green.

And the counterfactual doesn't hold for the problem cases:

> *Principle of Uniformity-Sampling-Counterfactual*
>
> All observed emeralds are grue and
>
> if they had not been observed, they would still have been grue
>
> justifies
>
> All unobserved Fs are grue

Jackson argued that if the emeralds had not been observed, they would *not* have been grue. For example, if they had not been observed, then they would still be underground, remain unobserved until after 2100, and therefore not be grue. So we get the correct verdict that we should not infer that unobserved emeralds are probably grue. And one more for good measure:

Principle of Uniformity-Sampling-Counterfactual

All observed Fs are observed and

if they had not been observed, they would still have been observed

justifies

All unobserved Fs are observed.

Trivially, if they had not been observed, they would *not* still have been observed. As the counterfactual condition fails, we get the correct verdict that we should not infer that unobserved Fs are observed.

7.5.2 Objection to Jackson's counterfactual solution

But there are cases for which Jackson's counterfactual holds, but for which we still don't think the inference is justified.[6] Recall the example of the food critic who has only seen dead chickens and infers that all chickens are probably dead. The relevant counterfactual to justify this inference is: if the chickens had not been observed, they would still be dead. To evaluate the counterfactual, we have to consider the closest possibility in which the (dead) chickens were not observed. Presumably these would be possibilities in which different chickens had been brought to her table, or where perhaps she had ordered fish instead. In those possibilities, the chickens would still have been dead. So Jackson's account gives the wrong verdict that the food critic's inference is justified:

Principle of Uniformity-Sampling-Counterfactual

All observed chickens are dead and

if they had not been observed, they would still have been dead

justifies

All unobserved chickens are dead.

Polling provides more realistic examples. Suppose I call people at home and ask who they'll vote for at the next election. I know that people at home are more likely to be unemployed, and unemployed people are more likely to vote Democrat. If 60 percent of my sample will vote Democrat, I should not infer that 60 percent of voters will vote Democrat. But I believe the counterfactual condition: for each person in my sample, if they had not been in my sample they would still vote Democrat. The reason is that the nearest possibility where they're not in my sample is one where they don't get to the phone in time, or the call doesn't go through, and so on—they will still have the same political preferences.[7]

This suggests that to solve the problem we need to make sure we have a representative sample.

7.5.3 *Random sampling*

In the problem cases, the sample was not representative of the population with respect to the property at issue. To make this more precise, say that a sample is representative with respect to property G if and only if the proportion of G in the sample is the same as the proportion of G in the population. Then we can strengthen the Principle of Uniformity as follows:

Principle of Uniformity-Sampling-Representative

All observed Fs are G and

the sample is representative

justifies

All unobserved Fs are G.

We finally have a true principle.

But to use this principle we would have to have a justified belief that the sample is representative. This requires information about what the unobserved parts of the population are like—but if we had that we wouldn't need to make an inference in the first place! So this principle demands so much of the agent that it ends up being useless.

However, we can know how the sample was *selected*. Every sample is selected by some procedure, and we often know what this selection procedure is. We want an *unbiased* procedure. We can define "unbiased" using the concept of probabilistic independence from Chapter 1:

"E is *independent* of H" means "$P(H|E) = P(H)$"

We can now say:

A selection procedure is *unbiased* with respect to property G if and only if being G is independent of being in the sample.

Intuitively, objects in the population with G have the same probability of being in the sample as those without G.

Now we can consider the following:

Principle of Uniformity-Sampling-Random

All observed Fs are G and

the selection procedure was unbiased with respect to G

justifies

All unobserved Fs are G

This gives us a usable principle. It also gives the right verdict in many problem cases. The food critic's selection process is biased with respect to being dead; a live chicken will not be brought to the table, so dead chickens have a higher probability of being observed than live ones. The polling procedure is biased with respect to voting intentions; Democrats are more likely to be at home, and so are more likely to be observed in a phone poll than non-Democrats. The procedure for observing shy chameleons is biased with respect to green; blushing green ones are more likely to be seen than blue ones. The procedure for observing emeralds is biased with respect to grue; by the definition of "grue," observed (green) emeralds are all grue, whereas nonobserved (green) emeralds are not grue. As all emeralds happen to be green (whether or not we know it), the result is that "grue" is effectively synonymous with "observed."

What makes the grue problem so clever is that the definition of "grue" builds a selection bias into the property. It's impossible to get a sample which is unbiased with respect to grue, because being in the sample affects whether something is grue.

The principle also seems to give the right verdict for nonproblem cases. Assuming that we think green emeralds are as likely to be observed as non-green emeralds, we should infer that unobserved emeralds are green.

7.5.4 Objections to random sampling

But do we have justification to believe that the selection procedure was unbiased with respect to G? It depends what G is. We shouldn't believe our procedure is unbiased with respect to being observed in the past. We can only observe things in the past (as opposed to the future), so we should believe that the procedure is biased toward observations made in the past. So far so bad. But there are other properties we might not be biased toward. Greenness seems to be such a property. There is no reason to think that we are more likely to observe green objects than non-green objects. This gives us hope that for familiar properties like greenness, we might have an unbiased procedure.

Still, is there a reason to think we are *not* more likely to observe green objects than non-green objects? (This question is subtly different from the last. The fact that there is no reason to think it will rain does not entail that there is a reason to think it won't rain.) It seems not. Perhaps God just wants us to observe green objects. Or perhaps the emeralds around here happen to be green whereas those far away are blue. If so, our procedure is biased. So it looks like we need *a priori* justification to believe that our selection procedure is unbiased. If we have this, we have reason to believe that the sample is representative, and both the new and old problems of induction would be solved.

Summary

We saw in this chapter that even if we grant that the world is uniform, the problem of induction remains, because there are lots of different ways the world could be uniform. One response is to identify a privileged set of properties as projectible, and only apply the Principle of Uniformity to those. But it is unclear how the privileged properties could be identified. Another response argues that the Principle of Uniformity can be applied only when the sample has been selected in the right way. This approach must steer a path between conditions that are too weak, and allow bad inferences, and conditions that are too strong, and are useless in practice. An unbiased procedure would solve the problem, but it is not obvious we have reason to think that our procedures are unbiased.

In the next chapter, we'll set aside these strange worries about grue and other bizarre possibilities. It turns out that even a sensible Principle of Uniformity applied only to familiar properties quickly leads to paradoxical results.

Study questions

1 What does "grue" mean?

2 What does "projectible" mean?

3 Explain Jackson's counterfactual solution to the grue problem.

4 How might random sampling solve the new problem of induction?

Advanced questions

5 The attempts to formulate the distinction between projectible and unprojectible properties were dismissed very quickly. Could any be made to work?

6 Are there more promising ways to define "bias"? (see Godfrey-Smith 2011)

7 Do the approaches of Jackson and Godfrey-Smith really fail for the same reasons as Stove's?

Further reading

See Vickers (2014) for a useful introduction. For some of the details, see the collection of papers in Stalker (1994) of which Sober's "No Model, No Inference" is most relevant to our discussion.

Maher has helpful lecture notes defending Carnap's inductive logic at: http://patrick.maher1.net/517/lectures/lecture7.pdf

8

The paradox of the ravens

In this chapter, we'll set aside the strange nonprojectible properties of the previous chapter, such as grue. Nevertheless, we'll see that a sensible Principle of Uniformity, combined with two further principles, leads to the Paradox of the Ravens (8.1). We'll consider whether one of these principles should be rejected (8.2). Then we'll make a distinction about how to understand the Principle of Uniformity: deductively (8.3) or inductively (8.4). In both cases, we'll find we need to put constraints on how the principle is applied.

8.1 The Paradox

The principles

Here are two plausible Principles of Uniformity:

> That an observed emerald is green justifies that all emeralds are green.[1]
> That an observed raven is black justifies that all ravens are black.

In an abstract schema, where F and G are properties:

Instance
That an observed F is G justifies that all Fs are G.

In the quest for substantive principles for inferring from the observed to the unobserved, *Instance* is one of the best candidates for a first step. It should seem obviously true.

(Comparison with previous chapter: Notice that the hypothesis confirmed is that *all* Fs are G. This is the conjunction of "observed Fs are G" and "unobserved Fs are G." The previous two chapters discussed only the latter. And indeed it is the unobserved that we are primarily concerned with. But it's useful to start with a hypothesis about *all* Fs because that's what the literature does, and because it makes one of the other principles (Equivalence) easier to understand. Hypotheses about the observed and the unobserved will be separated once more in 8.3. Also, the evidence earlier concerns only a single observed F rather than "all" the observed F, which follows the literature and makes things a bit simpler.)

But *Instance* quickly leads to paradox. We need two more principles to generate the problem. First:

Equivalence "All Fs are Gs" says the same as "All non-Gs are non-Fs."

Equivalence is not obvious, but some examples should make it intuitive. Consider "all humans breathe." This says the same as "all non-breathers are non-human." Both sentences are true if and only if there are no nonbreathing humans. (Careful: "All Gs are Fs" is different. The recipe to generate what's called the *contrapositive* is to reverse the F and G, and negate both.)

We can also give a cards example. Assume that every card in a special deck is either black or red, and either a club or a heart (we've removed the spades and diamonds for simplicity). Then, "all clubs are black" says the same as "all reds are hearts." Both of these sentences are true as long as there are no red clubs. A picture will help:

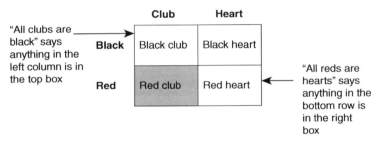

So both sentences make the same claim about the distribution of objects: there is nothing in the bottom left box.

The second principle for generating the ravens paradox is:

Substitution For any H1 and H2, if H1 and H2 say the same thing and E justifies H1, then E justifies H2.

Substitution is intuitive. If two sentences say the same thing then anything that justifies one must justify the other. Think of a Venn diagram—two sentences that say the same thing correspond to two areas that perfectly overlap, that is, there is really only one area, picked out in different ways. We won't question Substitution.[2]

The Paradox

Now let's use these principles to derive the paradox. Getting your head round the paradox is not easy, so we'll start with a cards example. Assume that everything is either black or red, and either a spade or a heart:

1   An observed red heart is an instance of a red heart

2   Therefore, that an observed red is a heart justifies that all reds are hearts (by *Instance*)

3   "All reds are hearts" says the same as "all clubs are black" (by *Equivalence*)

> *Conclusion* Therefore, that an observed red is a heart justifies that all clubs are black (by 2, 3, and *Substitution*).

This is a paradoxical conclusion. Why should observing a red heart justify that all clubs are black? Repeating the table from the previous page, why should finding something in the bottom right box justify that there is nothing in the bottom left box?

	Club	**Heart**
Black	Black club	Black heart
Red	Red club	Red heart E

We'll look at several examples of this problem, but the cards example is the most straightforward, so I recommend thinking hard about this case before moving on. Do you think the conclusion is true? If so, why does it seem odd? If you think the conclusion is false, which premise would you reject?

Here's another example that is relatively easy to get your head around. Suppose you're at a ride at the fairground where riders have to be taller than 4 ft. Let's divide everyone in the world into "riders," who are on the ride at a particular time, and "spectators," who are not. And divide everyone into those who are more than 4 ft tall and those who are less than 4 ft tall (pretend no-one is exactly 4 ft):

1   An observed 5 ft rider is an instance of a rider more than 4 ft tall.

2   Therefore, that an observed rider is 5 ft justifies that all riders are more than 4 ft tall. (By *Instance*)

3   "All riders are more than 4 ft tall" says the same as "everyone less than 4 ft tall is a spectator." (By *Equivalence*)

Conclusion Therefore, that an observed rider is 5 ft justifies that everyone less than 4 ft tall is a spectator. (By 2, 3, and *Substitution*)

Again, the conclusion is paradoxical—why should seeing someone on the ride of 5 ft justify that people less than 4 ft are not on the ride? You shouldn't be able to learn about spectators by observing riders.

At this point, you might be wondering why this chapter is called "the paradox of the ravens." The reason is that this paradox is usually presented in the following form, where we assume for simplicity that everything is either black or white, and either a sneaker or a raven:

1   An observed white sneaker is an instance of a white sneaker.

2   Therefore, that an observed white thing is a sneaker justifies that all white things are sneakers. (by *Instance*)

3   "All white things are sneakers" says the same as "all ravens are black." (By *Equivalence*)

Conclusion Therefore, that an observed white thing is a sneaker justifies that all ravens are black. (By 2, 3, and *Substitution*)

This conclusion is crazy. It says that if we go to the closet and see a white sneaker, it justifies that all ravens are black. Which means we don't need to go outside and look at birds to find out if ravens are black, we can just look in the closet—ornithology has become an indoor pursuit.

The argument says that finding something in the bottom right box justifies that there is nothing in the bottom left box.

	Raven	**Sneaker**
Black	Black raven	Black sneaker
White	White raven	White sneaker E

Can we reject a premise of the paradox? In 8.2 we discuss an attempt to deny *Equivalence*, and argue that the paradox is not avoided. In 8.3 and 8.4, we consider *Instance* and argue that there are several ways it can be false.

8.2 Deny equivalence

Equivalence is a principle of logic. But speakers don't always interpret the sentences expressing the paradox in such a way that they come out equivalent.[3] Recall the explanation of Equivalence:

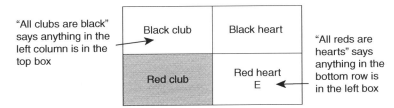

"All clubs are black" says anything in the left column is in the top box

| Black club | Black heart |
| Red club | Red heart E |

"All reds are hearts" says anything in the bottom row is in the left box

It was claimed earlier that both sentences make the same claim about the distribution of objects: there is nothing in the bottom left box.

But imagine that all the clubs have been removed from the deck. Many people say that "all clubs are black" is no longer true! But clearly "all reds are hearts" remains true. This means that people are not interpreting these claims as saying the same thing. Therefore when we interpret the hypotheses the way normal speakers do, Equivalence is false; "all clubs are black" does not say the same as "all reds are hearts."

(By contrast, philosophers interpret the claims in a way that makes Equivalence true, as they interpret "all F are G" as being true if there are no F. This oddity is a version of *the paradox of material implication*.)

Objection to denying equivalence

But once we make the intended interpretation explicit to ensure the truth of Equivalence, the paradox does not go away. We can replace "all clubs are black" with "there are no red clubs." Everyone agrees that the latter is true even if the clubs have been removed. Now the paradoxical argument is that a red heart justifies that there are no red clubs:

1 An observed red heart is an instance of a red heart.

2 Therefore, that an observed red is a heart justifies that all reds are hearts.

   (by *Instance*)

3 "All reds are hearts" says the same as "there are no red clubs" (by *Equivalence*)

   Conclusion Therefore, that an observed red is a heart justifies that there are no red clubs. (by 2, 3, and *Substitution*)

Paradox retained. Why should a red heart justify that there are no red clubs? Applying this to the ravens, we replace "all ravens are black" with "there are no white ravens":

1 An observed white sneaker is an instance of a white sneaker.

2 Therefore, that an observed white thing is a sneaker justifies that all white things are sneakers. (by *Instance*)

3 "All white things are sneakers" says the same as "there are no white ravens." (By *Equivalence*)

Conclusion Therefore, that an observed white thing is a sneaker justifies that there are no white ravens. (By 2, 3, and *Substitution*)

Still crazy. Does a white sneaker really justify that there are no white ravens?

8.3 Instance-observed

The real weak point of the paradox is *Instance*. To investigate it, we need to make a distinction. *Instance*, which says that an observed FG justifies that all F are G, can be broken up into two parts:[4]

Instance-observed

An observed F is G

justifies

All observed Fs are G.

Instance-un*observed*

An observed F is G

justifies

All *un*observed Fs are G.

Note: The object described in our evidence always counts as observed; the unobserved objects are those that remain unseen, and which we can only make inductive inferences about. This is slightly awkward use of language, but we'll just stipulate that that's how "observed" is to be understood.

We'll discuss *Instance-observed* here in 8.3 and *Instance-unobserved* in 8.4. The same pattern emerges in both sections. First, *Instance-observed* and *Instance-unobserved* both need to be restricted. Second, in cases where they hold and the conclusion that there are no white ravens is justified, we can explain why people find this paradoxical.

8.3.1 Deny Instance-observed

It might seem that *Instance-observed* is trivially correct.

Instance-observed

An observed F is G

justifies

All observed Fs are G.

Applying this to the ravens case, imagine going to your closet and observing a white sneaker (assume that this is all the evidence you have). The relevant inference looks undeniable:

Instance-observed, White Sneakers

An observed white thing is a sneaker

justifies

All observed white things are sneakers.

The relation between hypothesis and evidence is deductive; the hypothesis (all observed Fs are G) *entails* the evidence (an observed F is G): $P(E|H) = 1$. One might think it follows that the evidence justifies the hypothesis, that is, $P(E|H) = 1 > P(E)$.

But it doesn't. The reason is that the evidence was certain to be observed, $P(E) = 1$, and evidence that was certain to be observed can never justify anything.

Let's go through these two points. First, evidence that is certain to be observed can never justify anything. This is fairly intuitive. If you are certain a piece of evidence is about to be discovered, there is a sense in which you already have the evidence. The evidence doesn't tell you anything new, so you can't learn anything from it. Formally, if $P(E) = 1$, then $P(E|H) = P(E)$, so E does not justify H.[5]

Second, the evidence was certain to be observed. Here we have to be careful. It was not certain that you would observe a white sneaker. You might have observed a black sneaker. But as the relation between hypothesis and evidence is deductive, the possible evidence can be divided into that which will refute the hypothesis (a white raven) and that which will establish it (anything that's not a white raven). In the ravens paradox, your evidence is the latter. You were certain that you would obtain this evidence because you imagined looking in the closet, and you can be certain that there are no white ravens in the closet. So you were certain the evidence you have would be observed.

These two points together show that the observation of the white sneaker fails to justify that all observed white things are sneakers. To repeat, the evidence was certain to be observed, and evidence that is certain to be observed can never justify anything.

For contrast, imagine searching in a forest. You catch sight of something white in a tree. You rush toward it hoping to discover a white raven. But as you get to the tree, you see that it is just a sneaker sitting on a branch. "Hmm," you think, "still no observed white ravens." In this case, it's plausible that the white sneaker justifies that there are no observed white ravens. In this case, the evidence was not certain to be observed.[6]

Here's the diagram again:

	Raven	**Sneaker**
Black	Black raven	Black sneaker
White	White raven	White sneaker E

The hypothesis says there is nothing observed in the bottom left box. If you were certain all along that you were not going to observe something in the bottom left box, the hypothesis fails to be justified by observing something in the bottom right box. Thus *Instance-observed* is incorrect, and this removes the threat of indoor ornithology.

8.3.2 Instance-observed and the Wason selection task

Now we come to a different response to the paradox—accept the conclusion, and argue that it only *seems* paradoxical. For even when *Instance-observed* is correct, and the resulting inference that there are no observed white ravens is correct, people tend to be surprised that it is. There is a famous psychological experiment, the Wason selection task, which explains why:[7]

Each card has a number on one side and a colour on the other. Which cards do you need to turn over to justify that every observed card with an even number on one side is black on the other side i.e. there are no observed white evens?[8]

The Wason selection task.

Most subjects suggest only the eight and the black. *But the white card has to be turned over.* We have to check if the white card is even, as this would be a counterexample. An observed even white *refutes* the hypothesis that every observed even is black; an observed odd white *justifies* that every observed even is black, that is, no observed white evens.[9] Most people find this very odd when they first see it because they look for confirming instances and forget to look for counterexamples.

We can put the ravens paradox in this form using cards that have a type of object on one side and a color on the other. (Ravens are analogous to evens.) To check whether any observed ravens are white, we have to turn over the white card to check if it says "raven" on the other side. This would be a counter-example to the hypothesis that there are no observed white ravens. If instead it says "sneaker," then *this observation of a white sneaker justifies that there are no observed white ravens.*

The ravens paradox in the form of the Wason selection task.

This promises to give a resolution to the ravens paradox: *Instance-observed* is correct, and the white sneaker really does justify that there are no observed white ravens; and we find this puzzling because we forget to look for counterexamples.

8.4 Instance-unobserved

What about *Instance-unobserved*?

> *Instance-unobserved*
>
> An observed F is G
>
> justifies
>
> All unobserved Fs are G.

The labors of chapters 5 and 6 were motivated by the thought that something like *Instance-unobserved* must be true. But we saw in the last chapter that such a principle needs to be restricted, and a similar dialectic plays out here.

8.4.1 Natural Kinds

Quine (1969) argued that *Instance-unobserved* is only true when applied to *natural kinds*. Natural kinds are the type of thing that scientists investigate, and which cut reality at its joints. The best way to get a grip on them is with examples:

Natural kinds	Not natural kinds
Quark	Things owned by the Queen
Atom	People less than 4 ft tall
Molecule	White things
Acid	Non-ravens
Emerald	Things that tremble as if mad
Organism	Things that resemble flies from a distance
Raven	Fabulous things
Human	Sneakers

As ravens are natural kinds, we expect ravens to have the same properties, so an observed black *raven* suggests that unobserved *ravens* are black. By contrast, as white things are not natural kinds, we do not expect white things to have the same properties, so one observed *white* sneaker does not suggest that unobserved *white* things are sneakers. Pictorially, we expect everything in the shaded area to be in the same box.

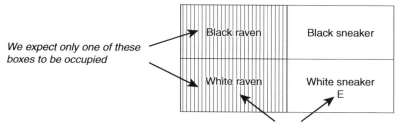

We expect only one of these boxes to be occupied

We do not expect only one of these boxes to be occupied

Using natural kinds, we can strengthen *Instance-unobserved* from:

Instance-unobserved
An observed F is G

justifies

All unobserved Fs are G.

to:

Instance-unobserved, Natural Kind

That an observed F is G and

F is a natural kind

justifies

all unobserved Fs are G.

As whiteness (F) is not a natural kind, an observed white (F) sneaker (G) fails to justify that all unobserved white things are sneakers.[10]

But it turns out that *Instance-unobserved, Natural Kind* is both too strong and too weak.

8.4.2 Objection to Natural Kinds: Too restrictive

One objection is that it isn't clear what a natural kind is. (This is analogous to the unclarity regarding what a projectible property is in 7.4.)

But even if it were, it seems too strong to say that *Instance-unobserved* is only true for natural kinds. That my observed pocket (F) contains francs (G) justifies that all my unobserved pockets (F) contain francs (G), even though my pockets are not a natural kind. So *Instance-unobserved* is not only true for natural kinds; *Instance-unobserved, Natural Kind* is too restrictive, telling us that there is no justification when in fact there is.

8.4.3 Objection to Natural Kinds: Not restrictive enough

The following possible distribution of objects suggests that *Instance-unobserved, Natural Kind* isn't restrictive enough.[11] Assume H and –H are the only possibilities.

	–H		H	
	Black raven	Black sneaker	Black raven	Black sneaker
B	◯			◯
	White raven	White sneaker	White raven	White sneaker
W	◯			◯

Observing a black raven entails that you are in the possibility on the left, where there are ravens, including a white one. So an observed black raven refutes the hypothesis that all unobserved ravens are black. But ravens are a natural kind, so *Instance-unobserved, Natural Kind* wrongly says that the hypothesis is justified.

The following examples make a similar point.

The 99 ft man

Hypothesis: Unobserved men are less than 100 ft tall

Instance: An observed 99 ft man

Additional details: Learning that a man could grow to 99 ft, you suddenly realize that a man could grow to 100 ft. So the hypothesis is "disjustified" by the instance (where "disjustified" means that the probability falls, by analogy with "disconfirmed").

The Grasshopper[12]

Hypothesis: Unobserved grasshoppers live south of Canada

Instance: An observed grasshopper 3 inches south of the Canadian border

Additional details: You previously thought grasshoppers could only survive in relatively mild climates. But if there are grasshoppers 3 inches from the Canadian border, there are almost certainly grasshoppers in Canada. So the hypothesis is disjustified.

In these cases, the distribution of properties means that the hypothesis is disjustified by the instance. Which constraints on the distribution of properties are necessary and sufficient for something like *Instance-unobserved* to be true remains an open question. (An application of Jackson's approach to the new problem of induction (7.5) would suggest that the properties of the observed objects must be representative of the population.)

Whatever the general answer to this question, we can consider the separate question of whether there is justification given the *actual* distribution of ravens, sneakers, whiteness, and blackness. We'll see that the hypothesis that unobserved ravens are black is justified, but only to a relatively small degree.

8.4.4 Instance-unobserved and degrees of justification[13]

Recall the inference at issue:

Instance-unobserved

An observed F is G

justifies

All unobserved Fs are G.

Even when *Instance-unobserved* is correct, the degree of justification might be relatively small. This leads us to what's called the Standard Bayesian Response to the paradox of the ravens. This response accepts the seemingly paradoxical conclusion, but softens the blow by showing that *the white sneaker justifies the hypothesis by less than a black raven would*.[14]

So far we have only talked about the existence or nonexistence of justification. But sometimes there is more rather than less justification, so we need the concept of *degree of justification*, that is, E justifies H to degree c. It then follows that one piece of evidence may confirm a hypothesis more than another piece of evidence does. So we need the concept of *comparative justification*, that is, E1 justifies H more than E2 justifies H. The Standard Bayesian Response makes this comparative claim: a black raven justifies H more than a white sneaker justifies H (where H = All unobserved ravens are black[15]). I'll explain intuitively how these concepts are put to work in the Standard Bayesian Response, then work through some numbers.

We're trying to decide between two ways the world might be: a world where some unobserved ravens are white (−H), and a world where all unobserved ravens are black (H). We can simplify a little by leaving "unobserved" implicit from now on: we are trying to decide between a world where some ravens are white (−H), and a world where all ravens are black (H). Each circle in the figure represents some fixed amount of credence that our evidence turns out to be in the corresponding box. You can also think of each circle as an object, for example, black raven, one of which is about to be selected at random. This distribution of objects is intended to reflect our actual beliefs about the distribution of ravens and sneakers given that there are white ravens (−H) and given that there aren't (H).

So where did this particular distribution come from? We've assumed that there are the same number of black and white objects, that there are more sneakers than ravens, and more white things than ravens. Check these hold across −H and H. Now what changes as we move from −H to H? The first change is that the white raven box is emptied. The credence from that box must be redistributed to the other boxes. How? Let's assume that H is independent of how likely you are to observe a raven, so the total credence in the ravens column must stay the same. Thus, the circle with the horizontal lines appears in the black raven box. Let's also assume that H is independent of how likely you are to observe a white thing, so the total credence in the white rows stays the same. Thus, the circle with the vertical lines appears in the white sneaker box. To keep the total number of circles the same, we have to remove one of the circles from the black sneaker box.

It turns out that on this distribution of objects, *an observed black raven justifies that (H) all ravens are black by more than a white sneaker would*. To see why, compare the change in black ravens to the change in white sneakers as we move from −H to H. Although credence in the black raven and white sneaker box have gone up by the same amount (one circle), the *proportion* increase of the black raven box is higher, that is, the black ravens go from 1 to 2 while the white sneakers go from 2 to 3. That is, the hypothesis (H) that all ravens are black gives a greater boost, proportionally speaking, to the black ravens than to the white sneakers. And it turns out, that's enough; if H gives a boost to E1 that is greater, proportionally speaking, than H gives to E2, then E1 justifies H more than E2 does. So a black raven justifies that all ravens are black by more than a white sneaker would.

Formally, and making explicit some assumptions left implicit above:

H = All ravens are black

B = This thing is black

R = This thing is a raven

E = −B−R = This thing is a white sneaker

The following can be proved:

If

(i) $P(-B) > P(R)$

(ii) $P(R|H) = P(R)$

(iii) $P(B|H) = P(B)$

(iv) $P(R\&-B) > 0$

then −B−R justifies H less than BR justifies H

Let's see how this plays out for the earlier example. We can compare the conditional credences:

P(BR|H) = 2/6

P(BR|−H) = 1/6

P(−B−R|H) = 3/6

P(−B−R|−H) = 2/6

At this point, we need a way to measure *degree of justification*. We will assume that the degree to which E justifies H is measured by

P(E|H)/P(E|−H)[16]

Intuitively, we compare how likely E is given H to how likely E is given −H. E justifies H if and only if this ratio is greater than 1. The greater the ratio, the greater the justification. Plugging in the numbers, BR justifies H to degree:

P(BR|H)/P(BR|−H) = 2/6/1/6 = 2.

Whereas −B−R justifies H to degree

P(−B−R|H)/P(−B−R|−H) = 3/6/2/6 = 1.5.

So −B−R justifies H, but less than BR does.

Summary

The paradox of the ravens is that plausible premises lead us from the evidence of a white sneaker to justification that all ravens are black. One way to block the argument is to deny *Equivalence*, but we saw the argument can be reformulated. A more promising way is to deny *Instance*. Even the deductive version of Instance, which says that the observed FG justifies that all observed Fs are G, is false if an FG is certain to be observed. And when it is true, people tend to overlook the possibility of a counter-example, leading them to see a paradox where there isn't one. The inductive version of Instance, which says that the observed FG justifies that all *un*observed Fs are G, has various counter-examples, and is only true given specific assumptions about the distribution of properties. Given the actual distribution of properties, the white sneaker justifies that all unobserved ravens are black by less than a black raven would, which partially explains why we might find the argument paradoxical.

In the next chapter, we consider another substantive principle of inductive reasoning—that our beliefs should match the known chances.

Study questions

1   Explain the paradox of the ravens.

2   What do you think is the best response to the paradox?

Advanced questions

3   Are the natural kinds solution to the ravens paradox and the projectibility solution to the grue paradox at root the same? Do they/ does it succeed?

4   The conditions stated for the Standard Bayesian Response give sufficient conditions for the claim that the white sneaker gives less justification than the black raven does. Are the conditions necessary? (Hint: No)

5   The distinction between *Instance-observed* and *Instance-unobserved* is not standard. Does it clarify or muddy the issue?

Further reading

The literature on the ravens paradox is vast and often technical. The classic source is Hempel (1945a), but this is difficult. Wikipedia is a good place to start for a detailed but accessible discussion plus a good list of references: http://en.wikipedia.org/wiki/Raven_paradox

9

Chance and credence

So far, probability has been closely connected to beliefs, be they actual beliefs (credence) or rational beliefs (inductive probability). But "probability" has another meaning. Sometimes, it refers to probabilities in the world that can be understood independently of what people do or should believe. We call these *chances*. Our two main questions are: What exactly is chance? And how does it connect to rational belief? We consider the two leading approaches to chance—the frequency theory and the propensity theory—and examine how each connects to rational belief.

We first clarify the distinction between chance and credence (9.1) and then discuss the actual frequency theory (9.2) and whether it is suitably connected to rational belief (9.3). An objection to the frequency theory (9.4) is motivated by an alternative metaphysical picture (9.5) which leads to the propensity theory (9.6). Finally, we discuss whether the propensity theory is suitably connected to rational belief (9.7).

9.1 Chance and credence

The best way to get a grip on *chance* is with examples. The most familiar example is the flip of a fair coin. The chance of Heads is 50 percent, as is the chance of Tails. More examples can be found in casinos—most gambling games produce chance outcomes. The chance of randomly selecting the Ace of Spades from a standard deck is 1/52, and the chance of the ball landing on Red 5 on a standard roulette wheel is 1/37.

Chances, unlike subjective or inductive probabilities, don't depend on what anyone believes, or what anyone's evidence is. For example, even if you think the coin will land Heads, that makes no difference to the chance of it landing Heads. And if you have evidence that the coin will land Heads, that also makes no difference to the chance that it will land Heads.

The contrast between chance and credence is nicely brought out by an example of Patrick Maher (2006). Suppose you have been told that a coin is either two-headed or two-tailed but you have no information about which it is. The coin is about to be tossed:

What is your *credence* that it will land Heads? 1/2.

What is the *chance* that it will land Heads? Either 0 or 1 but you don't know which.

So chance and credence are different, but there is an important connection between them. Suppose all you know about the flip of a coin is that the chance of Heads is 50 percent. What should your credence in Heads be? The obvious answer is 50 percent. Generally, if you assume that the chance of H is x, then your credence in H should be x. Formally, using Ch(H) as an abbreviation for "the chance of H":

Principal Principle (PP)[1]

If you are rational then $P(H| (Ch(H) = x)) = x$

Notice this rule tells us what we *ought* to do, not what we actually do. It was named the Principal Principle (PP) by David Lewis (1980) because he thought it was the central feature of our concept of chance. A useful way to get to grips with this principle is to think of chance as an *expert*, where an expert is someone to whom you should defer in your opinions. For example, if the weather forecaster tells you that it will rain tomorrow with 50 percent certainty, you ought to believe it will rain tomorrow with 50 percent certainty. Similarly, if the facts about chance tell you that there is a 50 percent *chance* of rain tomorrow, you ought to believe it will rain tomorrow with 50 percent certainty. The Principal Principle puts a constraint on our theory of chance—our theory should explain why it is true. In other words, our theory of chance should allow us to justify the Principal Principle.

It's important to realize that although the Principal Principle looks like it is connecting credence in H with chance of H, it isn't really. It's connecting credence of H with the agent's *beliefs* about the chance of H. The Principal Principle doesn't say anything about the real chance of H. It says approximately that if the agent believes the chance of H is x, she should have credence of x in H.

(There is a complication I will mention and set aside. Suppose a crystal ball that you know is accurate tells you a fair coin will land Heads tomorrow. This evidence seems to trump the chances; you should ignore the chances and believe it will land Heads. So the Principal Principle does not apply to such cases. But such cases are limited to exotic examples and we won't discuss it further. See Lewis (1994) for more.)

Two other constraints on a theory of chance are that chances must satisfy the rules of probability (Chapter 3) and that we must be able to discover what the chances are, at least in principle. Why are these constraints? Because we are trying to analyze a concept of ordinary language, *chance*, and it is part of our ordinary language concept that chances constrain rational belief, satisfy the rules of probability, and can be discovered.[2] To summarize:

Constraints on a theory of chance

A theory of chance should

1 allow a justification of the Principal Principle

2 ensure that chances are probabilities

3 allow us to discover what the chances are.

With this in mind, let's consider the two main approaches to chance: frequentism and the propensity theory.

9.2 Actual Frequency Theory

Frequentism comes in two versions, the first of which is the Actual Frequency Theory. Suppose a coin is flipped 10 times and then destroyed. It lands Heads six times, so the frequency of Heads is 6/10. The actual frequency theory of chance says that the chance of it landing Heads on each of the flips was 6/10. Generally, if an event of type *t* occurs *n* times in which outcome *O* occurs *m* times, then the chance of *O* on each occasion is *m/n*. In slogan form, chances are *identified* with actual frequencies.

Actual Frequency Theory

For each event of type *t*, the chance of outcome *O* occurring = The relative frequency of actual occurrences of *O* within all events of type *t*.

The theory is part of common sense, and has been the historically dominant theory of chance. Does it satisfy the constraints on a theory of chance? Actual frequentism allows us to discover what the chances of many events are. We can directly observe the actual frequencies of events, and chances are identified with actual frequencies, so we can directly observe the chances. Also, frequencies must satisfy the rules of probability due to the mathematics of frequencies, so actual frequentism automatically satisfies the rules of probability. Its relation to the Principal Principle is more complicated, but before we get to it we need to deal with a problem based on actual frequentism's use of the concept of a *type* of event.

The reference class problem

Using standard terminology, say that each type of event corresponds to a class of events. For example, the type of event *flipping a coin* determines the *class* of all the coin flips, which is just the collection of all the coin flips that ever take place. The problem is that every event is an instance of various types of event, and so it is a member of various classes. For example, as an English human, my death is a member of the class of English human deaths, and also a member of the wider class of all human deaths. This simple fact creates a problem when we try to apply actual frequentism.

What is the chance I will live past 80? Assuming actual frequentism, the chance is the actual frequency of deaths over 80 in the class in which my death belongs. But *my death belongs in more than one class*; it belongs in the class of all human deaths and the narrower class of all English human deaths. And the frequency of deaths over 80 in these two classes might not be the same. So actual frequentism doesn't answer the question of the chance of my surviving past 80; or rather, it gives us lots of answers, depending on the class we use (see Hájek 2009).

A natural response is to make chance relative to a reference class. Suppose 30 percent of all human deaths are past 80 and 50 percent of English human deaths are past 80. Then the chance that I will live past 80 given that I'm human is 30 percent and the chance that I will live past 80 given that I'm English is 50 percent. So far so good. But the problem reemerges when we try to apply the Principal Principle. What should my credence be that I live past 80 given this information? Recall the Principal Principle says (roughly) that my credence should match the chance. But there isn't just one chance—there are many, all relative to different reference classes. Which should we use when forming beliefs?

Reichenbach (1949, p. 439) argued that we should use the narrowest reference class for which we know the frequencies. In our example, if we know the frequencies for both, we should use the class of English humans, as this is narrower than the class of humans.

The problem is that this answer only applies when one class is a subclass of the other, the way the class of English deaths is a subclass of human deaths. But suppose we know that 40 percent of people with my genetic markers live past 80. And let's add that the reference class of people with my genetic markers is the same size as the reference class of English humans. As these two reference classes are the same size, the answer "use the narrowest reference class" can't be used.

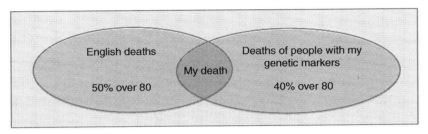

So the question remains: what credence should I have that I will live past 80? Some think this question has no good answer, and that actual frequentism should therefore be rejected. This seems to me an overreaction. We can answer that we should use both reference classes when assigning credence. Both reference classes are sources of evidence that should be taken into account and weighed up. There may not be any general rules for how to weigh them, but there is nothing new or mysterious about weighing evidence from various sources. If the chance of living past 80 is 40 percent relative to one reference class and 50 percent relative to another, I should take them both into account when forming beliefs. So it seems that there is no specific problem for chances here. We can now return to the question of whether we can justify the Principal Principle using actual frequentism.

9.3 Actual frequentism and the Principal Principle

Suppose all you know about a coin is that 50 percent of actual coin flips land Heads. With what credence should you believe that *this* flip will land Heads? The Principal Principle says: 50 percent. But why, given actual frequentism, should we accept Principal Principle?

Here's an argument, based on Strevens (1999). (The argument will go quickly, and will take for granted the concept of betting prices, so review Chapter 3 if it isn't at your fingertips.) Imagine a gambling game in which you have to bet on the outcome of a series of trials. Strevens proves that you will be best off in the long run if your betting prices match the frequencies. As actual frequentism identifies actual frequencies with chances, it follows that you are best off if your betting prices match the chances. Assuming that your betting prices match your credences, it follows that you are best off if your credences match the chances. And this is exactly what Principal Principle says: your credences should match the chances! QED.

But there is a problem. The argument only shows that you are best off *in the long run* if your credences match the chances. But the Principal Principle should apply to every case, including short run cases. To make this vivid, imagine you're only going to bet on one trial of a series of coin flips. Even if assigning 50 percent credence for Heads is a good *long-run* strategy over all the flips, it might not be a good *short-run* strategy for *this* flip. The earlier argument leaves it open that you might do better by assigning some other credence for this flip. Thus the argument fails to give a full justification of the Principal Principle.

One response is that if something is a good long-run strategy then it is a good short-run strategy, in the absence of specific information about the short-run event in question. As Hoefer (2007) puts it:

> It cannot be the case that [setting our credence for outcome A equal to a constant, x, over a series of n trials] is reasonable and justified, but . . . [setting our credence equal to x for each individual trial in the collection]— its identical sub-components—[is] unreasonable or unjustified. (p. 584)

But one strategy can be justified and the other unjustified if different constraints are in operation. When setting a long-run strategy, we are constrained to pick the same credence for every flip. When setting a short-run strategy, we are free to pick different credences for each flip. What is rational under the tougher constraints of a long-run strategy may not remain rational when the constraints are weaker.

So let's return to the question: even if assigning 50 percent credence in Heads for each event is a good long-run strategy over all the flips, why think it is a good short-run strategy for this flip?

It *is* a good short-run strategy if you should assign the *same* credence to each flip being Heads. For if each flip gets the same credence in Heads, then the only way to assign 50 percent credence in Heads as a long run strategy is to assign 50 percent credence for each flip. So we want something like the following principle:

> *Equal credence* Given that all we know about a class of events (e.g. flips) is that they have the same chance of being of type E (e.g. Heads), then we ought to assign the same credence to each of these events being of type E.[3]

This principle tells us to treat each individual event the same. So, can we defend *Equal credence*? *Equal credence* could be justified by appealing to the Principle of Indifference. Recall from Chapter 5:

> *Principle of Indifference* If there is no reason to assign one of the *n* possibilities a higher prior credence than any of the other possibilities, then each possibility should be assigned a credence equal to $1/n$.[4]

Let's work through how this applies here. The possibilities that get assigned the same credence are the permutations of Heads and Tails. Assuming the chance of Heads is 50 percent, the frequency of Heads must be 50 percent, so the permutations with two flips are: HT and TH. The Principle of Indifference assigns an equal credence to each permutation. So when faced with flip 1, you have 50 percent credence it is the H of HT, and a 50 percent credence it is the T of TH. The result is a credence of 50 percent that this particular flip is Heads, and we have justified the credence matching the chance (Principal Principle) as a short-run strategy.[5]

This argument of course relies on the Principle of Indifference, and we saw in Chapter 5 that attempts to justify this principle have not had much success. Still I think this discussion shows that the Principal Principle need not be taken as a primitive, brute constraint on rationality. Instead, it can be derived from the Principle of Indifference, for which there is independent motivation. And this is an advantage of actual frequentism.

9.4 Objections and hypothetical frequentism

The most serious objections to actual frequentism develop the intuition that actual frequencies can come apart from chances. A dramatic example is provided by the *problem of the single case*. This occurs when the event in question is an instance of a type of event that only occurs once. Suppose a coin is made, flipped once, it lands Heads, and then the coin is destroyed. Actual frequentism says that the chance of the coin landing Heads was 100 percent. And this seems wrong.

The problem remains when we increase the number of trials above 1. If there are two trials the only possible values of the chance of Heads are 0, 1/2, and 1, even if the coin is biased. This too seems wrong. So we have the problem of the double case. Similarly, we will have the problem of the triple case, and so on.

And no matter how large the number of trials, as long as it is a finite number, actual frequentism only allows chances that are fractions of integers (because chances are equal to m/n, the number of times the attribute occurred divided by the number of trials). But in fact there are scientific theories (namely quantum mechanics) that posit irrational chances such as $\frac{1}{\sqrt{2}}$. Actual frequentism is incompatible with such theories.

Hypothetical frequentism

To avoid these problems, hypothetical frequentists suggest that the chance is the frequency with which the outcome in question *would have happened*, if the type of event had occurred many times. For example, the chance that the single coin flip was Heads is the frequency with which it would have landed Heads if the coin had been flipped many times.

Hypothetical Frequentism

For each event of type t, the chance of outcome O occurring = The relative frequency of occurrences of O that *would have occurred in a large number of trials* of events of type t.

In slogan form, chances are identified with hypothetical frequencies. The actual frequencies are *evidence* for the chances. Hypothetical frequentism, like actual frequentism, automatically satisfies the rules of probability—hypothetical frequencies are frequencies, and frequencies satisfy the rules of probability.

One objection to hypothetical frequentism is that there is no such thing as what would have occurred in a large number of trials. Instead, there are a number of different things, each of which could have happened.

And even if there were a single thing that would have happened in a large number of trials, it isn't clear how we can discover what the chances are. We cannot simply observe what would have happened in the same way that we observe what did happen. A tempting response is that we can work out what would have happened using the chances. But this is circular—we are trying to discover the chances, so we cannot assume that we know the chances.

There are also problems with the entire frequency approach. For example, suppose an actual or hypothetical series of coin flips contains a lucky run of Heads toward the end. The frequency theories hold that these Heads will increase the chance of Heads overall. But a natural thought is that this is the wrong way round. Rather than the frequencies generating the chances, the chances should generate the frequencies. This thought leads to the *propensity theory of chance*. To understand this, let's back up and consider the metaphysical view that proponents of the frequency theory tend to have, and then contrast this with the metaphysical view proponents of the propensity theory tend to have.

9.5 Two metaphysical views

Frequency theorists tend to have something like the following view, associated with David Hume. At the most fundamental level, the world consists of local matters of fact. In one part of the universe, a star explodes. In another part of the universe, a cup falls. Add up all of these events, and you have a complete description of the entire universe. In slogan form, we might say that the universe is just one damn thing after another.[6]

This Humean picture does not include any *necessary* connections between these events. We let go of a cup and it falls. For a Humean, there is no necessary connection between these events. The cup might have floated away—nothing in the preceding events ensured that it would fall. If there is to be any *causation*, then it must be reducible to the pattern of events. Hume offered exactly such a reduction, identifying causation of E by C as the constant conjunction of C-type events with E-type events. Similarly, chance must be reduced to the pattern of events. And indeed actual frequency theorists identify the chance of O with the frequency of O in events of type t. So the actual frequency theory is compatible with an austere Humean metaphysics. One advantage of this view is epistemic—it is easy to explain how we can discover the chances.

On the competing, non-Humean, view, the events in the universe are bound together. The cup didn't just fall. It *had* to fall because it was pulled down by gravity. There was a necessary connection between the earlier state of the universe and the cup falling. This is the common-sense view. More generally, the universe does not just consist of a pattern of events at the fundamental level, it also consists of causes which connect events. On this view, *causes* are fundamental parts of the world, not reducible to patterns of events.

Furthermore, not all causes *entail* their effects. Some causes only make their effects more likely. Call these causes *propensities*. These propensities feature in a non-Humean theory of chance.

9.6 Propensity theory of chance

The key ideas behind the propensity theory are nicely put by Pierce (1910):

> I am, then, to define the meaning of the statement that the [chance], that if a die be thrown from a dice box it will turn up a number divisible by three, is one-third. The statement means that the die has a certain "would-be"; and to say that the die has a "would-be" is to say that it has a property, quite analogous to any *habit* that a man might have . . . [T]o define the die's "would-be" it is necessary to say how it would lead the die to behave on an occasion that would bring out the full consequence of the "would-be"; and this statement will not of itself imply that the "would-be" of the die consists in such behaviour. . . .
>
> Now in order that the full effect of the die's "would-be" may find expression, it is necessary that the die should undergo an endless series of throws from the dice box. (pp. 79–80)

What Pierce calls a "would-be," we call a "propensity." The key claim is that the propensity is more fundamental than the behavior. So whereas the hypothetical frequentist says that the chance is determined by what would happen if the die were thrown, the propensity theorist says that the chance is determined by an intrinsic property of the die—this intrinsic property is called a "propensity." The propensity *causes* the behavior, and is a part of the die even if it never finds expression in a series of throws. "Propensity" has the same meaning as "disposition" or "tendency," and I think the most helpful way of thinking about it is as a weakening of the concept of a cause. If events of type C *cause* events of type E, then a C event always leads to an E event; if events of type C have a *propensity* to cause events of type E, then a C event *tends/is disposed* to lead to an E event.

The propensity theory is most plausible where the chance is a fundamental part of the causal structure of the world. The best example of this in contemporary science is in quantum mechanics, and the most influential proponent of the propensity theory, Karl Popper (1959a), developed it to be applicable to quantum mechanics. In quantum mechanics, probabilities cause things to happen. For example, according to quantum mechanics, the chance of an atom of Uranium-238 decaying in 4.47 billion years is 50 percent. For the propensity theorist, this means that each such atom has a propensity—an intrinsic property—that causes decay within 4.47 billion years in half the atoms.

The propensity theory avoids the problem that the chance depends on any accidental features of the world. If there turn out to be a lucky run of uranium atoms that decay within 4.47 billion years, this won't change the propensity; the propensity causes the decay rather than the other way round.

The propensity theory also avoids the problem of the single case, and the related problems. Even if there were only one atom of Uranium-238 in the universe, it would still have a 50 percent chance of decaying in 4.47 billion years.

But the propensity theory has a problem with how we might *discover* the propensities. We cannot directly observe them, as we can with actual frequencies. How do we know that the world contains these connections between events? This is a general problem for non-Humeans—we see events, but we don't see connections between events, so why should we think such connections exist? But the non-Humean has a standard answer: we know about these necessary connections because they best *explain* our observations. We know that apples must fall to Earth because that would explain why they always do. Similarly, we know that atoms have a propensity to decay because that propensity would explain their decaying behavior. So although the propensity theorist does face some extra questions, they are questions that all non-Humeans must answer, so they aren't special problems for the propensity theory of chance.

A more serious problem is known as Humphreys' Paradox.[7] The root of the problem is that the rules of probability entail that if there is a probability of A given B, there is also a probability of B given A. Formally:

Symmetry P(A|B) has a numerical value if and only if P(B|A) has a numerical value.

But propensities are not symmetrical.

A = The die shows 6

B = The die is fair

According to the propensity theory of chance, Ch(A|B) = 1/6. But there is no value for Ch(B|A); there is no propensity that the die is fair given that it shows 6. For showing 6 has no effect on the fairness of the die. The problem is that probability is symmetrical but causation is not; as propensity is a type of causation, propensities are not symmetrical.

One propensity theorist response is to reject *Symmetry*. They can go on to explain that when it comes to the propensity theory, not all the rules of probability apply. Specifically, the mathematical development of probability theory does not map perfectly onto propensities. It is then incumbent on the propensity theorist to develop a theory of propensities, and to explain where and why it diverges from standard probability theory.[8]

9.7 Propensities and the Principal Principle

A major problem for the propensity theory is justifying the Principal Principle. Why should our beliefs match the propensities? Lewis puts the objection as follows:

> Be my guest—posit all the primitive unHumean whatnots you like . . . But play fair in naming your whatnots. Don't call any alleged feature of reality "chance" unless you've already shown that you have something, knowledge of which could constrain rational credence. I think I see dimly but well enough, how knowledge of frequencies . . . could constrain rational credence. I don't begin to see, for instance, how knowledge that two universals stand in a certain special relation N* could constrain rational credence about the future instantiation of those universals. (1994, p. 484)

Underlying this objection is the conflict between the two metaphysical views. Lewis is a Humean, and doesn't believe in the common-sense notion of a cause, whereby two events are necessarily connected—by universals, or by other "primitive unHumean whatnots." Similarly, he doesn't believe in a weakening of this notion of cause to a propensity. Propensities are just more whatnots. And the point Lewis is driving at in this passage is this: *even if these whatnots exist, why should they constrain our beliefs?* Actual frequencies are the sort of thing that might constrain our beliefs because actual frequencies describe actual patterns of events in the world. But why should we care about this whatnot called "propensity"?

Analytic Principal Principle

Hall (2004) suggests the following justification of the Principal Principle:[9]

> What I "have" are . . . *chances*, which, I assert, are simply an extra ingredient of metaphysical reality, not to be "reduced" to anything else. What's more, it is just a basic conceptual truth about chance that it is the sort of thing, knowledge of which constrains rational credence. Of course, it is a further question—one that certainly cannot be answered definitively from the armchair—whether nature provides anything that answers to our concept of chance. But we have long since learned to live with such modest sceptical worries. And at any rate, they are irrelevant to the question at issue, which is whether my primitivist position can "rationalize" the Principal Principle. The answer, manifestly, is that it can: for, again, it is part of my position that this principle states an analytic truth about chance and rational credence. (Italics original, 2004, p. 106)

The idea is that it is part of the *meaning* of "chance" that it refers to a propensity that constrains rational credence. We can make this explicit by defining "chance" as "the thing that causes events and constrains beliefs."

Objection to the analytic Principal Principle

The problem is that given Hall's beefed up concept of chance, we have no reason to think that there is anything in nature that satisfies it (and even if there is, it remains unclear why it satisfies it.) Hall suggests that it is irrelevant whether there is anything in nature that answers to this concept of chance. But if there isn't, this theory of chance isn't going to be of any interest.

Let's go through an analogy (this is like the "boche" example of Chapter 5). Suppose I introduce the name "SuperJulius" for the person who (a) invented the zip and (b) was infallible, if such a person exists. The fact that I have defined "SuperJulius" in this way gives you no reason to believe that someone infallible invented the zip. Instead, you should think it very unlikely that "SuperJulius" refers to anyone. Generally, the more analytic connections we add to a word, the less likely the word refers. And even if SuperJulius exists, we have no explanation of why he was infallible.

Hall faces a similar problem. He holds that it is analytic that chances (a) cause events, that is, are propensities and (b) constrain beliefs. So he is defining "chance" as "the thing that causes events and constrains beliefs." But this doesn't give us any reason to think that there really are things in the world that satisfy this definition. Instead, we should think that Hall's word "chance" fails to refer. Hall suggests that this is a skeptical worry, but far from being an outlandish scenario, it seems to be a scenario that may well be true. And even if we grant that there are propensities that constrain rational credence, it is still mysterious *why* they do so.[10]

If appeal to analyticities doesn't work, perhaps we have to argue that the Principal Principle is a primitive constraint on rationality. We have already seen that some such constraints are needed if we are to avoid crazy beliefs (Chapter 5). Whereas the frequency theorist can derive the Principal Principle from independently motivated Principles of Indifference (9.3), the propensity theorist cannot, which is perhaps a slight disadvantage of the propensity theory.

Reply to Lewis

Can this disadvantage be avoided? Can the Propensity Theorist justify the Principal Principle some other way? Let's have another look at Lewis's (1994) key claim:

> I don't begin to see . . . how knowledge that two universals stand in a certain special relation N* could constrain rational credence about the future instantiation of those universals. (p. 484)

Suppose that the relation, N*, was one of causation. Suppose universal (i.e. property) C is related to universal E in such a way that the instantiation of C *guarantees* the instantiation of E a second later. Perhaps C things always decay into E things. Would knowledge of this constrain rational credence about the future instantiation of those universals? Of course. Wherever you believe C is instantiated, you should believe E will be instantiated a second later. Now let's weaken the relation. Suppose that instead of C guaranteeing E, C *almost* guarantees E. That is, in the whole of history there is one instance of C that fails to generate E. Would knowledge of this still constrain rational credence about the future instantiation of those universals? Of course. Wherever you believe C is instantiated, you should have *very high credence* that E will be instantiated a second later. And this relation between C and E is one of propensity—C tends to produce E, but doesn't always. So knowledge of propensities does constrain rational credence.

This approach will need to piggy-back on the frequency theorist's justification of Principal Principle. Start by assuming that the frequency theorist can connect frequencies with rational belief. Now add that propensities provide evidence for frequencies. It follows that we can connect propensities with rational belief.

Summary

In this chapter, we've looked at the main options for a theory of chance—the frequency theory and the propensity theory. The frequency theory faces the problem of the reference class and the problem of justifying the Principal Principle, but we saw that both problems have promising answers. A more general problem with the frequency approach is the thought that frequencies are generated by chances rather than being identical to them. This thought leads to the propensity theory of chance, which says that chance is a fundamental part of the world. This faces Humphreys' Paradox, that not all the rules of probability apply to chance, and it also faces a problem justifying the Principal Principle.

The Principal Principle is a rationality constraint. In the next chapter, we'll consider two other candidates for rationality constraints—that your beliefs should match your expected future beliefs, and that your beliefs should reach a compromise with your epistemic peers.

Study questions

1 What is the Principal Principle? Why is it so-called?

2 What is the actual frequency theory?

3 What is the best argument against/in favor of the actual frequency theory?

4 What is the propensity theory?

5 What is the best argument against/in favor of the propensity theory?

Advanced questions

6 Is Lewis right that the Principal Principle is the central feature of our concept of chance?

7 Do you agree that the reference class problem doesn't create any special problem for chances?

8 Is hypothetical frequentism better or worse than actual frequentism?

9 Do the arguments regarding chance give us good reason to reject either of the "two metaphysical views"?

10 Is the criticism offered of Hall's view successful?

Further reading

The distinction between chance and credence can be traced to Carnap (1945). Lewis (1980) remains central to the contemporary debate; but see Hoefer (2007) for an accessible and improved version of the frequency theory. For more on propensity theories, see Gillies (2000).

The supplement to Eagle (2014) has a helpful overview.

10

Reflection and disagreement

The world is full of disagreement. How should we respond to those who disagree with us? And not only is there disagreement between different people, there can be disagreement between a person at one time and that same person at a later time. This happens whenever you change your mind. In this chapter, we'll look at two principles that aim to constrain beliefs given such disagreement.

The first, the Principle of Reflection (10.1), says roughly that your beliefs should match what you think you'll believe in the future. It says that you should defer to your future self. The second, the Equal Weight View (10.2), says that you should give the opinions of an epistemic peer the same weight as you give your own. Both these principles have initial plausibility, but face apparent counterexamples.

10.1 Reflection

If the weather forecaster tells you it will rain on Sunday, you should believe it will rain on Sunday. Generally, if you know what an *expert* thinks, you should defer to their opinion. That much is uncontroversial. But who counts as an expert? Van Fraassen (1984) made the suggestion that your future self counts as an expert. So if you know that in the future you will believe it will rain on Sunday, you should now believe that it will rain on Sunday. We can put the principle formally as follows, letting P1 represent the credences at the earlier time, t1, and P2 the credences at the later time, t2:

Reflection

If you are rational then $P1(H \mid P2(H) = x) = x$

This says that you should hold a particular conditional probability: Given that your later credence in H is x, your earlier credence in H should be x. A useful way to understand Reflection is to think of it as expressing *self-trust*. It says that you should trust your future self to form the right beliefs, and so you should defer to those future beliefs.

It's important to realize that although Reflection looks like it is connecting credences at two different times, it isn't really. It's connecting credences at one time, t1, with the agent's *beliefs* about her own credences at a later time, t2. Reflection doesn't say anything about what the agent will really believe at t2. It says approximately that if the t1 agent believes that she will believe-H-with-credence-x-at-t2, she should now believe H with credence x.

What can be said in favor of Reflection? There seems to be something right about it, and this is because your future self usually knows more than you do now. In the normal course of events you acquire evidence as time passes, so your future beliefs will be based on more evidence than you have now, and so will be more accurate.

But numerous purported counterexamples to Reflection have been given, which fall into two main classes: *belief in future memory loss* and *belief in future irrationality*.

Belief in future memory loss

William Talbott (1991) argues that you should not satisfy Reflection regarding what you have for dinner, because you will forget. Suppose at t1 you remember (S) having spaghetti for dinner on a particular day, so $P1(S) = 0.999$. By next year, you will have no idea what you had for dinner that day. You'll only know that you eat spaghetti, say, 10 percent of the time, so $P2(S) = 0.1$. Reflection says you should defer to your future self and have 10 percent credence in S, that is, $P1(S \mid P2(H) = 0.1) = 0.1$. But this is obviously wrong. You should ignore your later forgetful state and hold: $P1(S \mid P2(H) = 0.1) = 0.999$. So Reflection is not a constraint on rationality.

Notice that it doesn't matter whether you really do forget that you ate spaghetti. As long as you expect to forget you ate spaghetti, you should violate Reflection. And in fact you don't even need to fully believe that you will lose your memory—you should violate Reflection even if you believe there is just a possibility that you'll lose your memory.

Frank Arntzenius (2003) demonstrates this with a more exotic story. Suppose you are to be escorted to the city of Shangri-La either through the mountains (M) or over the sea (−M), depending on whether a fair coin lands Heads or Tails. If you travel over the mountains, you will arrive with memories of the mountains; but if you travel by sea your memories of the sea journey will be removed and replaced with memories of the mountains. Being told all this, when at t2 you arrive with memories of the mountains, you should only have a 0.5 credence in M. But when at t1 you're on the mountain path, you can be sure that M is true. So $P1(M \mid P2(M) = 0.5) \neq 0.5$; instead, $P1(M \mid P2(M) = 0.5) = 1$. So even if you end up traveling over the mountains and your memories aren't wiped, you should still violate Reflection because you don't fully trust your future memories.

Belief in future irrationality

David Christensen (1991) offers an example involving a drug, LSQ, that causes people to believe (F) they can fly by flapping their arms. So at t2, after taking the drug, $P2(F) = 1$, but knowing at t1 that you're about to take the drug, you should not believe you can fly, so $P1(F \mid P2(F) = 1) = 0.0001$, violating Reflection.

There are many similar examples. The ratio of people who think they are the Messiah to people who are the Messiah is high. So given that in the future you will think you are the Messiah, you should not now believe you are the Messiah. The same applies if you believe you're about to fall under the influence of people who can have undue influence on your beliefs, be they Monks, cults, hypnotists, or smooth-talking car salesmen. In such cases, you may expect to believe in the future that silence is holy, lizards rule Earth, you are a chicken, or this car is the best deal in town, but that doesn't mean you should believe it now. Again, Reflection is not a constraint on rationality.

Qualified Reflection

Despite these problems, there still seems to be something correct about Reflection. So rather than giving up on Reflection altogether, some philosophers have argued that it just needs to be qualified.

The two classes of counterexamples suggest that two qualifications have to be made to Reflection—agents should satisfy Reflection if and only if

(i) they are certain that they won't forget anything, and

(ii) they are certain that future changes in belief will be rational.[1]

Notice that it doesn't matter what will happen; what matters is what the agent thinks will happen. The suggestion is that they should satisfy Reflection when they think they will keep their memories and update rationally in the future.

(ii) requires clarification. What is it for future belief change to be rational? We can adopt the theory of Chapter 4 that the only way to rationally change belief is to conditionalize. So (ii) says that the agent is certain that all future changes in belief will be due to conditionalization. If so, (i) follows, as forgetting is a way of changing your beliefs that differs from conditionalization. So we can simplify the condition:

> *Qualified Reflection* Agents should satisfy Reflection if and only if they are certain they will always be conditionalizers.

Assuming this is correct, should we satisfy Reflection? Plausibly, we should not, for we should not be certain we will always be conditionalizers—we are flawed agents who are susceptible to drugs, cult leaders, hypnotists, and forgetting.

One interesting feature of this result is that it separates the question "what constraints *should my* credences satisfy?" from "what constraints does an *ideally rational* agent satisfy?" An ideally rational agent never forgets and is immune to drugs, cult leaders, and hypnotists, so an ideally rational agent satisfies Reflection. But that doesn't mean we should. We should take into account our fallibility and make allowances for it.

This is an instance of a general problem in arguing from ideals to constraints for humans. There are ways in which we should not emulate ideal agents. For a simple example, ideal agents should have credence 1 that they are ideal, but we should not. Similarly, ideal agents never need to apologize because they never do anything wrong. But that doesn't mean we should never apologize. To be as ideal as we can, we have to make allowances for our flaws.

This raises a complication for how we understand inductive probabilities. One way of understanding them is as the credence that an ideal agent would have. A different conception understands them as the probabilities that our degrees of belief *ought* to match. This discussion shows how these concepts can come apart. To the extent that we are concerned with ideal rationality, we are interested in the former. To the extent that we are concerned with what we ought to believe, we are concerned with the latter.

The motivation for Reflection was that there seemed to be something right about saying that you should defer to your own future opinions. But what about deferring to the opinions of other people? That doesn't seem as appealing. Someone else believing something doesn't give me a reason to believe it. Or does it?

10.2 Disagreement

A Rabbi and a Priest walk into a bar. Sadly nothing funny happens. Instead, each spends the evening trying to convince the other that they are right on matters theological. The Priest tries to convince the Rabbi that Jesus was the son of God. The Rabbi tries to convince the Priest that he wasn't. By closing time, several things have become apparent. First, each is rightly convinced that the other has all the same evidence, for example, they know all the same texts just as well. Second, each is rightly convinced that the other is just as intelligent as they are. When these two conditions hold—equal evidence and equal intelligence—say that the agents are *epistemic peers*. (And we'll assume the agents know they are epistemic peers.) Third, neither will budge. The disagreement between them remains. The question is:

Is it rational for this disagreement to remain?

This kind of case is not restricted to religious disagreement of course. Disagreement is everywhere, and the question of how we should respond is one of the most practical of epistemological problems. Here is a less profound case that is easier to think about:

Mental Math

After a restaurant meal, my friend and I decide to tip 20% and split the check, rounding up to the nearest dollar. As we have done many times, we do the math in our heads. We have long and equally good track records at this (in the cases where we've disagreed, checking with a calculator has shown us right equally frequently); and I have no reason (such as those involving alertness or tiredness or differential consumption of coffee or wine) for suspecting one of us to be especially good, or bad, at the current reasoning task. I come up with $43; but then my friend announces that she got $45.[2]

Is it rational for this disagreement to remain?

The *Equal Weight View* says no. It says that each should give the opinion of the other the same weight as they give their own. So each should alter their credence in the direction of the other's credence. If my initial credence that the bill comes to $43 is 0.8, and my friend's initial credence in $43 is 0.4, then after the announcements we should both end up with a credence half-way between, that is, 0.6. And if the Rabbi started with a credence of 0.1 that Jesus was the son of God and the Priest started with a credence of 0.98, then they should both end up with a credence of $(0.1 + 0.98)/2 = 0.54$.

For Equal Weight: Lack of arbitrariness

The main argument in favor of the Equal Weight View is that it seems arbitrary to deny it. To deny the Equal Weight View is to give your own verdict more (or less) weight than that of an epistemic peer. But as an epistemic peer has the same evidence and intelligence as you, surely you should give their verdict the same weight as your own.

We can make this intuition vivid by imagining that instead of the result being produced by mental math, it is produced by mechanical devices. Suppose each of us inputs the numbers into our own calculating device, each of which produces the wrong answer 10 percent of the time. If my device says "$43" and yours says "$45," then we should surely give both answers equal weight. To do otherwise would be to arbitrarily favor one device over the other. But they are equally reliable, so it would be wrong to favor one over the other. And it seems we should say the same when the device used to calculate the answer is the part of our own brain that does mental arithmetic. Let's now consider two arguments against the Equal Weight View.

Against Equal Weight 1: Spinelessness and self-trust

The main problem with the Equal Weight View is that it leaves us unable to hold any view on which there is disagreement, a consequence Elga (2007) calls *spinelessness*. (But be wary of letting an emotive name like "spinelessness" color our judgment; compare "the Patriot Act.") On any complicated issue, such as religion or politics, you are likely to have a large number of epistemic peers who hold a wide range of opinions. If you give all these opinions the same weight as your own, you will end up having a low credence that any one of them is right. Which means you should give up any convictions you might have, and be agnostic about pretty much everything.

Elga's response

Elga thinks the *problem of spinelessness* can be answered. That is, he thinks the Equal Weight View is compatible with holding strong beliefs on controversial issues. The reason is that people who disagree with you on controversial issues are likely to disagree with you on a host of related issues, so you should judge them wrong about these issues, and therefore judge them not to be epistemic peers after all. Elga offers the following case:

> Think of a smart and well-informed friend who has a basic political framework diametrically opposed to your own. Imagine that the two of you are both presented with an unfamiliar and tricky political claim. You haven't thought things through yet, and so have no idea what you will eventually decide about the claim. Still—*don't you think that you are more likely than your friend to correctly judge the claim, supposing that the two of you end up disagreeing?* If so, then however quick-witted, well-informed, intellectually honest, and thorough you think your friend is, you do not count her as an epistemic peer with respect to that claim. And if you do not count her as a

peer, the Equal Weight View does not require you give her conclusion the same weight as your own. (p. 493, Italics added)

Objection to Elga's response

But I don't think the Equal Weight Theorist can give this response. Consider the italicized question: "don't you think that you are more likely than your friend to correctly judge the claim, supposing that the two of you end up disagreeing?" I think the Equal Weight Theorist must answer: "No, I'm no more likely to be right that my friend." For the Equal Weight Theorist must give just as much weight to her opponent's belief in a diametrically opposed political framework as she does to her own. It follows that she must also give equal weight to any view that is derived from that framework, such as the tricky claim in question.

So let's suppose the Equal Weight View entails Spinelessness. Some philosophers take this consequence as sufficient reason to reject the Equal Weight View. But what's wrong with Spinelessness (other than its name)? Given the range of disagreements between well-informed people, surely the rational thing to do is to take a step back and withhold judgment on controversial matters on which your epistemic peers disagree. The human mind hates uncertainty, so it's considered normal, even desirable, to have opinions. But that doesn't make it rational. Perhaps beliefs, like everything else, should be held in moderation.

Against Equal Weight 2: Ignoring evidence

Some argue that the Equal Weight View amounts to ignoring evidence. Suppose that epistemic peers Alice and Bob initially assign credence of 0.5 to some proposition H. Then they acquire evidence E1, which Alice takes to justify credence of 0.8 in H, but Bob takes to justify credence of 0.2 in H. After discussing their disagreement, they both have the following evidence:

E1: The original evidence.

E2: Alice reached credence 0.8 on the basis of E1.

E3: Bob reached credence 0.2 on the basis of E1.

The Equal Weight View says that they should each end up with credence in H of 0.5.

Here is an analysis that results in a different verdict: E2 and E3 cancel each other out. E2 says Alice takes E1 to confirm H; E3 says Bob takes E1 to *dis*confirm H. With no reason to think Alice a better judge than Bob, or vice versa, E2 and E3 push us equally in opposite directions, thus canceling each other out. The only evidence left is E1, with which Alice reached a credence in H of 0.8. Supposing she was initially reasoning correctly to get a credence of 0.8 in H, she should end up with credence of 0.8 in H.[3]

Response: Opposing and undercutting defeaters

To defend the Equal Weight View, we can argue that the earlier analysis misdescribes the evidence. The analysis says that Alice should count E2 as evidence for H above and beyond E1. But that's double-counting; the only evidence Alice has for H is E1. Her belief that E1 supports H doesn't give her further evidence for H.

But if E2 doesn't count in favor of H, can E3 count against H, as the Equal Weight View says? Yes. Let's back up and consider why Alice believes H with 0.8 certainty. She believes H to degree 0.8 because she believes E1, and *takes E1 to be evidence for H*. But she might be wrong; she might have taken E1 to be evidence for H, when in fact it isn't. Learning of Bob's disagreement suggests that Alice is indeed mistaken, for Bob does not take E1 to be evidence for H. So on hearing Bob's disagreement, Alice should doubt that she has evaluated the evidence correctly. With the source of her belief in H thus undermined, Alice's credence in H should fall back to 0.5, just as the Equal Weight View says.

The evidence in this case is unusual. Usually evidence counts against a hypothesis by directly *opposing* it. For example, evidence that a coin landed Tails opposes the hypothesis that it landed Heads. But suppose you believed the coin landed Heads because Charlie told you, and you then discover Charlie lies. The discovery that Charlie lies *undercuts* your reason to believe the coin landed Heads, and therefore counts against Heads. Undercutting evidence typically comes in the form of evidence that your sources are unreliable, for example, the newspaper is inaccurate, your memory is failing, your eyesight is faulty. Peer disagreement is another undercutting case. On this analysis, E3 does not *oppose* H; it *undercuts* Alice's reason for believing H. That is, it undercuts Alice's belief that E is evidence for H. So Alice should revert to what she would believe if she had never learnt any of the evidence.[4]

Summary

In this chapter, we considered two plausible candidates for rationality constraints—Reflection and the Equal Weight View. I suggested that

Reflection is a plausible constraint on ideal agents who can be sure that they will always change their beliefs in a rational manner, but is too demanding for humans. On Disagreement, we considered the Equal Weight View, and looked at how two objections, Spinelessness and Ignoring Evidence, might be answered.

In the next chapter, we take a step back and consider more closely the probability-raising theory of justification introduced in Chapter 2.

Appendix: Sleeping Beauty

The Sleeping Beauty problem is a simple problem that interacts with conditionalization, chance, and Reflection, and brings out a limitation of the Bayesian framework. Here is the problem:

> It is Sunday night. Sleeping Beauty is about to be drugged and put to sleep. She will be woken briefly on Monday. Then she will be put back to sleep and her memory of being awoken will be erased. She might be awoken on Tuesday. Whether or not she is depends on the result of the toss of a fair coin. If it lands Heads, she will not be woken. If it lands Tails, she will be awoken on Tuesday. The Monday and Tuesday awakenings will be indistinguishable. Sleeping Beauty knows the setup of the experiment and is a paragon of probabilistic rationality. Her credence on Sunday that the coin will land Heads is 1/2. Should this change when she is woken?

> Some say no; her credence in Heads should stay at 1/2. Call these Halfers.

> Some say yes; her credence in Heads should fall to 1/3 (and her credence in Tails should rise to 2/3). Call these Thirders.

There are three possible wakings, all of which are subjectively indistinguishable, that is, the agent cannot tell which waking is taking place. The following picture shows the three possible wakings:

Sleeping beauty.

When Beauty is woken, she knows only that it is one of these three wakings. The question is whether being woken confirms Tails, as Thirders claim, or is irrelevant to Heads and Tails, as Halfers claim.

With many philosophical problems, common sense gives a clear answer, and the question is whether this answer survives scrutiny. But there are commonsensical arguments for both the opposing answers in the Sleeping Beauty problem.

Thirder argument

The simplest argument for 1/3 is a frequency argument. Suppose the experiment were repeated many times. Half the time the coin would land Heads and half the time Tails. The Heads landings would result in one waking and the Tails landings would result in two wakings. So overall there would be twice as many Tails wakings as Heads wakings. Assigning each waking equal credence, we get P(Heads) = 1/3:

Monday   Tuesday

Heads   1/3

Tails   1/3   1/3

Thirders.

The Halfer could respond by denying either of two assumptions. First, the Halfer could grant that Thirders are right about a *series* of experiments, but deny the same conclusion holds when the experiment only occurs *once*. For in a series of experiments there really are lots of Heads wakings *and* lots of Tails wakings, and it is reasonable to take today to be randomly selected from among them and therefore to assign equal credence. Whereas if there is only one experiment, there is either a Heads waking *or* Tails wakings. There aren't both Heads and Tails wakings; one of them remains a non-actual possibility. And it is less reasonable to take today to be randomly selected from among merely possible wakings.

A second Halfer response is to reject the Thirder argument even for the series of trials, by denying that Beauty is observing a randomly selected day. That assumption allows the Thirder to assign an equal credence to each waking, resulting in twice the credence in Tails. But the Halfer can argue that the correct way to assign credence is to first assign 50 percent each to Heads and Tails, a move which is endorsed by the Principal Principle. Then the 50 percent assigned to Tails is further divided equally among wakings. The resulting distribution looks like this:

Halfers.

Overall, we end up with 50 percent credence in Tails, which is the Halfer's preferred distribution.

Halfer argument

The main Halfer argument is that Beauty has not learnt anything new. All that's happened is that she has been woken, and she knew all along that she would be woken. So her credence should remain what it was before, that is, 1/2. This answer is supported by *conditionalization*, which says that the only rational way to change beliefs is to learn some evidence and eliminate the possibilities that the evidence rules out. But no new evidence has been learnt, so the beliefs should remain as they were.

Some object that Beauty has learnt something new—she has learnt that *now*—is a time when she is woken. She didn't know this on Sunday. On Sunday, before being put to sleep, Beauty knew that "now" was Sunday. After being woken, she no longer knows that "now" is Sunday—in fact she knows it is not, she knows that "now" is Monday or Tuesday. She has acquired a new belief: "it is now Monday or Tuesday." And she has acquired the belief in a way that brings out a limitation of the traditional Bayesian framework.

In the Bayesian framework, the objects of belief, propositions, are either true or false, eternally. This is why we update by conditionalization, which amounts to eliminating false possibilities. But beliefs like "it is now Monday" are not eternally either true or false; they are false at one time and true at a later time. So conditionalization is the wrong way to update these beliefs. Instead of eliminating false beliefs once and for all, we have to allow that something false now will be true later, and something true now will be false later. The Sleeping Beauty problem has drawn attention to this limitation, and there are now numerous suggestions for how to expand the Bayesianism framework to incorporate such beliefs.

Study questions

1 What is Reflection?

2 Describe a counterexample to Reflection.

3 Describe how Reflection can be modified to avoid the counterexample.

4 Explain the Equal Weight view.

5 Explain an objection to the Equal Weight view. Does it succeed?

Advanced questions

6 Are there counterexamples to Reflection other than the two discussed?

7 Can a version of Reflection be formulated if the agent only has a high degree of belief that they will always be conditionalizers? (see Briggs 2009)

8 Is the defense offered of spinelessness convincing?

9 Does the Equal Weight View ignore evidence?

Further reading

The Principle of Reflection was introduced by van Fraassen (1984). Weisberg (2007) offers an accessible and substantive discussion.

There has been growing interest in disagreement in recent years, and there are now two collections of papers on the topic (Feldman and Warfield 2010; Lackey and Christensen 2013).

The Sleeping Beauty problem was introduced by Elga (2000), which remains the central paper, together with Lewis's (2001) reply. See Titelbaum (forthcoming) for a useful overview of the many responses.

11

Confirmation and the old evidence problem

Consider the probability-raising theory of confirmation, versions of which have been in use throughout this book:

Probability-raising theory of confirmation[1]

E *confirms* H relative to B means $P(H|E) > P(H)$

E *disconfirms* H relative to B means $P(H|E) < P(H)$

E is *independent* of H relative to B means $P(H|E) = P(H)$

It's time to consider this theory more closely. We'll compare our probability-raising theory of confirmation to two competing theories, *falsificationism* and *hypothetic-deductivism*, and argue that it retains the best bits of them (11.1). Then we'll elaborate on some other appealing features of the probability-raising account (11.2) before discussing the most prominent objection—the old evidence problem (11.3).

11.1 Deductive theories

The probability-raising theory of confirmation is neutral about whether the probability used is subjective (credence) or inductive. But there are reasons to be unhappy with both. On the one hand, some think that inductive probability is a myth borne of wishful thinking (see Chapter 5). On the other hand, some think that credences are not the sort of thing that can be used in a theory of confirmation. The problem is that credences, being simply degrees of belief, are not objective enough to play a role in science. As Jaynes (1968) put it:

the notion of [credence] belongs to the field of psychology and has no place in applied statistics. Or, to state this more constructively, objectivity requires that a statistical analysis should make use, not of anybody's personal opinions, but rather the specific factual data on which those opinions are based. (p. 228)

This gives us reason to consider theories not based on probabilities, but on deductive logic alone. Two such theories have been historically important, *falsificationism* and *hypothetico-deductivism*. But they are no longer popular among philosophers because they are silent when there is no deductive relation between evidence and hypothesis, and because, as we'll see, their insights can be incorporated into the probability-raising theory.

Falsificationism

Popper (1959b) argued that we should try to *falsify* theories rather than confirm them. We falsify a theory by finding evidence that is incompatible with it. Falsified hypotheses should be rejected; surviving hypotheses should be retained and subjected to further attempts to falsify them. But we should not believe that these hypotheses are likely to be true—their survival does not increase their inductive probability. We can say no more than that they have survived possible refutation, or as Popper put it, they have been *corroborated*.[2] So this isn't so much an alternative theory of confirmation as an alternative that rejects our concept of confirmation altogether.

Let's go through an example. Suppose we want to evaluate the hypothesis that all ravens are black. Clearly a white raven would falsify the hypothesis, so it is valuable to look for white ravens. Popper and Bayesians can agree on that. What if we found a black raven? Bayesians tend to hold that finding a black raven confirms that all ravens are black. Popper disagrees. As he doesn't expect unobserved ravens to resemble observed ravens (as the problem of induction has not been solved), there is nothing especially useful about a black raven. It is important only to the extent that it doesn't refute the hypothesis. So it is exactly as useful as a white sneaker, or a yellow banana—they don't refute the hypothesis either.

We won't discuss induction in this chapter. We'll just focus on an insight that Popper seems to be right about—that we should reject theories if evidence is found that entails their falsity.

The probability-raising theory of confirmation retains this insight. The main task is to translate "falsification" into probabilistic terminology, which we can do as follows:

"E falsifies H" means "P(H|E) = 0."

That is, E falsifies H when the probability of H given E is 0. Assuming P(H) > 0, P(H|E) = 0 < P(H), so E disconfirms H.

Furthermore, a probability of 0 means the theory is impossible, which would amount to a rejection of the theory. So the probability-raising theory of confirmation retains the insight that a theory should be rejected if falsifying evidence is found. Let's move on to another theory of confirmation that uses only deductive logic.

Hypothetico-deductivism

Hypothetico-deductivism says that a hypothesis H is confirmed by evidence E if and only if E is deductively *entailed* by H.[3]

Hypothetico-deductivism: E confirms H if and only if H deductively entails E[4]

For example, suppose H = All ravens are black, and E = All observed ravens are black. The truth of H deductively entails the truth of E, so according to Hypothetico-deductivism, E confirms H. This is intuitively the correct result.

The probability-raising theory of confirmation keeps this insight. The main task is to translate "deductively entails" into probabilistic terminology. We can do so as follows:

"H deductively entails E" means "$P(E|H) = 1$."

Assuming that $P(E) < 1$, we get the result that $P(E|H) > P(E)$, so E confirms H.

So *falsificationism* and *hypothetico-deductivism* are special cases of the probability-raising account of confirmation. *Falsificationism* describes cases where $P(H|E) = 0$ and *hypothetico-deductivism* describes cases where $P(E|H) = 1$. The probability-raising account deals correctly with both.

11.2 Surprising and unsurprising evidence

The probability raising theory of confirmation gives intuitively correct results for other cases too. Recall that Bayes Theorem shows us how to derive the value of P(H|E) from P(H):

$$P(H|E) = P(H)\frac{P(E|H)}{P(E)}$$

To obtain P(H|E), P(H) gets multiplied by *the multiplier* P(E|H)/P(E). The size of the difference between P(H|E) and P(H) reflects the *degree of confirmation*.

Surprising evidence

The smaller the credence of E, the greater the multiplier, so the greater the value of P(H|E). This reflects the natural thought that surprising evidence strongly confirms hypotheses that predict it. For example, Einstein's theory of relativity (H) predicted that light would be deflected by gravity (E). This was a very surprising result, so P(E) was extremely small, say 0.0001; yet E was entailed by the theory of relativity, so P(E|H) = 1. So the multiplier, P(E|H)/P(E), was huge (perhaps 1/0.0001 = 10,000), giving a massive boost to P(H|E). Sure enough, when E was discovered, there were headlines around the world proclaiming the revolution in science.

Unsurprising evidence

Similarly, the greater the probability of E, the lower the value of P(H|E). This is demonstrated in the following dialogue from the Simpsons:

Homer: Not a bear in sight. The Bear Patrol must be working like a charm.

Lisa: That's specious reasoning, Dad. By your logic I could claim that this rock keeps tigers away [H].

Homer: Oh, how does it work?

Lisa: It doesn't work.

Homer: Uh-huh.

Lisa: It's just a stupid rock.

Homer: Uh-huh.

Lisa: But I don't see any tigers around [E], do you?

pause

Homer: Lisa, I want to buy your rock.

In this example,

H = The rock keeps tigers away

E = There are no tigers around

H entails E, so P(E|H) = 1, which is greater than P(E) as long as there might have been tigers around, that is, P(E) < 1. Thus P(E|H) > P(E), so the multiplier is greater than 1, so E does confirm H; Homer is right.

So what's Homer got wrong? He's missed that the *degree of confirmation* is tiny because the evidence is very unsurprising. We would not expect to see tigers around in Springfield, so P(E) is almost 1. Therefore the multiplier is only just above 1, so P(H) gets multiplied by a number only just above 1 to generate $P(H|E)$. So $P(H|E)$ is only very slightly bigger than $P(H)$; there is confirmation, but to a very low degree (compare 8.4.4).

11.3 The old evidence problem

Recall the probability-raising-theory-of-confirmation can be interpreted using inductive probability or degrees of belief. Inductive probabilities have received a lot of criticism (Chapters 5–7) whereas degrees of belief have so far got away unscathed. But can we really use degrees of belief to define confirmation? One worry we mentioned in passing at the beginning of this chapter is that degrees of belief are too subjective to be used to define confirmation. A different worry that has received much more attention is called the *old evidence problem* (Glymour 1980), and we turn to this now.

The old evidence problem arises when E was believed before H was formulated. For example, a long-standing problem in the study of the Solar System was that Newton's equations did not correctly describe the orbit of Mercury. There was a small deviation from the path predicted. Call the description of the non-Newtonian orbit of Mercury, E. E was known when Einstein first formulated the (general) theory of relativity (H) in 1915. And the theory of relativity *does* correctly describe the orbit of Mercury (E), so it was widely agreed that the orbit of Mercury, E, confirmed the theory of relativity, H.

But now we have a problem. For according to the credence-raising theory of confirmation, E does not confirm H, for it was not the case that $P(H|E) > P(H)$. The reason is that if E is already believed, it makes no difference to your credences to suppose it is true, so $P(H|E) = P(H)$. The point can be best seen by noting that, due to the rules of probability:

If $P(E) = 1$ then $P(H|E) = P(H)$

Adding the assumption that if E is believed then $P(E) = 1$, we get the result that nothing believed can confirm anything.

To see intuitively why $P(H|E) = P(H)$ if E is already believed, just take something you already believe, call it E, and consider the probability that it will rain tomorrow given E—it will be the same as your unconditional probability that it will rain tomorrow. For example, suppose your credence that it will rain tomorrow is 0.5. What's your credence that it will rain tomorrow given that grass is green? Still 0.5.

As well as old evidence cases, a similar problem arises in cases where H is already believed. We might call these *old hypothesis* cases. For example, suppose we all believe with 100 percent certainty that (H) the butler did it, so $P(H) = 1$. It seems perfectly correct to say "The butler's fingerprints on the murder weapon (E) confirm that he did it." But it is not the case that $P(H|E) > P(H)$, for if $P(H) = 1$ then $P(H|E) = P(H) = 1$.

11.3.1 Less than certainty response

The problem cases involve believing propositions with certainty. In fact very little is believed with certainty, so perhaps this is a way out of the problem. Suppose that the probability of E (Mercury's orbit) for Einstein in 1915 was 0.999. It would then be true that even according to the probability-raising theory of confirmation, the perihelion of Mercury (E) would confirm relativity (H), as P(E|H) = 1 > P(E) = 0.999, making the multiplier (P(E|H)/P(E)) larger than 1.

Objections to the Less than certainty response

One objection is that the degree of confirmation that E gives H will be much less than we think it should be. We're imagining a case where P(E) goes from 0.999 to 1, so this would have only a tiny effect on other beliefs, as Lisa Simpson pointed out. But as E led to headlines about the revolution in science, we want the verdict that E confirms H to a very large degree.

Another objection is that even if the less-than-certainty-response works for most cases, it won't work for all. There will still be examples, real or imagined, where P(E) = 1, and the probability raising theory of confirmation will wrongly say that E fails to confirm H in these examples. One counter-example is all it takes to refute an analysis.

11.3.2 Logical learning response

Garber (1983) suggests admitting that E does not confirm H. Instead, he thinks that what confirms H is the discovery that H entails E. For example, once Einstein had worked out his theory, he believed both the theory of relativity and what the orbit of Mercury was. But he did not believe that the one implied the other. He had to work out what results his theory gave for the orbit of Mercury. Once he did this, he discovered that his theory entailed the evidence, and this is what confirmed his theory.

Write "H entails E"' as "H ⊢ E." Let the new evidence be "H ⊢ E." Plugging this in to our theory of confirmation, "H ⊢ E confirms H" means "P(H| H ⊢ E) > P(H)." E is part of the background beliefs, so we get the correct verdict that H ⊢ E confirms H.

Objections to the logical learning response

The main objection is that the Logical Learning Response changes the subject. Even if "H ⊢ E" confirms H, E does not confirm H. So this response just bites the bullet.

A further objection is that the Logical Learning Response works only if we start off ignorant of some logical facts, that is, that H entails E. The problem is that if we are ignorant of logical facts, we must violate the rules of probability, which requires that all logical facts are believed with certainty (see the discussion of logical omniscience in Chapter 3).

11.3.3 Objective chance response

Hawthorne (2005) and Fitelson (2006) argue that we can base our judgments of confirmation on *chance* (Chapter 10). For example, suppose someone takes a pregnancy test that gives a positive result (E). This confirms that they are pregnant (H), and it does so even if they already believe with certainty that they are pregnant, $P(H) = 1$. This is because facts about the reliability of the test generate chances, and these chances ground our judgments of confirmation. For example, if the statistics show that $Ch(E|H) = 0.99$ and $Ch(-E|H) = 0.02$, then we can use these statistical probabilities to vindicate the judgment that E confirms H. We can express the probability raising theory of confirmation as: "E confirms H" means "$Ch(E|H) > Ch(-E|H)$."

So instead of saying that "E confirms H" means "$P(E|H) > P(-E|H)$" where P expresses *the beliefs of an agent at a time*, the suggestion is that "E confirms H" means "$Ch(E|H) > Ch(-E|H)$" where Ch expresses *chance*. Our judgment that E confirms H is then based on our belief that $Ch(E|H) > Ch(-E|H)$.

Objection to the objective chance response

The problem is that there will be cases where there are no chances to be used. For example, suppose E is a unique event like the Big Bang, and H is, say, the hypothesis that the universe will survive for exactly 30 billion years. We want the verdict that E confirms (or disconfirms) H, even when E was discovered before H was formulated, creating the old evidence problem. But neither the frequency theory nor the propensity theory of chance can provide a suitable chance of E given H. The frequency theory needs a class of similar events to give reasonable verdicts about chance, and the propensity theory needs some kind of causal tendency. So there are no chances in the vicinity to ground our judgments of confirmation.

11.3.4 Counterfactual response

Perhaps the dominant response to the old evidence problem is Colin Howson's (1991) counterfactual response. Howson says that we should *imagine* what the agent would have believed if, counterfactually, E were not believed. Let's express this counterfactual credence function with $P_{Counterfactual}$. Then "E confirms H" means "$P_{Counterfactual}(H|E) > P_{Counterfactual}(H)$."

We can think of this act of imagination as the inverse of making a supposition. Whereas to obtain the conditional probability of H given E, we suppose that E is true by *eliminating* all the not E possibilities, in old evidence cases we believe E and want to suppose that we don't, so we *uneliminate* all the not E possibilities.

Let's go through an example. Say you already fully believe the evidence, E, that the die landed with an even number showing (*Even*). The question is whether this confirms that Two is showing (*Two*).

E = *Even* = An even number is showing

H = *Two* = A two is showing

As P(Even) = 1, *Even* can't confirm anything. This is a problem, as it seems that *Even* confirms *Two*. The suggested solution here is that by an act of imagination, you uneliminate Even, and then consider whether $P_{Counterfactual}(Two|Even) > P_{Counterfactual}(Two)$.

A diagram will help show what's going on. The eliminated odd possibilities are shaded on the left. You can uneliminate them by imagining you don't believe *Even*. After this act of imagination, you end up with the counterfactual credences shown on the right.

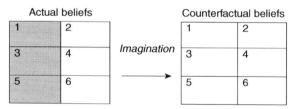

$P_{Counterfactual}(Two|Even) = 1/3 > P_{Counterfactual}(Two) = 1/6$, so *Even* confirms *Two*.

Similarly, we imagine that Einstein in 1915 did not believe that Mercury violates Newton's laws and ask whether $P_{Counterfactual}(H|E) > P_{Counterfactual}(H)$. If so, E confirms H for Einstein in 1915.

Actual beliefs			Counterfactual beliefs	
Mercury follows Newton's laws (–E)	Mercury violates Newton's laws (E)	*Imagination* →	Mercury follows Newton's laws (–E)	Mercury violates Newton's laws (E)

And indeed we would expect that given the counterfactual beliefs, the supposition that Mercury violates Newton's laws greatly decreases credence in Newton's theory and increases credence in the theory of relativity.[5]

First objection to the counterfactual response: Indeterminacy and subjectivism

But what value should the new possibilities have? That is, when the 1, 3, and 5 possibilities get unelimated, they go from 0 to . . . what exactly? We hid this problem by using a dice example, where it's natural to say that each possibility gets credence of 1/6. But what about cases where there are no chances to base these credences on, as in the case of Mercury's orbit?

An inductivist can answer the question, as the inductivist thinks there is a fact of the matter about what priors one should have.[6] But the subjectivist cannot give a determinate answer. The subjectivist endorses the view that credences can take any values, as long as they are probabilistically coherent. Similarly, the subjectivist will endorse the view that these new unelimated possibilities can take any values, as long as they are probabilistically coherent.

But with no constraints on how to unelimate possibilities, the counterfactual response is too vague to be useful. That is, the counterfactual response doesn't determine what values $P_{Counterfactual}$ will take, so it won't tell us whether $P_{Counterfactual}(H|E) > P_{Counterfactual}(H)$.

Response: Determinacy

The subjectivist can respond that for a given agent at a time, there will be determinate values for $P_{Counterfactual}$. As Howson (1991) puts it:

> It may take some exercise of the imagination to evaluate what your degree of belief in H would be were you, counterfactually, not to [believe] E, but there is no reason in principle to think that it can't be done. Indeed, it seems to be done all the time: "if I hadn't seen him palm that card, I'd think he had paranormal powers," for example. (p. 548)

The values will vary from one person to another, but this is exactly as the subjectivist expects. And to the extent that it is indeterminate what the counterfactual values would be, it is indeterminate whether E confirms H.

Second objection to counterfactual response: Problematic counterfactuals

But there are a range of cases where the beliefs in the counterfactual situation are problematic. For a start, maybe there are no such beliefs. Perhaps if Einstein in 1915 had not believed Mercury violated Newton's laws, he would not have pursued science at all. Then he would never have formulated the theory of relativity, so $P_{Counterfactual}(H)$ would not have any value at all. It follows that there is no answer to whether $P_{Counterfactual}(H|E) > P_{Counterfactual}(H)$, so there is no answer to whether E confirms H.[7]

And here's a particularly tricky case from Maher (1996):

> Suppose Mr. Schreiber is the author of novels that are **popular** (E), though it is important to him that he is making important contributions to **literature** (H). Schreiber basks in his success, taking his popularity to be evidence of the importance of his work; that is, he takes E to confirm H. However, he is well aware that the many aspiring serious novelists whose work is unpopular tend to rationalize their failure by supposing that the public taste is so depraved that nothing of true value can be popular. Schreiber thinks this reaction to unpopularity is unjustified and due merely to an inability to admit that one's work lacks merit. However, we can suppose that if Schreiber did not know of his own work's popularity, he too would share this opinion. We can even suppose that Schreiber, aware of his own foibles, is aware of this fact. Then it is true, and Schreiber knows it is true, that were he not to know E, he would have a probability function P such that P(H|E) < P(H). However, Schreiber now thinks that his judgment in this counterfactual situation would be irrational. Thus he now judges that E confirms H though the counterfactual analysis implies the contrary.[8] (p. 156)

The diagram shows how *Literature* is correlated with, and so is confirmed by, *Popular* in the actual belief function, but not in the counterfactual belief function.

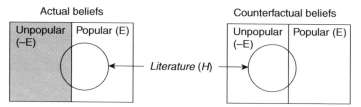

Actual beliefs   Counterfactual beliefs

In this case there exists a counterfactual belief function, but it doesn't match Schreiber's judgments of confirmation.

Maher is making an appeal to irrationality that the subjectivist might reject. But the irrationality is not an essential part of the example. What's essential is that Schreiber's actual beliefs about whether E confirms H don't match his counterfactual beliefs about whether E confirms H. Schreiber actually believes that E confirms H, but in the counterfactual situation he doesn't believe E confirms H, and the mismatch means that his counterfactual beliefs don't reflect his judgments about confirmation.

Response to problematic counterfactuals: Insulated reasoning

So to solve this problem we need to imagine counterfactual reasoning where we hold fixed Schreiber's beliefs about whether E confirms H. To do this, we need a principled distinction between beliefs about whether E confirms H and other beliefs. And this is not as hard as it looks. Beliefs about whether E confirms H are inference principles. They are higher-order beliefs—they are beliefs about beliefs—specifically, about whether the belief that E confirms the belief that H. By contrast, the beliefs that E and that H are first-order beliefs about the world. So when we consider the counterfactual beliefs where E is uneliminated, we simply hold fixed the higher-order beliefs (inference principles). Following Chalmers (2012, pp. 101–7), call this *insulated reasoning,* and express the resulting probability function with $P_{Counterfactual\ Insulated}$. Then the modified theory says that "E confirms H" means "$P_{Counterfactual\ Insulated}(H|E) > P_{Counterfactual\ Insulated}(E)$."

Let's now apply this to the Schreiber example. Schreiber currently believes that E confirms H. When he uneliminates not E, he holds fixed his higher order, that is, inferential beliefs, including the belief that E confirms H. So when not E gets uneliminated and Schreiber considers the effect of supposing E, the resulting probability function gives the correct verdict that $P_{Counterfactual\ Insulated}(H|E) > P_{Counterfactual\ Insulated}(H)$.

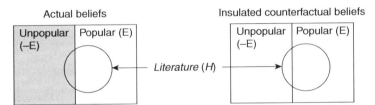

Summary

In this chapter, we compared the probability-raising theory of confirmation to two rival theories that do not make use of probability theory—hypothetico-deductivism and falsficationism—and saw that the core of these accounts can be translated into probabilistic concepts. Then we saw how the probability-raising theory vindicates our intuitions about surprising and non-surprising evidence. Finally, we looked at a problem for the probability-raising theory—the old-evidence problem—and considered five suggestions for how to solve it—the noncertainty, logical learning, objective chance, counterfactuals, and insulated reasoning responses.

In the next two chapters, we apply the probabilistic approach to epistemology to two traditional epistemological problems—justification-skepticism and knowledge-skepticism.

Study questions

1 Compare and contrast the probability-raising theory of confirmation with Popper's theory or hypothetico-deductivism.

2 Explain the old evidence problem.

3 What do you think is the best response to the old evidence problem? Does it succeed?

Advanced questions

4 How do falsificationism and/or hypothetico-deductivism deal with the problems of grue and the ravens?

5 Is the old evidence problem still a problem if we use inductive probability?

6 Three responses to the old evidence problem were dismissed fairly quickly. Could they be made to work?

7 Does insulated reasoning solve the old evidence problem?

Further reading

Hájek and Joyce (2008) and Huber (2014) have detailed overviews of the main theories of confirmation. Maher (1996) has a wide-ranging discussion in defense of an inductive theory of confirmation.

Glymour (1980) is the seminal paper on old evidence and remains a good guide to this and other objections to subjective Bayesianism.

12

Justification and probability

The problem of induction raised the question of how one belief could justify another. Let's assume this problem has been solved, and help ourselves to inductive probabilities. A deeper problem remains—how do any beliefs get justified *in the first place*? In this chapter, we'll consider the three main positions: foundationalism (12.1), coherentism (12.2), and infinitism (12.3).

Let's start with an example. Suppose after your physical, the doctor tells you: "You're going to live to 100." Cautiously optimistic, you ask your doctor how he could know such a specific piece of information. "Simple—I can read palms and your lifeline is spectacular."

You would suddenly have grave concerns about the doctor's optimistic estimate of your life span. Why? Because it turns out that the doctor's belief that you would live to 100 is not justified. The doctor's belief that your lifeline is spectacular does not justify his belief that you will live to 100. What we need from the doctor is a relevant justify*ing* belief. For example, the belief that you are the healthiest specimen ever examined is the sort of belief that would justify his belief that you will live to 100.

But even this isn't sufficient for justification. Suppose your doctor says you are the healthiest person ever examined, and, being the suspicious type, you ask him how he knows. He replies: "Oh I didn't do any tests, I just had a dream that you were the healthiest person ever examined." Once again, the doctor has no justification for believing that you will live to 100. The problem now isn't that he doesn't have a justify*ing* belief—he does (he believes you are the healthiest person ever examined). The problem now is that he ought not to! That is, he ought not to believe that you are the healthiest person ever examined, as he has no justification to believe it.

It seems that in order to have a justified belief, that belief must itself be based on a justified belief. Let's put this more generally. Take some arbitrary justified belief, B1. In order for B1 to be justified, there must be some other justified belief, B2, which justifies B1. This leads to the following principle.

1   A belief can only be justified by another justified belief.

This principle seems plausible. But it quickly gets us into trouble. To see how, we just need to ask: what justifies B2? It must be some other belief, B3. But what justifies B3? Some other belief B4, and so on to infinity. This is called *the epistemic regress*. The problem is that if the regress cannot be stopped, it looks like none of our beliefs are justified.

To state the problem of the epistemic regress more precisely, the following plausible statements are incompatible:

1   A belief can only be justified by another justified belief.

2   There can be no circular chains of justification.

3   Any justificatory chains must have a finite length.

4   Some beliefs are justified.

Denying each of these statements results in the four main responses to the problem of the epistemic regress: foundationalism, coherentism, infinitism, and justification-skepticism.

Foundationalism (12.1) denies 1. It says that the regress eventually comes to an end with some special *basic* beliefs that are justified by something other than beliefs—perhaps they are justified by experiences or sensations. Foundationalism can be pictured as an upside down pyramid, with the basic beliefs at the bottom justifying all the other beliefs. In the following diagram, B3 is a basic belief. (The arrows represent justification.)

Coherentism (12.2) denies 2 and says roughly that there can be circular chains of justification. (Precise definition in 12.2.) B1 can justify B2 while B2 justifies B1. Coherentism can be pictured as a raft or, better, as a metal boat—the boat stays afloat though each part alone would sink.

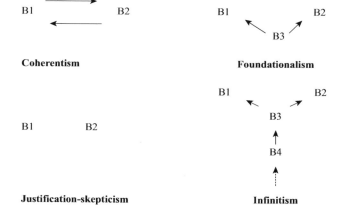

Infinitism (12.3) denies 3 and says that justificatory chains can have infinite length. B2 is justified by B3, which is justified by B4, and so on to infinity. All the beliefs in an infinitely long chain are justified.

Justification-skepticism denies 4 and says that none of our beliefs are justified. Justification-skepticism can be pictured as box of marbles, in which each floats around independently of the others. This is the position philosophers work hard to avoid—it is almost unthinkable that none of our beliefs are justified. Notice that justification-skepticism only says that our beliefs *are* not justified; it doesn't make the stronger claim that it is *impossible* they be justified.

If follows that all four positions are compatible. One could deny more than one of 1–4, and so, for example, be a foundationalist and a coherentist, holding that justification flows from special basic beliefs and also from circular sets of belief. Or one could be an infinitist and a skeptic, holding that our beliefs *would* be justified if there were a never-ending chain of justifying beliefs, but as it happens there *is* not. We won't dwell on these possibilities though, as only one of 1–4 need be denied in order to answer the epistemic regress. And as we'll see, denying each is problematic, so there is little motivation to deny more than one of them.

12.1 Foundationalism

Foundationalism says that a belief can be justified by something other than a justified belief. Call these basic beliefs.

Basic beliefs = Beliefs that are justified, but not by other beliefs.

What could justify basic beliefs? The best way to think about this question is to run through a dialogue between a normal agent and a skeptic. Here is one way the conversation might go. (There are lots of other ways too, and I recommend trying your own.)

Stage directions: A skeptic and Fred the Foundationalist are in an apparently normal store, looking at a red table

Fred: That table is red

Skeptic: Why do you believe the table is red?

Fred: Because it looks red

Skeptic: But why do you believe that it looks red?[1]

Fred: That's a baffling question, but having thought about it for many years, I can give you the obvious answer—I believe it looks red because I'm having a red *experience*. You might call it a red *sensation*. Whatever you call it, everyone with normal colour vision and a little experience in the world knows what I'm talking about. The experience I'm now having justifies my belief that it looks red.

This dialogue sets the terms of the controversy, and is worth dwelling on. The agent is expressing a version of foundationalism, suggesting that what justifies basic beliefs are *experiences*.[2] (There are other candidates, but we'll focus on experiences. It is important to understand that experiences are neither justified nor unjustified. You simply find yourself having them. For a useful contrast, babies have experiences but they don't have beliefs.)

The key foundationalist claim is that the experience justifies the belief. What arguments are there in favor of foundationalism? The main argument is that it stops the epistemic regress in a natural way. Fred's claim that experiences justify our beliefs seems obviously true. So foundationalism is the default choice unless it runs into a serious problem. Unfortunately, it does run into a serious problem.

The problem is that we are fallible. Our senses might be misleading. We might be brains-in-vats controlled by an evil scientist. Or we might be in the Matrix, living in a computer simulation. Or we might be deceived by an evil demon. In all these cases, our senses are inaccurate—we can have a red experience without there being a red object before us. We'll see how this problem applies in the first instance to the simplest version of foundationalism—naïve foundationalism. Then we'll see how two modifications, *a priori* foundationalism and dogmatist foundationalism, try to solve the problem.

12.1.1 *Naïve foundationalism*

Naïve foundationalism is the boldest version of foundationalism. It says that no matter what other beliefs you have, if you have a red experience, then you are justified in believing that the object is red.[3] So according to naïve foundationalism, justification has the following structure at the bottom level:

The object is red   (Basic belief)

justified by   ↑

Experience of redness

We can put the principle as follows, where R stands for the type of experience, for example, red.

Naïve foundationalism

Whatever other beliefs you have,

if you have an R experience then the belief that the object is R is justified.

This says your justification is independent of your other beliefs.

Problem for Naïve foundationalism

But your senses might be misleading.

Suppose for simplicity that some object before you is either red or white, and that you can have either a red or a white experience. Suppose you believe that your senses are *inaccurate*. Suppose you now have a red experience. Should you believe that there is a red object before you? No; it is likely that there is a *white* object before you. Thus, the naïve foundationalist position is refuted—given the belief that your senses are inaccurate, the belief that the object is red is not justified. The justification is not independent of your other beliefs.[4]

Let's work this through and connect it to probability and conditionalization. There are two possible types of experience—Looks-red and Looks-white—and two possible states of the world—Is-red and Is-white.

In the following Venn diagram, the possibilities where your experiences are accurate are on the left. In the possibilities on the right, your experiences are inaccurate. These are the bad possibilities—the skeptical possibilities—where your experiences *inaccurately* represent the world, for example, you have a red experience and the object is white.

Supposing you believe that there is a fair chance your senses are inaccurate, you shouldn't assign high probability to the Accurate possibilities. In fact, a reasonable prior probability assignment is to assign each possibility a probability of 1/4.[5]

	Accurate	**Inaccurate**
Looks-red	Looks-red and Is-red	Looks-red and Is-white
Looks-white	Looks-white and Is-white	Looks-white and Is-red

It follows that P(Is-red|Looks-red) = P(Is-red) = 1/2. (For the conditional probability, just eliminate the bottom half of the diagram.) The probability of Is-red is exactly the same as it was before! Assuming that justification requires an increase in probability (Chapter 5), as we will throughout this chapter,

Probability-raising theory of justification[6]

"E justifies H relative to B" means "P (H|E) > P (H)"

the experience has not justified the belief. This is incompatible with foundationalism, which says that the experience does justify the belief.

This failure is caused by two underlying problems with naïve foundationalism. Naïve foundationalism is most attractive when thinking about an agent who doesn't have any background beliefs, for example, they have an experience and nothing else in their stock of mental states. But this doesn't fit with our probabilistic framework. According to the probabilistic framework, you must always begin with some prior probabilities or other. Furthermore, these prior probabilities encode relations of justification. Specifically, if the agent is going to get justification for believing that the object is red, then the prior probabilities need to encode beliefs such as "If I have a red experience then it probably is red." These thoughts lead us to *a priori foundationalism*.

12.1.2 A priori foundationalism

A priori foundationalism says we have *a priori* justification that our senses are accurate. The structure of justification now looks like this:

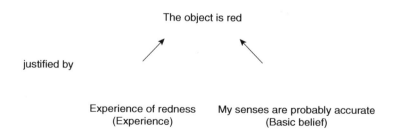

According to *a priori* foundationalism, the basic belief is not "The object is red"; the basic belief is "My senses are probably accurate," and this belief is justified *a priori*. The prior credences now look like this:

	Accurate	Inaccurate
Looks-red	Looks-red and Is-red	Looks-red and Is white
Looks-white	Looks-white and Is-white	Looks-white and Is-red

The vertical line has shifted to the right to indicate that Accurate is more likely than Inaccurate. Now P(Is-red|Looks-red) > P(Looks-red) = 1/2, so the red experience justifies the belief, as desired.

Problem for a priori foundationalism

The obvious problem is: does the agent really have *a priori* justification that her senses are probably accurate? Recall that subjectivists say that there is no *a priori* justification (beyond the rules of probability), and so will reject *a priori* foundationalism, whereas inductivists think that agents should have *a priori* credences with particular values, and so can accept *a priori* foundationalism. And we are granting inductivism in this chapter.

But the chief problem of inductive probabilities—where do these probabilities come from?—is especially severe. The inductive *a priori* foundationalist claim is that we have justification to believe, based on no evidence whatsoever, that "My senses are probably accurate." Why should we believe that? The two possible answers we saw in Chapter 5 don't look very plausible. The first was that we have some faculty that allows us to "see" (metaphorically) that certain arguments are inductively valid. The second was that it is part of the meaning of the words that some inferences are valid. Neither looks plausible for justifying the belief that my perceptual beliefs are probably accurate.

What we would like is for justification to be provided by our experiences, even when there is no prior belief that our senses are accurate. According to *dogmatist foundationalism*, that is exactly what we can have.

12.1.3 Dogmatist foundationalism

Dogmatist foundationalists hold that in the right conditions, if it appears that H then you have justification to believe H.[7] And this justification exists even if you don't have independent justification to believe your senses are accurate. All you need is the absence of undermining beliefs:

> *Dogmatist Foundationalism* Given the absence of undermining beliefs such as "My senses are *in*accurate,"
>
> if you have an R experience then the belief that the object is R is justified.

Notice the conditional (if you have an R experience then the belief that it is R is justified) is the same as for naïve foundationalism. The dogmatist just adds a necessary condition that restricts the contexts in which the conditional holds. Dogmatism is motivated by the natural thought that we can take appearances at face value—if it looks red then you have justification to believe it is red. We don't need to do anything fancy or respond to any philosophical worries to have this justification. Admittedly, we can't *always* take appearances at face value—on occasions when we worry we are being deceived, or have reason to think we are being deceived, or when nothing obviously follows from appearances, the dogmatist strategy may not be applicable. Nevertheless, on many occasions we can make instinctive and obvious inferences from appearances, and the dogmatist idea is that these occasions suffice to generate justified beliefs. So dogmatists hold that prior probabilities matter . . . a bit! You mustn't have skeptical beliefs that your senses are inaccurate, but you need not have prior justification to believe your senses are accurate!

Let's run through the example. The dogmatist doesn't invoke any specific *a priori* beliefs, so assume all four possibilities start with a probability of 1/4:

	Accurate	**Inaccurate**
Looks-red	Looks-red and Is-red	Looks-red and Is white
Looks-white	Looks-white and Is-white	Looks-white and Is-red

These priors have the same values we plugged into the naïve foundationalism example, and so do the conditional probabilities:

P(Is-red|Looks-red) = P(Is-red) = 1/2.

But according to dogmatism, if you actually *have* a red experience, the probability of Is-red rises above 1/2:

	Accurate	**Inaccurate**
Looks-red	Looks-red and Is-red	Looks-red and Is white

Expressing the probability after having the red experience with $P_{Red\ experience}$:

$P_{Red\ experience}$ (Is-red) > P(Is-red) = 1/2,

so after the red experience the belief that the object is red has greater probability than it did before.

(Notice that our probability raising definition of justification is not satisfied—as we saw earlier, P(Is-red|Looks-red) = P(Is-red) = 1/2. But nevertheless, when the experience actually occurs, it increases the probability of the belief. And this, the dogmatist claims, is what we really care about.)

Objections to dogmatist foundationalism

The main objection is that dogmatism violates conditionalization.[8] Recall conditionalization says that

$P_E(H) = P(H|E)$.

But dogmatism says that

$P_{Red\ experience}$(Is-red) > P(Is-red|Looks-red) = 1/2

Conditionalization is a widely held principle that is supported by arguments and intuition (Chapter 4), so having to reject it is a major cost.[9]

Secondly, according to dogmatism, before the experience the agent does not have a justified belief that her beliefs are accurate, but after the experience she does. The experience itself generates justification. This can be seen from the diagrams—the vertical line shifts to the right after the experience, indicating that Accurate has become more likely than before. And this is very odd—the agent has apparently justified the belief that her senses are accurate merely by using them. This is called the *bootstrapping argument*.[10] Imagine this in practice: "That truck looks red, so I believe it looks red, so my senses are accurate, and that dove looks white, so I believe it looks white, so my senses are accurate. Wow, aren't my senses terrific!" But clearly the agent has no idea whether her senses are accurate.

We can press this objection a bit further. According to dogmatism, whatever experience the agent has, it will lead to her increasing her probability that her senses are accurate. The agent can say "I don't have any evidence that my senses are accurate at the moment. But in a moment I will perceive something or other and this will give me justification to believe that they are. Still, I don't believe they are yet!" This is crazy.[11]

As noted in 6.3, the same objections apply to Max Black's defense of induction. He wanted to justify induction without relying on any *a priori* principles. Black claimed that using a rule to confirm itself is acceptable, even when there is no independent justification to think it a good rule. That's what's going on in the bootstrapping argument; the rule is something like "form beliefs that say things are as they appear." The rule begins with no justification, gets used, and ends up with justification! (The insignificant difference is that Black infers from belief to belief, whereas dogmatist foundationalists infer from experience to belief).

There is a further objection which is hard to make precise, but which afflicts *all* versions of foundationalism. The objection is that "nothing can count as a reason for holding a belief except another belief" (Davidson 1986, p. 310). Why not? The idea is that as beliefs are made of concepts, the only things that can justify beliefs are also made of concepts. But experiences are not made of concepts, so they are not in the business of justifying beliefs. So only other beliefs can justify, which leads us to coherentism.

12.2 Coherentism

Coherentism says roughly that there are circular chains of justification. More precisely, the coherentist introduces the concept of *coherence*, then argues that a set of beliefs is justified (or not) in virtue of the coherence of the beliefs.

So what is coherence? The first thing to say is that *coherence* is being used as a technical concept, and philosophers disagree about the best version of it. But we can get a grip on the concept with the following example:

S1 = {Bob likes to party; Bob is 19}
S2 = {Bob likes to party; Bob is 91}

Whatever the exact definition, we can agree that the first set coheres better than the second set. So the coherentist says that someone who holds the first set is better justified than someone who holds the second set (other things equal). Each belief is justified in virtue of being part of a set of cohering beliefs. Notice that coherence comes in degrees, and likewise justification comes in degrees. (See the appendix for further discussion of coherence.)

For the coherentist, the structure of justification is something like this:

Belief1   Belief2

Here the arrows represent the relation of coherence. As Belief1 and Belief2 cohere, they are both justified.

A natural question for the coherentist is: how do any beliefs get justified in the first place? The short answer is: gradually. Imagine a baby with a set of experiences but no beliefs. As the baby develops, she will acquire some beliefs, but we can suppose that initially none of these beliefs are justified. As the child's mental capacities develop, the set of beliefs grows, and, we can assume, becomes increasingly coherent. When the beliefs are sufficiently coherent, each belief in the system will be justified. So rather than justification being acquired one belief at a time, it spreads slowly across the entire set of beliefs—light dawns gradually over the whole.[12]

There is plenty of intuitive motivation for coherentism. Suppose it looks like there is an object in front of you, but it's dark and you aren't sure. How would you find out? You would stick your hand out and see if you could feel the object. If you could feel it, this would very strongly confirm that there was an object in front of you. Why? Because the beliefs "it looks like an object," "it feels like an object," and "there is an object" all *cohere*. Given this coherence, you seem to have overwhelming justification to believe that there is an object in front of you. As the saying almost goes, if it looks like a duck and feels like a duck, it's probably a duck.

Bertrand Russell (1997) points out that although we have experiences in dreams that are in some ways similar to those in real life, we don't believe our dreams are real, and the reason is that dreams don't cohere:

> If our dreams, night after night, were as coherent one with another as our days, we should hardly know whether to believe the dreams or the waking life. As it is, the test of coherence condemns the dreams and confirms the waking life. (p. 140)

Or suppose, to take an example often used by coherentists, that two witnesses to a crime say the same thing. Even if you initially had no reason to believe that they were telling the truth, the fact that they agree makes it very likely that they are. As BonJour (1985) puts it:

> . . . [A]s long as we are confident that the reports of the various witnesses are genuinely independent of each other, a high enough degree of coherence among them will eventually dictate the hypothesis of truth

telling as the only available explanation of their agreement—even, indeed, if those individual reports initially have a high degree of negative credibility, that is, are much more likely to be false than true. (p. 148)

We'll now consider two objections to coherentism.

12.2.1 First objection to coherentism: Isolation

One objection to coherentism is that there can be sets of beliefs that cohere, but which have no connection to the agent's *experiences*. Coherentism says the beliefs are justified, but it seems clear they are not.

To see the problem, consider two people, 1 and 2, who have acquired a number of experiences (E) and beliefs (B). Suppose to start with that the beliefs are exactly those we would expect people to form given the experiences.

Now suppose that we swap the beliefs but keep the experiences the same. That is, we give person 1 the beliefs of person 2 and vice versa, but don't swap the experiences.

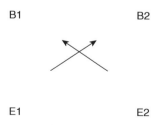

According to coherentism, the only thing relevant to justification is the degree of coherence of the beliefs. As they cohere just as much as before the swap, the coherentist says they remain just as justified. But this seems to be the wrong verdict. The problem is that the justification of beliefs has become isolated from experiences.

Response: Cognitively spontaneous beliefs

To avoid this problem, the coherentist needs to provide an account of how experiences play a role in justifying beliefs. The most detailed coherentist theory is offered by Laurence BonJour (1985).[13]

BonJour (p. 117) first introduces *cognitively spontaneous beliefs*:

> *Cognitively spontaneous beliefs* Beliefs which are not inferred from other beliefs, but which strike the agent in a spontaneous, involuntary way.

The key distinction is that cognitively spontaneous beliefs are *caused* by experiences, but not *justified* by them. A plausible example would be the belief that there is a red object in front of you, while looking at a red object in normal conditions. This belief is not inferred from anything; instead, it is *caused* by your experiences. The challenge for the coherentist is to explain how the manner in which the belief was caused plays a role in the way it is justified.

BonJour (p. 123) argues that an agent can reason her way to a justified belief as follows:

1　I have a cognitively spontaneous belief that H.

2　Cognitively spontaneous beliefs are very likely to be true.

3　Therefore H is very likely to be true.

4　Therefore (probably) H.

If this works, experiences play a role in justification, without justifying any beliefs on their own. The experiences get into the picture by causing cognitively spontaneous beliefs, the contents of which are then justified by other beliefs.

The question now is whether the coherentist can give an account of how the agent can be justified in believing 1 and 2. Belief 1 can be divided into two parts—there is (a) the belief that I believe H and (b) the belief that the belief in H is cognitively spontaneous. For (a) to be justified, I must have justified beliefs about what I believe. For (b) to be justified, I must have justified beliefs about the nature of my beliefs—in particular, that my belief that H was not inferred from other beliefs. Both parts therefore rely on us having (second-order) justified beliefs about our own (first-order) belief system. BonJour assumes that we do, calling this the *Doxastic Presumption*. Many philosophers took the Doxastic Presumption to be the weak point of the theory, not least BonJour himself (1999).

I think it's at least as difficult to justify belief 2, that cognitively spontaneous beliefs are very likely to be true. BonJour argues that this can be justified in the same way other beliefs are—empirically, by making observations and learning from experience.

But this looks circular. BonJour is trying to show that experiences can play a role in justification, even though they don't justify anything themselves. So he can't simply assume that beliefs can be justified by observation and experience.

12.2.2 *Second objection to coherentism: No probability raising*

The second challenge for coherentism is to show how beliefs that are individually unjustified manage to acquire justification if they cohere with each other. After all, if one information source is completely unreliable, and a second information source is also completely unreliable, it seems that they must remain just as unreliable even if they agree with each other.

We can formalize this by applying the probability raising theory of justification, which says that E justifies H if and only if $P(H|E) > P(E)$. It can be proved that if sources are (i) probabilistically independent and (ii) don't increase the probability of a hypothesis alone, then they don't increase the probability of a hypothesis when they agree.[14] Suppose two witnesses, A and B, report on the color of a table—which can be either red or white—saying either "red" or "white." We can formally express the probabilistic independence condition (i) as follows:

Probabilistic Independence

P(B says "red" | A says "red" & Red) = P(B says "red" | Red)

P(B says "red" | A says "red" & White) = P(B says "red" | White)

Intuitively, this says that if we hold fixed the color of the table, whether A says "red" is independent of whether B says "red."

We can formally express the condition (ii) that the sources don't increase the probability of the hypothesis individually as follows:

Non-foundationalism

P(Red | A says "red") = P(Red) P(Red | B says "red") = P(Red)

It then follows that A and B agreeing does not confirm the truth of what they say:

No Coherence Justification

P(Red | A says "red" & B says "red") = P(Red)

This seems to refute coherentism, which requires:

Coherence Justification

P(Red | A says "red" & B says "red") > P(Red)

We can see what's going on by filling in the story a little. Let's add that you know that A and B tell the truth 50 percent of the time, plus you initially assign each of Red and White a probability of 50 percent. Now you get the evidence that both A and B report "Red." Thus, the reports cohere. Does this increase the probability of Red? No. Initially there are eight possibilities. After the reports of A and B, all but the top two rows of the diagram are eliminated. But this leaves Red and White with the same probability as before, 50 percent. (The shaded areas are eliminated by the reports.)

	Red	White
Agreement	A: "Red" B: "Red" (Both tell the truth)	A: "Red" B: "Red" (Both lie)
	A: "White" B: "White" (Both lie)	A: "White" B: "White" (Both tell the truth)
Disagreement	A: "Red" B: "White" (A tells truth, B lies)	A: "Red" B: "White" (A lies , B tells truth)
	A: "White" B: "Red" (A lies, B tells truth)	A: "White" B: "Red" (A tells truth, B lies)

P(Red| A says "red" and B says "red") = P(Red), so the reports have not justified Red. And this objection seems to be fatal to coherentism.

Nevertheless, there is a strong intuition that reports that agree with each other provide justification to believe them. If the objector is to deny this intuition, she should explain why it seems so plausible.

Here are two reasons the coherence intuition is so appealing. The first is that if the individual sources begin with some credibility, then their coherence can increase the justification they provide. And this is the kind of case we are more familiar with. After all, we would expect that more witnesses tell the truth than lie (otherwise, we should rarely believe anyone's testimony).

The second reason is that if two witnesses agree, then the probability they are telling the truth does go up. But this doesn't give us justification to believe them—for the probability that they are both lying goes up as well. What gets eliminated is the possibility that one is lying and the other is telling the truth. This too can be seen in the earlier diagram. The prior probability that they both tell the truth is 1/8, and this goes up to 1/2 after they give the same report (the possibility they both tell the truth occupies 1/2 of the top row). The coherentist is right about that. But the probability that they are both lying also goes up from 1/8 to 1/2, so you have no more reason to believe them now than before. (This result is sensitive to the value of the priors though.)

12.3 Infinitism

Few philosophers have been brave enough to defend infinitism. But it has been prominently defended in recent years by Peter Klein (1999, and many other places). Recall infinitism says that justificatory chains have infinite length. So if an agent has justification for believing B1, it comes from the agent's justified belief in B2, which justifies B1. And if that agent is justified in believing B2, it comes from the agent's justified belief in, B3, and so on to infinity. If there really is an infinitely long chain of justifying beliefs, B1 is justified.

What is to be said in favor of infinitism? The motivation comes largely from the problems with foundationalism and coherentism. But it is highly counterintuitive, and we'll look at two objections: that we don't have an infinite number of beliefs, and that even if we do, they are not of the right kind.

12.3.1 First objection to infinitism: Finite minds

According to infinitism, in order for any belief to be justified, the agent must have an infinite number of beliefs. But we are only finite creatures—we have a finite number of neurons in our brain and live for a finite length of time, so we cannot have an infinite number of beliefs. Therefore, according to infinitism, none of our beliefs are fully justified. So infinitism leads to justification-skepticism.

Infinitist responses

The first thing an infinitist should say in response is that infinitism and justification-skepticism are compatible, as noted at the beginning of this chapter. So it is no objection that infinitism leaves open that none of our beliefs are justified. Infinitism is about what it would take to be justified; skepticism is about whether our beliefs are actually justified. But most philosophers want to avoid justification-skepticism, so let's see if infinitism allows us to do so. The infinitist must argue that we really do have an infinite number of beliefs, and they might do so as follows.

Do you believe that 1 + 1 = 2? Yes. What about 1 + 3 = 4? 1 + 4 = 5? 1 + 5 = 6? You believe all such propositions, of which there are an infinite number, so you do have an infinite number of beliefs. Or consider your belief that there isn't a dinosaur in the room. You also believe that there isn't a rhino in the room, or a chimp. . . . Again, it becomes plausible that you really do have an infinite number of beliefs. Of course, you haven't consciously considered each of these beliefs, but surely you believe lots of things that you have never consciously considered.

The infinitist idea is something like: if S has a *disposition* to endorse the conscious thought that H given enough time and encouragement, then S believes H. So the infinitist is invoking what we might call a *dispositional belief*. This can be contrasted with an *occurrent belief*, which is a belief that you are consciously thinking at a particular time. The infinitist then argues that it is asking too much of us to hold that beliefs are only justified by occurrent beliefs; dispositional justifying beliefs are sufficient.

This seems correct in many cases. For example, when I pick up a textbook I might never have the occurrent belief "this book is accurate." Nevertheless, if I am disposed to believe that the textbook is accurate were I to think about it, then I seem to be justified in believing what I read in the textbook.

Some philosophers object at this point that, first, these dispositional beliefs are not sufficient for justification, and, second, that we do not have an infinite number of them. But I think our probabilistic framework helps assuage these worries.

First, the probability raising theory of justification says that probabilities encode justification relations. For example, if according to S's prior probabilities, $P(H|E) > P(H)$, then that probability function encodes the belief that E justifies H. So it's plausible to say that S believes that E justifies H, even if S has never consciously thought about it.

Second, it's plausible that S has an infinite number of such dispositional beliefs encoded by the prior credences. For example, the prior probabilities might encode that: E justifies H more than E justifies J, for some competing hypothesis J. There seem to be no end of such dispositional beliefs.

More generally, the idea of holding a finite number of beliefs is undermined as soon as we start thinking about the way we represent the world. Our brain stores representations of the world, but not as a list that can be counted. Asking how many things you believe seems a bit like asking how many facts are represented by a painting. If forced to choose, we'd surely say that any painting represents an infinite number of facts (the Mona Lisa's mouth is longer than her nose, and longer than half her nose, and longer than a quarter of her nose . . .). Similarly, if forced to choose we'd surely say that the brain represents an infinite number of beliefs.

Let's grant that we have an infinite number of beliefs; this is not sufficient to vindicate infinitism though, as they have to be the right kind of beliefs.

12.3.2 Second objection to infinitism: What are these beliefs?

What exactly are these infinite beliefs? When we ask for justification, we seem to arrive at beliefs about appearances before long, and these don't seem to be justified by further beliefs—they seem to be justified by experiences. We saw this in the dialogue with Fred on p. 171—we quickly run out of beliefs that do any justifying. The challenge for the infinitist is to explain how an infinite number of justifying beliefs can get into the story.

Infinitist response: Infinitism about inference principles

I think the best infinitist response is that there are an infinite number of *inference principles*—beliefs stating that one belief justifies another. Let me explain.

Let's start with the following foundationalist structure, where E is an experience:

The infinitist complains that E is not sufficient for justification of H—they also want an inference principle connecting E with H, for example, E justifies H:

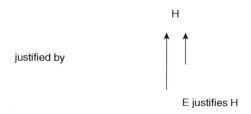

The infinitist now complains that E and "E justifies H" is not sufficient for justification of H—they also want an inference principle such as "E and 'E justifies H' justify H":

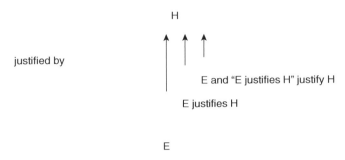

And we can't stop there. The infinitist now wants "E and 'E justifies H' and E and 'E justifies H' justify H." And so on to infinity. So an infinite number of beliefs are needed for H to be justified, as the infinitist wanted.[15]

Objections to infinitism about inference principles

But this theory doesn't fit with the description of infinitism earlier. There, the claim was that B1 was justified by B2, which in turn was justified by B3, and so on all the way down. But here the infinite chain of beliefs is not ever-descending vertically, but ever-expanding horizontally. This is significant because each member of this new chain of beliefs requires justification, and the infinitist still needs to tell us how. For example, consider "E justifies H" in the diagram. The extra beliefs the infinitist adds on the right do not justify "E justifies H." So the infinitist has not justified "E justifies H," and presumably needs to use either a foundationalist or coherentist strategy to do so. So this version of infinitism isn't really an alternative, but an addition, to foundationalism or coherentism. This threatens the motivation for infinitism, which was dissatisfaction with foundationalism and coherentism.

Summary

In this chapter, we discussed whether any beliefs can be justified, and considered foundationalism, coherentism, and infinitism. Foundationalism says that beliefs can be justified by nonbeliefs, and we focused on the version that says beliefs can be justified by experiences. Foundationalism was divided into three versions, which disagree about the range of cases where experiences justify beliefs: naïve, *a priori*, and dogmatist foundationalism.

Naïve dogmatism looks absurd, *a priori* foundationalism is committed to controversial *a priori* principles and dogmatist foundationalism is committed to violations of conditionalization and problematic circular reasoning.

Coherentism says that beliefs can be justified in virtue of cohering with each other. This faces the problem of connecting beliefs with experience, which BonJour attempted to solve using *cognitively spontaneous beliefs*. It also faces the problem that probability theory seems to show that if two sources fail to confirm a hypothesis individually, then they fail to confirm a hypothesis when they cohere.

Finally, infinitism says that beliefs can be justified by forming an infinitely long chain of justification. One objection is that we do not have an infinite number of beliefs. A more difficult objection concerns what these beliefs might actually be.

In the final chapter, we assume that all these problems about justification have been solved, and ask whether we can therefore know anything.

Appendix: What is coherence?

What exactly does "coherence" mean? We can start to give an answer using our probabilistic framework and supposing that coherence amounts to probabilistic coherence, where the probability is inductive probability.[16] So what exactly does "probabilistic coherence" mean? One of the open questions for coherentists is to develop a formal account that captures the concept of coherence, and it turns out to be surprisingly difficult to do so. Let's take a look at one suggestion and a criticism of it.

Shogenji's measure of coherence

Recent interest in defining coherence was sparked by Shogenji's (1999) suggestion of the following:

For any set of beliefs, $S = \{B1, B2, \ldots, Bn\}$:

$$Coh(S) = \frac{P(B1 \text{ and } B2 \text{ and } \ldots \text{ and } Bn)}{P(B1) \times P(B2) \times \ldots \times Bn}$$

The function *Coh* compares the joint probability of the members of S (the numerator) with the value that this joint probability would take were these members statistically independent of one another (the denominator). It thereby provides a measure of the degree to which the members of this set are statistically relevant to one another.

Let's see how this works using the earlier example. To keep things simple, assume that the population consists of an equal number of 19 and 91 year olds (and no-one else). And 10 percent of 91 years olds like to party while 90 percent of 19 year olds like to party:

P(Bob is 19) = 0.5

P(Bob is 91) = 0.5

P(Bob likes to party) = 0.5

P(Bob is 19 and Bob likes to party) = 0.45

P(Bob is 91 and Bob likes to party) = 0.05

S1 = {Bob likes to party; Bob is 19}

S2 = {Bob likes to party; Bob is 91}

$$Coh\ (S1) = \frac{P(\text{Bob is 19 and Bob likes to party})}{P(\text{Bob is 19}) \times P(\text{Bob likes to party})} = \frac{0.45}{0.5 \times 0.5} = 1.8$$

$$Coh\ (S2) = \frac{P(\text{Bob is 91 and Bob likes to party})}{P(\text{Bob is 91}) \times P(\text{Bob likes to party})} = \frac{0.5}{0.5 \times 0.5} = 1.2$$

So the first set, S1, has a coherence measure of 1.8, whereas the second set, S2, has a coherence measure of only 0.2.

Schupbach's objection to Shogenji's measure

Schupbach (2011) points out that adding an irrelevant belief to a set should make the set less coherent. But on Shogenji's measure the level of coherence stays the same. Example:

S2 = {Bob likes to party; Bob is 91}

S3 = {Bob likes to party; Bob is 91, my niece has the measles}

$$\begin{aligned} Coh\ (S3) &= \frac{P(\text{Bob is 91 and Bob likes to party and my niece has the measles})}{P(\text{Bob is 91}) \times P(\text{Bob likes to party}) \times P(\text{my niece has the measles})} \\ &= \frac{P(\text{Bob is 91 and Bob likes to party}) \times P(\text{my niece has the measles})}{P(\text{Bob is 91}) \times P(\text{Bob likes to party}) \times P(\text{my niece has the measles})} \\ &= \frac{P(\text{Bob is 91 and Bob likes to party})}{P(\text{Bob is 91}) \times P(\text{Bob likes to party})} \\ &= Coh\ (S2) \end{aligned}$$

My niece having the measles is independent of whether Bob is 91 or likes to party. So both the numerator and the denominator are multiplied by the same number—the probability that my niece has the measles. This cancels out, so Coh(S3) = Coh(S2). But the intuitive verdict is that Coh(S3) < Coh(S2).

Study questions

1 Explain the epistemic regress.

2 Explain foundationalism, coherentism, and infinitism.

3 Which is the best response to the epistemic regress. Does it succeed?

Advanced questions

4 Compare and contrast the discussion of foundationalism with the discussion of inductive probabilities (Chapter 5).

5 Compare the three versions of foundationalism. Which is best? Are there others?

6 The text suggests that coherentism has similar commitments to *a priori* foundationalism. Is this right?

7 The text says: "B1 can justify B2 while B2 justifies B1." Coherentist complaint: "No. B1 and B2 *cohere*. They are both justified, but in virtue of their coherence, not by justifying each other." Discuss.

8 Do BonJour's cognitively spontaneous beliefs solve the problem of isolation?

9 Is there any response to Huemer's argument (see footnote 7 to this chapter) that agreeing unreliable reports don't confirm the hypothesis?

10 Can the infinitist give a different answer to the challenge concerning what the infinite beliefs are?

Further reading

Smithies (2014) gives a helpful overview of foundationalism; BonJour (1985) remains an excellent account of coherentism and Murphy (2014) and Klein and Turri (2014) discuss infinitism.

The most lively area of research in recent years has probably been on dogmatism, of which Morreti (forthcoming) gives a helpful overview.

13

Knowledge and probability

People talk about what they know all the time, and for examples we need go no further than singers dispensing wisdom: "You wanna go where everybody knows your name," "Everybody knows that the dice are loaded," "You gotta know when to hold 'em," "If I knew then what I know now." But do we know as much as we think we do?

You've probably had at least one conversation with someone who thinks JFK was killed by an elaborate conspiracy, and at some point the conversation may go something like this:

> **Annoying person**: So you think you know JFK was killed by a lone gunman?
>
> **Sensible person**: Yes
>
> **Annoying person**: But how can you know this? Isn't it *possible* there was a conspiracy?
>
> **Sensible person**: Well anything's possible . . .
>
> **Annoying person**: So you don't know! If you think it's possible JFK was not killed by a lone gunman then you don't know he was. I win, and accept your apology.

The argument turns on the connection between knowledge and credence, and implicitly uses two premises, which we'll call *Conspiracy* (13.1) and *Knowledge-requires-certainty* (13.2). These premises entail that we don't know anything, *Knowledge-skepticism* (13.3). We'll consider whether *Knowledge-skepticism* is tenable (13.4), then whether *Knowledge-requires-certainty* can be rejected (13.5 and 13.6).

13.1 Conspiracy

The first premise says that all your beliefs have credence less than 1. Formally,

Conspiracy
For all H, P(H) < 1

Is this plausible? Conspiracy theories provide a useful motivation, hence the name of the principle. Are you certain that JFK was killed by a lone gunman? Surely not—it's possible he was killed by a conspiracy. Are you certain who the President is right now? Surely not—it's possible that the President resigned 10 seconds ago. Let's get serious. Are you certain you are awake right now? No—you could be dreaming. In fact, it's possible that your entire life is a dream. As Zhuangzi put it:

> Once upon a time, I dreamt I was a butterfly . . . Now I do not know whether I was then a man dreaming I was a butterfly, or whether I am now a butterfly, dreaming I am a man.[1]

Let rip the paranoid fantasies and there is no telling where we can stop. Descartes famously considered the possibility that there was an evil demon that had consistently deceived him, and concluded that he could not be certain that he was holding a piece of paper. The modern equivalent is the possibility that we are in the Matrix, a computer-simulated reality that provides us with misleading experiences. These possibilities seem to show that we cannot be certain of anything.

Conspiracy is widely agreed upon, but there are two qualifications that should be noted. First, what about someone who simply *is* certain of things? For example, someone who says "It is impossible that there was a conspiracy, I am 100% certain, and there's nothing you can do about it." The best response to such an unyielding interlocutor is to shift to what they *ought* to believe. Surely even if they are 100 percent certain, they shouldn't be. And knowledge requires justified belief, not merely belief. Thus, Conspiracy could be strengthened to say that all beliefs *should* have credence less than 1 (i.e. inductive probability less than 1). I will stick with actual credences for simplicity.

Second, is Conspiracy really true for *all* beliefs? In earlier chapters, we saw arguments that tautologies such as "grass is green or grass is not green" have credence 1. These arguments could be questioned, but we won't do so here. For even if there are some beliefs that we are 100 percent sure of, they will be limited to logical and mathematical beliefs, and perhaps beliefs about our experiences. All scientific beliefs, beliefs about the world around us, and any information we find in an encyclopedia seem to have credence less than 1, and so remain a target of the skeptical argument.

13.2 Knowledge-requires-certainty

The second premise of our argument for Knowledge-skepticism we call *Knowledge-requires-certainty*; it says exactly what you'd expect:

Knowledge-requires-certainty If P(H) < 1 then you don't know H

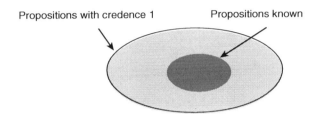

Propositions with credence 1   Propositions known

Knowledge-requires-certainty sets a high bar on knowing; to know something, you have to be certain. It says that a necessary condition on knowing H is that P(H) = 1. We can re-state the principle (as the contra-positive):

Knowledge-requires-certainty If A knows H then P(H) = 1

Another way to put it is that *Knowledge-requires-certainty* says that every *alternative* must be eliminated. Understanding "alternative" as a possibility in which not H, and "has eliminated" as "has zero credence in," we can reformulate Knowledge-requires-certainty in ordinary language:

Knowledge-requires-certainty reformulated If A knows H then A has eliminated all the alternatives.

This way of putting it will be useful later when we talk about *relevant* alternatives.

(Careful: *Knowledge-requires-certainty* does *not* say that if P(H) = 1, then H is known. That's the wrong way round. You cannot come to know something merely by being certain of it, e.g. H might be false.)

Knowledge-requires-certainty is more controversial than Conspiracy, so we'll discuss three arguments in its favor—the Lottery Paradox, a story about a detective, and concessive knowledge claims (if you're already convinced, you can skip to the next section, but be warned that these three arguments will be revisited shortly).

First argument for Knowledge-requires-certainty: The Lottery

Suppose you buy a lottery ticket. You know there are 100 tickets and that exactly one will win, so the probability your ticket will *lose* is 99/100. That's pretty high, but do you *know* it will lose? Knowledge-requires-certainty says no. And there are several reasons to think this the correct verdict—the opposite verdict, that you know the ticket will lose, leads to trouble.

First, if you did know the ticket was going to lose, it would have been completely crazy to buy it. But it isn't completely crazy to buy the ticket—it might be a foolish bet, but it is not completely crazy. Compare someone buying a ticket to *last week's* lottery, after the jackpot is known to have been paid out to someone else. *That* would be crazy.

Second, imagine that instead of the ticket being for something good, it is for something terrible, such as being drafted to Vietnam, or to be executed. No-one would say that they know the ticket will lose in that situation, but again, the degree of belief is 0.99.

Third, *Knowledge Closure* is a plausible principle:

Knowledge Closure

If A knows H1 and A knows H2 then A is in a position to know H1&H2.

Knowledge Closure is very plausible—it would be odd to say that you know it is sunny and know it is warm but are not in a position to know whether it is sunny and warm. But *Knowledge Closure* soon leads to contradiction if you know your ticket will lose. We're supposing the 0.99 probability your ticket will lose is enough for you to know it will lose. But every ticket has a 0.99 probability of losing, so you must know that every ticket will lose. By *Knowledge Closure* you are in a position to know the conjunction: ticket 1 will lose and ticket 2 will lose and . . . and ticket 100 will lose. But in fact you know that one ticket will win—contradiction! (We saw a similar argument for the view that rationally accepting H requires certainty in H in Chapter 2.)

These lottery-based arguments all indicate that to know your ticket will lose you must have a degree of belief of 1 that it will lose. And, more generally, that to know H, you must have a degree of belief of 1 that H.

Second argument for Knowledge-requires-certainty: Detective

Dr. Black has been murdered and Poirot is on the case. Numerous suspects have been eliminated from the enquiry, and Poirot's evidence is pointing at the butler. But the cook was also in the house at the time of the murder and has no alibi. Does Poirot *know* that the butler did it? Surely not. As long as it is a live possibility that the cook did it, Poirot cannot know the butler did it. He can strongly believe the butler did it, but it seems he cannot know the butler did it. Why not? The natural answer is that there is a possibility that the cook did it; P(The butler did it) < 1, therefore he cannot know the butler did it, that is, *Knowledge-requires-certainty*.

What would it take for Poirot to know the butler did it? Plausibly, he would have to eliminate the possibility that the cook did it, indeed, eliminate every possibility incompatible with the butler having done it. And this is exactly what *Knowledge-requires-certainty* tells us he must do. As *Knowledge-requires-certainty* gives the right verdict in this kind of example, we have an argument for *Knowledge-requires-certainty*.

Third argument for Knowledge-requires-certainty: Concessive knowledge claims

Concessive Knowledge Claims are statements that attribute knowledge of H to an agent (perhaps oneself) and also claim that H might, from the agent's perspective, be false. For example,

> *Concessive Knowledge Claim 1*
> I know it is raining but it might not be raining.

Or, to give a third-person example,

> *Concessive Knowledge Claim 2*
> Bob knows it is raining but it is possible for Bob that it is not raining.

Or, to put it abstractly,

> *Concessive Knowledge Claim 3*
> A knows H but it is possible for A that not H.

There seems to be something wrong with *Concessive Knowledge Claims*. Their oddity is explained by *Knowledge-requires-certainty*, which effectively says that A knowing H requires that it is not possible for A that not H. *Concessive Knowledge Claims* therefore contradict themselves by effectively saying "it is not possible for A that not H but it is possible for A that not H."

That's the case for *Knowledge-requires-certainty*.

13.3 Knowledge-skepticism

Let's now put together *Conspiracy* and *Knowledge-requires-certainty* to get an argument for *Knowledge-skepticism*:

1 *Conspiracy* P(H) < 1

2 *Knowledge-requires-certainty* If P(H) < 1 then you don't know H

Therefore

3 *Knowledge-skepticism* you don't know H

This simple argument is easy to confuse with others, so let's make some clarifications.

i Knowledge-skepticism does not say that H is false. The skeptic is not saying that you really are dreaming. She's saying that you *might* be, and that that possibility destroys knowledge.

ii Knowledge-skepticism does not say that you don't have justification (which was the focus of the last chapter). Knowledge-skepticism can allow that your beliefs are justified; knowledge-skepticism denies that your justification is sufficient for knowledge. So knowledge-skeptics can have conversations in which they assert H and explain how their belief in H is justified. They just think it falls short of knowledge.

iii Relatedly, the knowledge-skeptic does not say "I know we don't know anything." That would be inconsistent. But no such second-order knowledge claim should be made. The knowledge-skeptic can just give us her reasons to believe that we don't know anything, without going so far as to say she knows we know nothing.

Nevertheless, knowledge-skepticism is not an appealing thesis. There are two big problems. The first is linguistic—knowledge-skepticism says that many of the things people say are false. People makes claims about knowing things all the time—just think of the examples at the opening of this chapter. If knowledge-skeptics are right, then all of these claims are false, which means people are systematically misguided about what they know. We would need a very good argument to accept such a surprising conclusion.

The second problem with knowledge-skepticism is epistemic. Knowing things is a desirable state to be in—the quest for knowledge is a noble goal. But if the skeptic is right, the quest must be abandoned—we can never know anything. It seems to follow that we should stop trying—all libraries and universities can be shut down. Some philosophers like crazy theses, but this seems too much for anyone to swallow.

13.4 Defense of knowledge-skepticism: Assertibility

Let's consider whether knowledge-skepticism could be defended from these two problems. A promising strategy can be found in the work of Unger (1971, 1975) and Schaffer (2004a). We need two concepts to understand this strategy. Start with the concept of *absolute terms*. These are best explained by examples such as "flat" or "empty." Strictly speaking, an object is flat only if it has no bumps on it whatsoever. So almost nothing is really flat—there will nearly always be some bumps, even if only at the microscopic level. Similarly, an object is empty if and only if it has nothing at all in it. So almost nothing is really empty—there are molecules of oxygen in an otherwise empty fridge. So why do we so often say things are flat or empty?

Our answer is that some things are false, but acceptable to say in a conversation. It is acceptable to say that the fridge is empty when the hearer can be expected to understand that you aren't talking about air molecules. The air molecules aren't relevant. And it is acceptable to say that Kansas is flat when the hearer can be expected to understand that you mean that there are no mountains. The hills aren't relevant. We'll say these sentences are *assertible*, where we understand assertible as "acceptable to say in a conversation."[2] *Assertibility* is the second concept we need.

The result is that we can now hold that although it is false that the fridge is empty, the sentence "the fridge is empty" is assertible. And although it is false that Kansas is flat, the sentence "Kansas is flat" is assertible. Now we can apply this to "knows." The result will be that although it is false that A knows H (skepticism), the sentence "A knows H" is assertible.

It is plausible that "knows" is an absolute term, in the sense that in order to know something, *all* alternative possibilities must be eliminated, so most attributions of knowledge are literally false. But they can be close to being true, such as when the *relevant* possibilities have been eliminated. Under such circumstances, an attribution of knowledge is assertible, even though it is false.

So this skeptical strategy still holds knowledge to the highest standard:

Knowledge-requires-certainty If A knows H then A has eliminated all the alternatives.

But the strategy adds that the *assertibility* of "A knows H" requires less:

If "A knows H" is *assertible* then A has eliminated all the *relevant* alternatives.

So agents don't know anything because they don't eliminate all the alternatives, but the claim that agents know is assertible when the agents eliminate all the *relevant* alternatives.

Let's work through an example. Suppose, Poirot has eliminated everyone who was in the house other than the butler, who had motive, opportunity, and a history of killing his employer. It seems that Poirot knows the butler did it. But let's consider a skeptical possibility. Suppose Poirot hasn't eliminated the possibility that Dr. Black was murdered by an alien. Given *Knowledge-requires-certainty* and *Conspiracy*, Poirot does not know the butler did it.

Our knowledge-skeptic says: Poirot does not know the butler did it but "Poirot knows that the butler did it" is assertible. Poirot has not eliminated all the alternatives, but he has eliminated all the *relevant* alternatives.

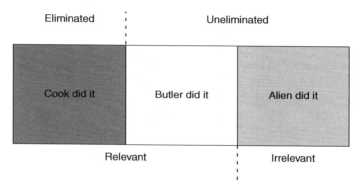

The same applies to other skeptical scenarios, such as dreaming, or being in the Matrix, that destroy knowledge. Our skeptic claims that such possibilities prevent the agent from knowing, but don't prevent the sentence "the agent knows . . ." from being assertible.

This skeptical theory provides an answer to both the problems for knowledge-skepticism earlier. The first problem was that knowledge-skepticism makes many of the things we say about knowledge false. Our skeptic accepts this and explains why it isn't a problem—lots of the things we say are false (e.g. the fridge is empty), but they are still assertible.

The second problem was that knowledge-skepticism threatens the whole enterprise of the quest for knowledge. On this version of knowledge-skepticism, it doesn't. Even if we rarely achieve knowledge, we can improve our epistemic state by eliminating possibilities. Poirot, who has eliminated the gardener, is in a better epistemic position than his assistant, who has not. So even if knowledge is unobtainable, we can get closer to a state of knowledge by eliminating possibilities as our inquiry proceeds, and this is clearly a worthwhile enterprise.

In explaining this skeptical theory, we have used a model of epistemic inquiry on which the aim is to eliminate *possibilities*. In addition, we have used the concept of a *relevant possibility*. But now we have the concept of a relevant possibility, we can use it for a more ambitious purpose—*what if the elimination of relevant possibilities was sufficient for knowledge itself?*

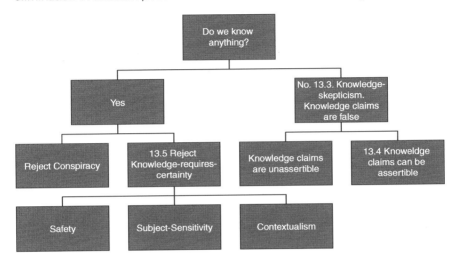

13.5 Relevant Alternatives Theory of Knowledge

This section discusses an answer to the skeptical argument: reject *Knowledge-requires-certainty*. According to this answer, knowledge requires only that the *relevant* alternatives are eliminated, not that all alternatives are eliminated.

Let's go back to Poirot. All the suspects other than the butler have been eliminated. Any normal person would say Poirot knows the butler did it, but the skeptic is worried about the possibility of an alien murderer. So perhaps we should ignore this possibility. Perhaps this possibility does not destroy knowledge. Perhaps knowledge requires eliminating the *relevant* possibilities, and irrelevant possibilities can be ignored. Thus Poirot does know the butler did it because he has eliminated the possibility that the other suspects did it, and ignores the possible alien. This is the Relevant Alternatives Theory of knowledge:[3]

Relevant Alternatives

If A knows H then A has eliminated all the *relevant* alternatives.

The diagram below, repeated from earlier, now represents Poirot knowing the butler did it. The possibility that the cook did it has been eliminated by the evidence and the possibility that an alien did it is not relevant. There are no uneliminated relevant possibilities in which the butler did not do it; therefore, Poirot knows the butler did it.

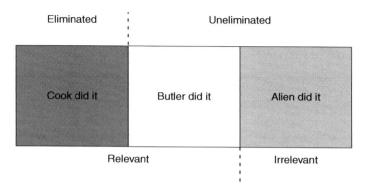

Relevant Alternatives denies *Knowledge-requires-certainty*. The alien possibility has a credence greater than 0, so the credence the butler did it is less than 1; but Poirot still knows the butler did it because the alien possibility is irrelevant. *Relevant Alternatives* does justice to many of the arguments and intuitions motivating *Knowledge-requires-certainty*. To see how, we need to look more closely at *Relevant Alternatives*. We need to ask: which possibilities are relevant?

Safety, Subject-Sensitivity, and Contextualism

We'll look at three main theories of what determines which possibilities are relevant. I explain the theories, then compare how they fare against the arguments for *Knowledge-requires-certainty*.

To understand the first two theories, we need some new apparatus. We need to imagine all the possibilities arranged in order of how similar they are to actuality. Close to actuality are possibilities that are only slightly different. These are possibilities where a fly survived for 1 second longer, or where you had an extra chip at lunch today. A bit further away are possibilities where the Greeks were defeated by the Persians, or Columbus never made it to America. And far away are possibilities where the dinosaurs were never wiped out, or where there are no planets, or where we only exist in a computer simulation.

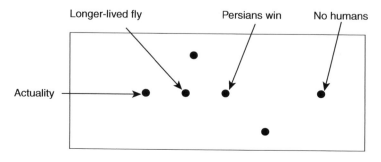

That's the apparatus. Now for the three theories for what determines which possibilities are relevant: Safety, Subject-Sensitivity, and Contextualism.

(i) *Safety* says that the relevant possibilities are those that are similar to actuality (which is usually called "the actual world"). Think of these as the possibilities that could easily have been actual; they will form a circle of fixed radius around the actual world.

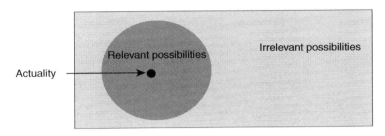

Safety is motivated by the thought that you cannot know something if you could very easily have been wrong. For example, someone who luckily looks at a clock stuck at 12, at exactly 12, does not thereby know that it is 12. The belief is true only by luck, and could easily have been false, such as if she'd looked at the clock at 1. Safety says this possibility (looking at the clock at 1) is relevant, and as it is uneliminated, the possibility destroys knowledge; Safety gives the correct verdict that the agent doesn't know. By contrast, the possibility in which you are a butterfly dreaming that you are a human, though uneliminated, is so distant that it is not relevant, so you still know that you are a human.[4]

(ii) *Subject-Sensitivity* modifies Safety by adding that the radius of the circle can vary, and it varies depending on what is at stake for the knower. The higher the stakes, the more possibilities are relevant.

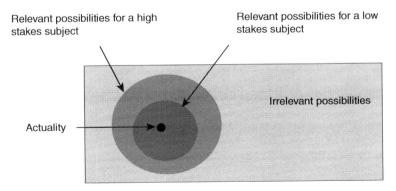

On this view, whether someone knows the time by looking at their watch depends on how important it is that they get the right time. If it doesn't matter what time it is, only the nearby possibilities matter; as long as their watch is fairly reliable, they know the time. But if they are coordinating a bank raid requiring perfect timing, they don't know unless they have eliminated more distant possibilities, such as those where the batteries have run out.[5]

(iii) *Contextualism* agrees with Subject-Sensitivity that the relevant possibilities vary, but says that they vary depending on the context of the *speaker*, that is, the person ascribing knowledge, not the knower. So Contextualism primarily makes a claim about the meaning of a speaker's utterance of a knowledge ascription like "A knows H." Different versions of Contextualism then give different answers to the question of what it is about the speaker's context that determines which possibilities are relevant. Let's consider the version that says that a possibility is relevant if it is being considered in the conversation.[6]

To understand Contextualism, it's best to start with an analogy to a word like "tall." If a basketball coach says "Bob is short," when Bob is 6'1', he really means "Bob is short for a basketball player" and speaks truly. If someone else says "Bob is short," and means "Bob is short for a normal human" he speaks falsely. This shows that "short" means different things in different conversational contexts; *the same sentence expresses different propositions when uttered in different contexts.*

Contextualism says the same applies to "knows." If Poirot is asked whether the butler *or the cook* did it, Poirot is right to say "I know the butler did it." But if Poirot is asked whether Dr. Black was murdered by the butler *or an alien*, Poirot would say something false if he said "I know the butler did it." That latter question changes the conversational context, and *makes* the alien possibility relevant. The same sentence expresses a true proposition in the first context and a false proposition in the second context.[7]

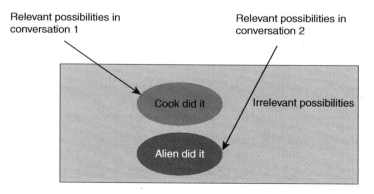

So those are three versions of the relevant alternatives theory. They are three different ways of rejecting *Knowledge-requires-certainty*. They all say that A can know H while P(H) < 1, while telling different stories about why some possibilities are irrelevant. Which is of the three is best?

13.6 Evaluating theories of relevant alternatives

In this section, we'll consider how each of the three versions of the relevant alternatives theory fares against the three arguments for *Knowledge-requires-certainty*—the Lottery, the Detective, and concessive knowledge claims. The issues here get very complicated and we will only be able to give a sense of how the arguments will go.

Safety

Recall that Safety says that a possibility is relevant if and only if it is similar to the actual world. Can this handle the arguments for *Knowledge-requires-certainty*?

(a) *Safety and the Lottery*. Earlier we saw that *Knowledge-requires-certainty* delivers the verdict that you don't know your lottery ticket will lose. Does Safety deliver this verdict? It does. The Safety theorist just needs to hold that the possibility where you win is *nearby*, and therefore relevant, and therefore destroys any knowledge that your ticket will lose. And it is plausible that the possibility where your ticket wins is nearby. Getting your numbers drawn might be very unlikely, but it would not have taken significant changes to the world to get it to happen—you'd just need the balls drawn to be in slightly different positions.

But we can raise an objection to Safety by rigging the lottery. Suppose that it's the New Jersey state lottery and the governor has secretly fixed it so his mistress's ticket will win. There is no nearby possibility where your ticket will win. So according to Safety, there is no nearby possibility where your ticket wins, so you know your ticket will lose. This is a problematic result.

(b) *Safety and the Detective*. Recall that the intuition that Poirot has to eliminate all the alternatives before knowing that the butler did it supported *Knowledge-requires-certainty*. The Safety theorist replies that not *all* alternatives need to be eliminated; distant possibilities need not be eliminated, such as the possibility of an alien murderer. So Safety correctly predicts that the alien does not need to be eliminated from inquiry. The alien example supports Safety over *Knowledge-requires-certainty*.

(c) *Safety and Concessive Knowledge Claims*. Recall the intuition that there is something wrong with saying "Bob knows H but it is possible for Bob that not H." According to *Knowledge-requires-certainty*, concessive knowledge claims are always false, which explains why there seems to be something wrong with them. By contrast, Safety says that the Concessive Knowledge Claims can be true, as long as the H possibility is far away.

But Concessive Knowledge Claims seem wrong no matter how far away the H possibility is, for example, "Poirot knows it was the butler, but it is possible for Poirot that it was an alien." The Safety theorist needs to explain why such Concessive Knowledge Claims seem false.

Subject-Sensitivity

Recall that Subject-Sensitivity says that a possibility is relevant if and only if it is sufficiently similar given what's at stake for the subject—the higher the stakes, the more possibilities are relevant. Can this handle the arguments for *Knowledge-requires-certainty*?

(a) *Subject-Sensitivity and the Lottery.* Subject-Sensitivity says that Bob knows his ticket will lose only if he doesn't care too much about whether it will lose. If a lot is at stake, more possibilities become relevant, perhaps including the possibility that his ticket will win, in which case he doesn't know his ticket will lose. Whereas if Bob is a millionaire for whom it doesn't matter if he wins the lottery, he knows his ticket will lose.

This is problematic. Surely even millionaires don't know their ticket will lose. And the general principle is worse: the less you care, the more you know. So it looks like according to Subject-Sensitivity, you can increase your knowledge by smoking lots of weed and not caring about anything.

(b) *Subject-Sensitivity and the Detective.* We get the same pattern in the murder mystery. Poirot, who is already rich and famous, has a relatively narrow range of relevant possibilities to eliminate in order to know the butler did it, while the ambitious young attorney battling for his career has to eliminate more possibilities, and therefore knows less. This is another application of: the less you care, the more you know.

(c) *Subject-Sensitivity and Concessive Knowledge Claims.* What does Subject-Sensitivity say about: "Bob knows H but it is possible for Bob that not H"? According to Subject-Sensitivity, the sentence is true if the possibility that H doesn't matter much to Bob. This conflicts with the intuitive verdict that the sentence is always false, so the Subject-Sensitivity theorist, like the Safety theorist, has to explain away the appearance of falsity.

Contextualism

Recall that contextualism says that that a possibility is relevant if it is being considered in the conversation. Can this handle the arguments for *Knowledge-requires-certainty*?

(a) *Contextualism and the Lottery.* Does Contextualism give the verdict that Bob doesn't know his ticket will lose? It does, as long as the possibility of the ticket winning is being considered in the conversation. And it's plausible that given the structure of lotteries, the possibility of each ticket winning is always considered in a conversation about lotteries.

(b) *Contextualism and the Detective.* According to Contextualism, whether Poirot knows the butler did it depends on the conversation. If the question is "did the butler or the cook do it?" then Poirot knows the butler did it. But if someone in the conversation raises the question "did the butler or an alien do it?" then Poirot does not know the butler did it.

This kind of case is one of Contextualism's main selling points, as it allows a plausible response to the knowledge-skeptic. The contextualist says that when the knowledge-skeptic raises his bizarre possibilities, they become relevant to the conversation, and therefore many knowledge claims are false in a conversation with a knowledge-skeptic. But when the knowledge-skeptic goes away, such knowledge claims become true. So the knowledge-skeptic is right when he says we don't know we're awake. But when we stop talking about skepticism, we are right when we say "I know where we should go for lunch."

(c) *Contextualism and Concessive Knowledge Claims.* What does Contextualism say about: "Bob knows H but it is possible for Bob that not H"? Contextualism declares such sentences false. Once the not H possibility is introduced into the conversation, it becomes relevant, so Bob doesn't know H. This explains why there seems to be something wrong with Concessive Knowledge Claims.

Synthesis

As if this isn't complicated enough, we can combine elements of Safety, Subject-Sensitivity, and Contextualism. For example, David Lewis (1996) argues that possibilities that are sufficiently similar to the actual world are relevant (a version of Safety); that possibilities that the agent ought to have sufficiently high credence in, given what's at stake, are relevant (a version of Subject-Sensitivity); and that possibilities the speaker pays attention to are relevant (a version of Contextualism).[8]

Summary

This chapter discussed whether we can know anything. There is a powerful skeptical argument that we cannot, based on our lack of complete certainty, and the condition that knowledge requires certainty. One response is to accept knowledge-skepticism, and argue that it isn't as bad as it seems, by explaining how knowledge claims are still assertible. A more ambitious response is to deny *Knowledge-requires-certainty*. This requires an account of how someone can know H when alternatives are uneliminated, and we compared three strategies for ruling these alternatives irrelevant—Safety, Subject-Sensitivity, and Contextualism. Whether any such strategy can succeed remains a lively topic in contemporary epistemology.

Study questions

1 Explain *Knowledge-requires-certainty*.

2 Explain *Knowledge-skepticism* and give an argument in its favor.

3 Explain the relevant alternatives response to *Knowledge-skepticism*. Does it succeed?

4 Explain Safety, Subject-Sensitivity, or Contextualism. How does it answer *Knowledge-skepticism*?

Advanced questions

5 Compare the argument given for *Knowledge-skepticism* with more traditional skeptical arguments.

6 Compare and contrast Safety, Subject-Sensitivity, and Contextualism. Which is best?

7 How does the version of Contextualism described here compare to other versions in the literature?

Further reading

The classic source for knowledge-skepticism is Descartes (1641/1996). Dodd (2011) has a helpful discussion in the same spirit as my own.

Dretske (1981) gives a wonderfully readable argument for relevant alternatives, which is developed in Lewis's more rigorous but more difficult 1996. Schaffer (2005) offers a useful overview of the options for the relevant alternatives.

Good overviews of the issues in the final subsection can be found in Black (2014) and Rabinowitz (2014).

Notes

Chapter 1

1 It is arguable that credence 1 does not suffice for certainty. I might have credence 1 that the value of a random real number between 0 and 10 is not π, without being certain of it. We'll set aside this complication.

2 This only holds when $P(E) > 0$, as you can't divide by 0.

3 The *degree-of-belief-raising theory of confirmation* is usually called the *probability-raising theory of confirmation*. But "probability" can mean different things, so I will use the more specific expression here. See Chapter 11.

4 The first three are drawn from http://www.mathgoodies.com/lessons/vol6/conditional.html, the last three are drawn from www.math.uconn.edu/~feinberg/math1030f11/Bayes%20Solns.pdf. More can be found at both.

Chapter 2

1 It's called this due to its connection to the concept of closure in logic.

Chapter 3

1 http://www.youtube.com/watch?v=d8IBnfkPsM

2 See Cresswell (1975) for work on these complications.

3 This assumption is discussed in the appendix.

4 The proof is explained at Vineberg (2011).

5 See Lehman (1955) and Kemeny (1955).

6 See also Skyrms (1987) and Armendt (1993).

7 Thanks to Branden Fitelson for helping me figure out how to explain this section.

8 Adapted from Kahneman (2011, p. 313).

Chapter 4

1 And be careful not to confuse *prior* with *a priori*, which will be introduced in the next chapter; the earlier time (prior) need not be at the beginning of enquiry (*a priori*).

2 See Vineberg (2011) for various proofs.

3 See Skyrms (1993).

4 I will use the version described by Elga (2007).

Chapter 5

1 This isn't quite true. If the agent ought not to believe P1 (or P2) then they plausibly should not believe C. But we'll set aside this complication, which is about the *scope* of the requirement.

2 Technically, we need to add that P1 and P3 express everything relevant to C that the agent believes. This rules out a belief in P4: "Socrates is an atypical human with respect to mortality" which defeats the argument.

3 See White (2005).

4 See van Fraassen (2010).

Chapter 6

1 We only really need: The future will *probably* resemble the past. But I'll suppress this for simplicity.

2 To be precise, this is the bit of the Principle of Uniformity concerned with the future, but that's the bit we need to justify (we already know that in the past the "future" resembled the past).

3 It is controversial how much appearances need to *resemble* reality to generate true beliefs (Russell 1927). In Chapter 12, I will fudge this issue by talking about "accuracy."

4 These cross-cut Hume's famous distinction between demonstrative and nondemonstrative reasoning (the former demonstrate that the conclusion must be true, the latter only that the conclusion is probably true). There could be demonstrative *a posteriori* reasoning and nondemonstrative a priori reasoning, for example, Strawson's argument in 6.4. All the responses we'll consider offer nondemonstrative reasoning.

5 Black did not think it answered Hume's problem, but others do; see van Cleve (1984).

6 Technically, this is true only if we understand the conclusion to say that R will be successful in the future *and present*.

7 Indurkhya (1990).

8 To be clear, we would have justification to make some inductive inference or other, which would solve the problem of induction as broadly defined at the end of 6.1. But we would also like specific beliefs to be justified, for example, the belief that the next emerald is green. This specific belief fails to be justified.

9 See De Pierris, Graciela and Friedman, Michael, "Kant and Hume on Causality," *The Stanford Encyclopedia of Philosophy* (Winter 2013 Edition), Edward N. Zalta (ed.), http://plato.stanford.edu/archives/win2013/entries/kant-hume-causality/

10 BonJour (1998, chapter 7) offers a defence of a nonanalytic a priori principles of induction. But he seems to rely on a priori rationality constraints on conditional probabilities and it's not clear where these come from. Also, be warned that "intuition" is used in different ways by different philosophers, and is often used to refer to something less controversial than Kantian intuition.

Chapter 7

1 The word "probably" has been made explicit here. Chapter 6, note 1.

2 In fact, I give a simplified version of Goodman's example.

3 Projectibility is often applied to predicates rather than properties, but we will ignore this distinction.

4 This is related to the view that only *nautral kinds* are projectible. I will leave discussion of natural kinds to the next chapter (8.4).

5 We're using a slightly different definition of "grue" here, but you get the point (hopefully).

6 See Godfrey-Smith (2003).

7 This way of putting things is based on the standard similarity semantics for counterfactuals (Lewis 1973a). But I think we can get the same result with any theory of counterfactuals.

Chapter 8

1 Remember we are using "justifies" in the probability-raising sense. A more natural expression in English is "is some evidence for."

2 The following plausible statements are jointly incompatible with Substitution: (i) "Hesperus is Phosphorus" says the same thing as "Hesperus is Hesperus." (ii) The Babylonians made observations that justified "Hesperus is Phosphorus." (iii) The Babylonians did not make observations that justified "Hesperus is Hesperus."

3 Cohen (1987).

4 We're now expressing it as a rule rather than a principle, but as noted in 6.3, we're not going to fuss about this.

5 This is an instance of the old evidence problem of 11.3.

6 Compare Horwich (1982). We can also see this as an application of Popper's (11.1) insight that scientists should attempt to falsify hypotheses.

7 Humberstone (1994) made the connection to the ravens paradox.

8 Think of the "observed" cards as being all the cards on display. The issue is complicated when you get to choose what you observe, as in this case.

9 The black card cannot falsify the hypothesis, so doesn't need to be turned over if we are only looking for counter-examples. Whether turning the black card can justify the hypothesis depends on the background. If evens are monogamous and are found only with black or only with white, then finding an even with a black proves that all evens are black.

10 We assume that G is projectible. Natural kinds and projectibility are closely related—it is plausible they can be interdefined, and both face the same objections. I've talked about projectibility in the last chapter and natural kinds in this chapter to keep the discussion as clean as possible. But this was a somewhat arbitrary decision, and my treatment is based on my suspicion that there is no deep distinction. An FG is a GF; we observe two correlated properties, F and G, and the question is what to infer about their correlation among unobserved objects.

11 Compare Good (1967).

12 Swinburne (1971). I also like the following example, although it doesn't involve natural kinds: Three people leave a party, each with a hat. Hypothesis: None of the three leaves with his own hat. Instances: Person 1 is observed leaving with person 2's hat, and person 2 is observed leaving with person 1's hat. Additional details: Assuming there are no other hats at the party, and that person 3 leaves with a hat, he must leave with his own hat, refuting the hypothesis.

13 The Bayesian literature talks about confirmation rather than justification, but little turns on this so I've continued the thread of the previous chapters. The problems of grue and the ravens are problems for both objectivists and subjectivists, as they result from Principles of Uniformity that look compelling. We can focus on the probabilities without worrying about their interpretation.

14 Hosiasson-Lindenbaum (1940, p. 140). I use the phrase "relatively small" because I will focus on the comparative claim "E1 justifies H more than E2 does." It's not hard to extend the argument to the qualitative claim "E justifies H to a tiny degree." See Fitelson (2006).

15 Notice we are directly evaluating the *Conclusion*: Therefore, that an observed white thing is a sneaker justifies that all observed ravens are black. It makes things simpler at this point to take for granted *Equivalence*, thus moving straight though *Instance* to the *Conclusion*. We also won't worry about using "there are no observed white ravens" rather than "all observed ravens are black."

16 Fitelson (2006). This is called the I-measure, which has the advantage that priors are not needed.

Chapter 9

1 Actually this isn't quite what the Principal Principle, as named by David Lewis, says. Lewis restricted the Principal Principle to initial credence functions, but we'll ignore this for simplicity.

2 The most contentious of these is that they can be discovered. Argument for: Chances are used by scientists who take chances to be discoverable. So nondiscoverable chances would be at best a revisionary theory of chance.

3 Howson and Urbach (1996, p. 345) seem to make implicit use of such a principle.

4 Strevens objects that the required Principle of Indifference is just a special case of Principal Principle. "[T]he principle [of indifference] really says: assign equal [credences] to outcomes that are produced with the same objective probability. This, of course, is just a special case of [Principal Principle]" (1999, p. 26). But our principle of indifference above only requires that we have no reason to assign different credences to the outcomes; it doesn't require that the outcomes are produced with the same objective probability. And even Streven's principle is weaker than Principal Principle, rather than stronger as a special case would be; Streven's principle only says that the possibilities should have the same credence, not that that credence should match the chance.

5 What if the chance of Heads were 60 percent? Then there would have to be at least five flips, for example, TTHHH, and each of the 32 permutations would get equal credence.

6 Based on Elbert Hubbard's definition of history.

7 Humphreys (1985).

8 See Lyon (2014).

9 I am interpreting Hall uncharitably for pedagogical purposes. It is clear from his later discussion that he means to endorse the Principal Principle as a primitive constraint on rationality. But the appeal to conceptual and analytic truths of the quoted passage makes this look more palatable than it is. Nevertheless, I recommend Hall's (challenging) paper as one of the most enlightening on the topic.

10 These issues are most familiar to contemporary philosophy from John Mackie's (1977) error theory of ethics. Mackie held that it followed from the concept of "good" that if there is a property of goodness, it is able to motivate all agents, irrespective of their desires. Mackie thought there was no such property, and therefore held an error theory of goodness. Hall argues that it follows from the concept of "chance" that if there are chances they constrain beliefs. My point is that this makes an error theory of chance very plausible.

Chapter 10

1 See Weisberg (2007) and Briggs (2009).

2 See Christensen (2007, p. 193).

3 See Kelly (2010). Does an analogous argument apply to Bob? Should he end up back at 0.2? Perhaps not. Plausibly, Bob should not end up back at 0.2 because he should not have been at 0.2 in the first place. This is why it matters who was initially reasoning correctly. Thus, Kelly defends the "right reasons view" rather than the "stick-to-your-guns view."

4 See Christensen (2011). See Pollock (1986, pp. 38–9) for more on undercutting evidence.

Chapter 11

1 I've earlier used "confirmation" for the relation between subjective probabilities and "justification" for the relation between inductive probabilities. Technically we should use a third term for when we are neutral about the type of probability. But that would be overkill, so I follow the literature by using "confirmation" here as well. In this chapter, we will suppress reference to background beliefs.

2 Popper combined this normative claim with the descriptive claim that this is what scientists actually do. See 6.5.2.

3 Ayer (1936) and Hempel and Oppenheim (1948).

4 Technically, we also need to assume that –H doesn't also entail E, that is, if E is entailed by everything then H does not confirm E.

5 The counterfactual response is often put in terms of the agent having different background *knowledge*. But talk of background knowledge is usually a casual way of talking about background beliefs. We won't get to knowledge until Chapter 13.

6 Arguably some features of the old evidence problem are also problems for inductivists. For example, when we imagine not believing that the die showed Even, do we also imagine not believing the die is unbiased? No. Do we also imagine not believing it showed less than three? Yes. Why the difference? The inductivist has to explain exactly which beliefs are imagined away and which remain.

7 See van Fraassen (1988).

8 Notation altered; notice Maher uses the natural locution of "knows," but what matters to the example are Schreiber's beliefs.

Chapter 12

1 We'll actually focus on the belief from the earlier step: the table is red. The problems this belief faces are also faced by the belief that it looks red, but the latter belief is more confusing.

2 The presence of "it" might be problematic, as we perhaps shouldn't presuppose that there is any object to be the referent of "it." This problem can be avoided by using the basic belief "I am being appeared to redly," so feel free to substitute this in.

3 See Smithies (2012).

4 See Sellars (1956), BonJour (1978), and Klein (2007).

5 Typically, probabilities are only assigned to propositions; but experiences (e.g. Looks-red) are not propositions. Nevertheless, there are possibilities with a red experience and possibilities without, and I suggest that probabilities can be assigned to these possibilities.

6 Technically this should be "Inductive-probability-raising theory of justification" as we are assuming inductive probabilities solve the problem of induction and finding that the epistemic regress remains.

7 See Huemer (2000) and Pryor (2000) for recent explicit defenses.

8 White (2005).

9 Someone might object that conditionalization only applies to beliefs, not experiences. But the justifications for conditionalization seem to apply just as well to experiences.

10 So named by Vogel (2000). Such worries have a long and distinguished history (see van Cleve 1979; Alston 1986).

11 This also violates the Principle of Reflection (Chapter 10), but I think the craziness here is much worse than a mere counterexample to Reflection.

12 The analogy is from Wittgenstein (1969, §141), though not in aid of the same idea.

13 I will omit qualifications Bonjour makes that we won't be concerned with.

14 See Huemer (1997) and Olsson (2005, chapter 2). I'm picking out one strand of a literature summarized by Olsson (2014).

15 Fumerton (2010) suggests a regress of this form. A similar problem, though perhaps not the same one, can be found in Lewis Carroll's classic (1895).

16 Why inductive? Because coherentists don't say that anything goes. They say there is objective justification of coherent beliefs. Subjectivists won't criticize someone for taking experiences to confirm beliefs, so won't criticize foundationalists. And coherentists do criticize foundationalists. Yet inductive probabilities would not obviate the need for coherentism, as inductivist coherentists may deny that there are inductive relations between propositions and *experiences*.

Chapter 13

1 Zhuangzi, translated by Giles (1901, p. 63).

2 In the background here are Paul Grice's (1967, 1981) ideas about the rules of conversation which determine what is acceptable, for example, be informative, be relevant. Assertible sentences follow these rules. Note some sentences can be true but unassertible. For example, if I know Bob is at the pub then saying "Bob is either at the pub or the library" is unassertible because it is insufficiently informative.

3 See Dretske (1981).

4 See Sosa (1999), Williamson (2000), and Pritchard (2009).

5 See Hawthorne (2004) and Stanley (2005).

6 A different version of Contextualism says that what shifts in different contexts is the degree of justification needed (see Schaffer 2005 for discussion). A cousin sometimes called "Contextualism" says that "knows" always means the same thing, but requires a further parameter to determine which proposition is expressed (Schaffer 2004a, b). A more distant cousin sometimes called "Contextualism" says that a sentence always expresses the same proposition, but the truth-value of the proposition depends on a further parameter (MacFarlane 2009). So be warned: "Contextualism" is used in different ways by different philosophers.

7 Notice the actual world isn't shown in this diagram. For what's relevant for the contextualist is independent of the actual world. This means that the contextualist will need to add an extra clause about truth to their analysis of knowledge, whereas Safety and Subject-Sensitivity theorists have the option of using their theory of relevance to obtain the truth condition on knowledge.

8 These are Lewis's Rules of Resemblance (combined with the Rule of Actuality), Rule of Belief and Rule of Attention respectively. I don't want to imply that Lewis's theory takes the best bits of the other theories. Lewis's theory is important because it was the first to give a detailed account of what makes an alternative relevant.

References

Alston, W. (1986) "Epistemic Circularity," *Philosophy and Phenomenological Research*, 47(1), 1–30.

Armendt, B. (1993) "Dutch Books, Additivity and Utility Theory," *Philosophical Topics*, 21(1), 1–20.

Arntzenius, F. (2003) "Some Problems for Conditionalization and Reflection," *The Journal of Philosophy*, 100(7), 356–70.

Ayer, A. J. (1936) *Language, Truth and Logic*. London: Victor Gollancz.

Bentham, J. (1789/1961) "An Introduction to the Principles of Morals and Legislation," in *Utilitarianism*. Garden City, NY: Doubleday, pp. 7–398.

Black, M. (1954) *Problems of Analysis*. Ithaca, NY: Cornell University Press.

Black, T. (2014) "Contextualism in Epistemology," *The Internet Encyclopedia of Philosophy*, ISSN 2161–0002, http://www.iep.utm.edu/contextu/

BonJour, L. (1978) "Can Empirical Knowledge have a Foundation?" *American Philosophical Quarterly*, 15, 1–13.

— (1985) *The Structure of Empirical Knowledge*. Cambridge, MA: Harvard University Press, pp. 38–52.

— (1998) *In Defense of Pure Reason: A Rationalist Account of a priori Justification*. Cambridge: Cambridge University Press.

— (1999) "The Dialectic of Foundationalism and Coherentism," in J. Greco and E. Sosa (eds), *The Blackwell Guide to Epistemology*. Malden, MA: Blackwell, pp. 117–44.

Bradley, D. J. (2011) "Self-Location is no Problem for Conditionalization," *Synthese*, 182(3), 393–411.

Briggs, R. (2009) "Distorted Reflection," *Philosophical Review*, 118(1), 59–85.

Carnap, R. (1945) "The Two Concepts of Probability," *Philosophy and Phenomenological Research*, 5, 513–32.

— (1950) *Logical Foundations of Probability* (Second Edition 1962). Chicago: University of Chicago Press.

— (1971) "A Basic System of Inductive Logic Part 1," in R. Carnap and R. C. Jeffrey (eds), *Studies in Inductive Logic and Probability*, Vol. I. Berkeley and Los Angeles: University of California Press, pp. 33–165.

— (1980) "A Basic System of Inductive Logic," in R. C. Jeffrey (ed.), *Studies in Inductive Logic and Probability*, Vol. II. Berkeley and Los Angeles: University of California Press, pp. 7–155.

Carroll, L. (1895) "What the Tortoise Said to Achilles," *Mind*, n.s., 4, 278–80.

Chalmers, D. J. (2012) *Constructing the World*. Oxford: Oxford University Press.

Christensen, D. (1991) "Clever Bookies and Coherent Beliefs," *The Philosophical Review*, 100(2), 229–47.

— (2001) "Preference-Based Arguments for Probabilism," *Philosophy of Science*, 68(3), 356–76.

— (2004) *Putting Logic in its Place: Formal Constraints on Rational Belief.*
    New York: Oxford University Press, pp. xii–187.
— (2007) "Epistemology of Disagreement: The Good News," *Philosophical Review*, 116(2), 187–217.
— (2011) "Disagreement, Question-Begging, and Epistemic Self-Criticism," *Philosophers' Imprint*, 11(6), 1–22.
Cohen, Y. (1987) "Ravens and Relevance," *Erkenntnis*, 26(2), 153–79.
Cresswell, M. J. (1975) "Hyperintensional Logic," *Studia Logica*, 34(1), 25–38.
Davidson, D. (1986) "A Coherence Theory of Truth and Knowledge," in E.
    LePore (ed.), *Truth and Interpretation: Perspectives on the Philosophy of Donald Davidson.* Oxford: Blackwell, pp. 307–19.
de Finetti, B. (1937) "La Prévision: Ses Lois Logiques, Ses Sources
    Subjectives," *Annales de l'Institut Henri Poincaré*, 7, 1–68; translated as "Foresight. Its Logical Laws, Its Subjective Sources," in H. E. Kyburg, Jr. and H. E. Smokler (eds.), *Studies in Subjective Probability.* Robert E. Krieger Publishing Company, 1980.
De Pierris, G. and Friedman, M. (2013) "Kant and Hume on Causality," in E. N.
    Zalta (ed.), *The Stanford Encyclopedia of Philosophy* (Winter 2013 Edition), http://plato.stanford.edu/archives/win2013/entries/kant-hume-causality/
Descartes, R. (1641/1996) *Meditations on First Philosophy*, translated by John
    Cottingham. Cambridge: Cambridge University Press.
Dodd, D. (2011) "Against Fallibilism," *Australasian Journal of Philosophy*, 89(4),
    665–85.
Dretske, F. (1981) "The Pragmatic Dimension of Knowledge," *Philosophical Studies*, 40(3), 363–78.
Dummett, M. (1981) *Frege: Philosophy of Language* (Second Edition).
    Cambridge, MA: Harvard University Press.
Eagle, A. (2014) "Chance versus Randomness," in E. N. Zalta (ed.), *The Stanford
    Encyclopedia of Philosophy* (Spring 2014 Edition), http://plato.stanford.edu/archives/spr2014/entries/chance-randomness/
Earman, J. (1992) *Bayes or Bust: A Critical Examination of Bayesian Confirmation
    Theory.* Cambridge, MA: MIT Press.
Elga, A. (2000) "Self-Locating Belief and the Sleeping Beauty Problem,"
    Analysis, 60(266), 143–7.
— (2007) "Reflection and Disagreement," *Noûs*, 41(3), 478–502.
— (2010a) "Subjective Probabilities should be Sharp," *Philosophers' Imprint*,
    10(5), 1–11.
— (2010b) "How to Disagree about How to Disagree," in Feldman and Warfield
    (eds), *Disagreement.* Oxford: Oxford University Press, pp. 175–86.
Feldman, R. and Warfield, T. (eds) (2010) *Disagreement.* New York: Oxford
    University Press.
Fitelson, B. (2006) "Logical Foundations of Evidential Support," *Philosophy of
    Science*, 73(5), 500–12.
Fitelson, B. and Easwaran, K. (2015) "Accuracy, Coherence and Evidence," in
    T. Szabó Gendler and J. Hawthorne (eds), *Oxford Studies in Epistemology*,
    Vol. 5. Oxford University Press.
Foley, R. (2009) "Beliefs, Degrees of Belief, and the Lockean Thesis," in
    F. Huber and C. Schmidt-Petri (eds), *Degrees of Belief.* Synthese Library 342,
    Springer Science + Business Media B.V, pp. 37–47.
Fumerton, R. (2010) "Foundationalist Theories of Epistemic Justification,"
    in E. N. Zalta (ed.), *The Stanford Encyclopedia of Philosophy* (Summer

2010 Edition), http://plato.stanford.edu/archives/sum2010/entries/justep-foundational/

Garber, D. (1983) "Old Evidence and Logical Omniscience in Bayesian Confirmation Theory," in J. Earman (ed.), *Testing Scientific Theories*, *Midwest Studies in the Philosophy of Science*, Vol. X. Minneapolis, MN: University of Minnesota Press, pp. 99–131.

Giles, H. A. (1901) *A History of Chinese Literature*. New York: D. Appleton.

Gillies, D. (2000) "Varieties of Propensity," *British Journal for the Philosophy of Science*, 51(4), 807–35.

Glymour, C. (1980) *Theory and Evidence*. Princeton, NJ: Princeton University Press.

Godfrey-Smith, P. (2003) "Goodman's Problem and Scientific Methodology," *The Journal of Philosophy*, 100(11), 573–90.

— (2011) "Induction, Samples, and Kinds," in J. Campbell, M. O'Rourke, and M. Slater (eds), *Carving Nature at Its Joints: Topics in Contemporary Philosophy*. Cambridge, MA: MIT Press, pp. 33–52.

Good, I. J. (1967) "The White Shoe is a Red Herring," *British Journal for the Philosophy of Science*, 17, 322.

Goodman, N. (1955) *Fact, Fiction, and Forecast* (Third Edition 1973). Indianapolis, IN: Bobbs-Merrill.

Greaves, H. and Wallace, D. (2006) "Justifying Conditionalization: Conditionalization Maximizes Expected Epistemic Utility," *Mind*, 115(459), 607–32.

Grice, H. P. (1967) *Logic and Conversation*. William James Lectures, Cambridge, MA: Harvard University.

— (1981) "Presupposition and Conversational Implicature," in P. Cole (ed.), *Radical Pragmatics*. New York: Academic Press, pp. 183–98.

Haack, S. (1976) "The Justification of Deduction," *Mind*, 85(337), 112–9.

Hall, N. (2004) "Two Mistakes About Credence and Chance," in F. Jackson and G. Priest (eds) *Lewisian Themes*. Oxford: Oxford University Press, pp. 94–112.

Hájek, A. (2003) "What Conditional Probability Could Not Be," *Synthese*, 137(3), 273–323.

— (2008a) "Arguments For-or Against-Probabilism?" *British Journal for the Philosophy of Science*, 59, 793–819.

— (2008b) "Dutch Book Arguments," in P. Anand, P. Pattanaik, and C. Puppe (eds), *The Oxford Handbook of Rational and Social Choice*. Oxford: Oxford University Press, pp. 173–95.

— (2009) "Fifteen Arguments against Hypothetical Frequentism," *Erkenntnis*, 70(2), 211–35.

Hájek, A. and Joyce, J. (2008) "Confirmation," in S. Psillos and M. Curd (eds), *The Routledge Companion to the Philosophy of Science*. New York: Routledge, Taylor & Francis Group, pp. 115–29.

Harman, G. (2008) *Change in View: Principles of Reasoning*. Cambridge, MA: Cambridge University Press.

Hawthorne, J. (2004) *Knowledge and Lotteries*. Oxford: Oxford University Press.

— (2005) "Degree-of-Belief and Degree-of-Support: Why Bayesians Need Both Notions," *Mind*, 114(454), 277–320.

Hempel, C. G. (1945a) "Studies in the Logic of Confirmation (I)," *Mind*, 54, 1–26.

— (1945b) "Studies in the Logic of Confirmation (II)," *Mind*, 54, 97–121.

Hempel, C. G. and Oppenheim, P. (1948) "Studies in the Logic of Explanation," *Philosophy of Science*, 15, 135–75.

Hoefer, C. (2007) "The Third Way on Objective Probability: A Sceptic's Guide to Objective Chance," *Mind*, 116, 549–96.

Horwich, P. (1982) *Probability and Evidence*. Cambridge, MA: Cambridge University Press.

Hosiasson-Lindenbaum, J. (1940) "On Confirmation," *The Journal of Symbolic Logic*, 5(4), 133–48.

Howson, C. (1991) "The 'Old Evidence' Problem," *British Journal for the Philosophy of Science*, 42(4), 547–55.

Howson, C. and Urbach, P. (1996) *Scientific Reasoning: The Bayesian Approach* (Second Edition). Chicago: Open Court Publishing.

Huber, F. (2014) "Confirmation and Induction" | *Internet Encyclopedia of Philosophy*, http://www.iep.utm.edu/conf-ind/

Huemer, M. (1997) "Probability and Coherence Justification," *Southern Journal of Philosophy*, 35, 463–72.

— (2000) "Direct Realism and the Brain-in-a-Vat Argument," *Philosophy and Phenomenological Research*, 61(2), 397–413.

Hume, D. (1739/1987) *A Treatise of Human Nature*. London: Penguin Books.

Humphreys, P. (1985) "Why Propensities Cannot be Probabilities," *Philosophical Review*, 94, 557–70.

Humberstone, I. L. (1994) "Hempel Meets Wason," *Erkenntnis*, 41(3), 391–402.

Indurkhya, B. (1990) "Some Remarks on the Rationality of Induction," *Synthese*, 85(1), 95–114.

Jackson, F. (1975) "Grue," *Journal of Philosophy*, 72(5), 113–31.

Jaynes, E. T. (1968) "Prior Probabilities," *Systems Science and Cybernetics, IEEE Transactions on*, 4(3), 227–41.

Jeffrey, R. C. (1970) "Dracula Meets Wolfman: Acceptance vs. Partial Belief," in M. Swain (ed.), *Induction, Acceptance and Rational Belief*. Netherlands: Springer, pp. 157–85.

— (1983) *The Logic of Decision*. Chicago, IL: Chicago University Press.

Joyce, J. (1998) "A Non-Pragmatic Vindication of Probabilism," *Philosophy of Science*, 65, 575–603.

— (2009) "Accuracy and Coherence: Prospects for an Alethic Epistemology of Partial Belief," in F. Huber and C. Schmidt-Petri (eds), *Degrees of Belief*. Synthese Library 342, Springer Science + Business Media B.V, pp. 263–97.

— (ms) "Why Evidentialists Need Not Worry About the Accuracy Argument for Probabilism."

Kahneman, D. (2011) *Thinking Fast and Slow*. London, UK: Penguin Books.

Kant, I. (1786/2004) *Metaphysical Foundations of Natural Science*, translated and edited by M. Friedman. Cambridge, MA: Cambridge University Press.

Kelly, T. (2005) "The Epistemic Significance of Disagreement," *Oxford Studies in Epistemology*, I, 167–96.

— (2010) "Peer Disagreement and Higher-Order Evidence," in R. Feldman and T. Warfield (eds), *Disagreement*. Oxford: Oxford University Press, pp. 111–74.

Kemeny, J. (1955) "Fair Bets and Inductive Probabilities," *Journal of Symbolic Logic*, 20(3), 263–73.

Keynes, J. M. (1921) *A Treatise on Probability*. Courier Dover Publications, http://www.gutenberg.org/files/32625/32625-pdf.pdf

— (1937) "The General Theory of Employment," *The Quarterly Journal of Economics*, 51(2), 209–23.

Klein, P. (1999) "Human Knowledge and the Infinite Regress of Reasons," in J. Tomberlin (ed.), *Philosophical Perspectives*, 13, 297–325.

— (2007) "Human Knowledge and the Infinite Progress of Reasoning," *Philosophical Studies*, 134(1), 1–17.

Klein, P. and Turri, J. (2014) "Infinitism in Epistemology," *The Internet Encyclopedia of Philosophy*, http://www.iep.utm.edu/inf-epis/

Kyburg, H. E. (1961) *Probability and the Logic of Rational Belief.* Middletown, CT: Wesleyan University Press.

Lackey, J. and Christensen, D. (eds) (2013) *The Epistemology of Disagreement: New Essays.* Oxford: Oxford University Press.

Lange, M. (2011) "Hume and the Problem of Induction," in D. M. Gabbay, S. Hartmann, and J. Woods (eds), *Handbook of the History of Logic: Inductive Logic*, Vol. 10. Oxford: Elsevier, pp. 43–91.

Lehman, R. (1955) "On Confirmation and Rational Betting," *Journal of Symbolic Logic*, 20, 251–62.

Lewis, D. (1973a) *Counterfactuals.* Oxford: Blackwell.

— (1980) "A Subjectivist's Guide to Objective Chance," in his *Philosophical Papers*, Vol. 2. Oxford: Oxford University Press (1986), pp. 83–132.

— (1996) "Elusive Knowledge," *The Australasian Journal of Philosophy*, 74, 549–67.

— (2001) "Sleeping Beauty: Reply to Elga," *Analysis*, 61(271), 171–6.

— (1994) "Humean Supervenience Debugged," *Mind*, 412, 471–90.

Lyon, A. (2014) "From Kolmogorov, to Popper, to Renyi: There's No Escaping Humphreys' Paradox (When Generalised)," in A. Wilson (ed.), *Chance and Temporal Asymmetry.* Oxford: Oxford University Press.

MacFarlane (2009) "Nonindexical Contextualism," *Synthese*, 166, 231–50.

Mackie, J. L. (1977) *Ethics: Inventing Right and Wrong.* Harmondsworth: Penguin.

Maher, P. (1992) "Diachronic Rationality," *Philosophy of Science*, 59, 120–41.

— (1996) "Subjective and Objective Confirmation," *Philosophy of Science*, 63(2), 149–74.

— (2006) "The Concept of Inductive Probability," *Erkenntnis*, 65(2), 185–206.

Moretti, L. (forthcoming) "Recent Work on Phenomenal Conservatism," *Analysis*.

Murphy, P. (2014) "Coherentism in Epistemology," *The Internet Encyclopedia of Philosophy*, http://www.iep.utm.edu/coherent/

Olsson, E. (2005) *Against Coherence: Truth, Probability, and Justification.* Oxford: Oxford University Press.

— (2014) "Coherentist Theories of Epistemic Justification," in E. N. Zalta (ed.), *The Stanford Encyclopedia of Philosophy* (Spring 2014 Edition), http://plato. stanford.edu/archives/spr2014/entries/justep-coherence/

Pierce, C. S. (1910) "Notes on the Doctrine of Chance," re-printed in "Essays in the Philosophy of Science," The American Heritage Series, Indianapolis, IN and New York: Boobs-Merrill (1957), pp. 74–84.

Pollock, J. (1986) *Contemporary Theories of Knowledge.* Savage, MD: Rowman & Littlefield.

— (1995) *Cognitive Carpentry: A Blueprint for How to Build a Person.* Cambridge, MA: MIT Press.

Popper, K. R. (1959a) "The Propensity Interpretation of Probability," *British Journal for the Philosophy of Science*, 10(37), 25–42.

— (1959b) *The Logic of Scientific Discovery*. London: Hutchinson.

Pritchard, D. (2009) "Safety-Based Epistemology: Whither Now?" *Journal of Philosophical Research*, 34, 33–45.

Pryor, J. (2000) "The Skeptic and the Dogmatist," *Nous*, 34(4), 517–49.

Quine, W. V. (1969) "Natural Kinds," in *Ontological Relativity and Other Essays*. New York: Columbia University Press, p. 114.

Rabinowitz, D. (2014) "The Safety Condition for Knowledge," *The Internet Encyclopedia of Philosophy*, ISSN 2161–0002, http://www.iep.utm.edu/safety-c/

Ramsey, F. P. (1926) "Truth and Probability," in R. B. Braithwaite (ed.), *The Foundations of Mathematics and Other Logical Essays*. London: Routledge (1931), pp. 156–98.

Reichenbach, H. (1949) *The Theory of Probability*. Berkeley, CA: University of California Press.

Resnik, M. D. (1987) *Choices: An Introduction to Decision Theory*. Minneapolis, MN: University of Minnesota Press.

Russell, B. (1927) *The Analysis of Matter*. London: Routledge Kegan Paul.

— (1946) *A History of Western Philosophy*. London: George Allen & Unwin.

— (1997) *The Problems of Philosophy*. Oxford: Oxford University Press.

Salmon, W. C. (1979) *The Foundations of Scientific Inference*, Vol. 28. Pittsburgh, PA: University of Pittsburgh Press, http://www.csulb.edu/~cwallis/100/articles/salmon.html

Schaffer, J. (2004a) "Skepticism, Contextualism, and Discrimination," *Philosophy and Phenomenological Research*, 69(1), 138–55.

— (2004b) "From Contextualism to Contrastivism," *Philosophical Studies*, 119(1), 73–103.

— (2005) "What Shifts? Thresholds, Standards, or Alternatives?" in G. Preyer and G. Peter (eds), *Contextualism in Philosophy*. Oxford: Oxford University Press, pp. 115–30.

Schupbach, J. N. (2011) "New Hope for Shogenji's Coherence Measure," *British Journal for the Philosophy Science*, 62, 125–42.

Sellars, W. (1956) "Empiricism and the Philosophy of Mind," *Minnesota Studies in the Philosophy of Science*, 1, 253–329.

Shogenji, T. (1999) "Is Coherence Truth Conducive?" *Analysis*, 59(264), 338–45.

Skyrms, B. (1975) *Choice and Chance: An Introduction to Inductive Logic*. Belmont, CA: Dickinson Publishing Company.

— (1984) *Pragmatics and Empiricism*. Yale University.

— (1987) "Dynamic Coherence and Probability Kinematics," *Philosophy of Science*, 54(1), 1–20.

— (1993) "A Mistake in Dynamic Coherence Arguments?" *Philosophy of Science*, 60(2), 320–8.

Smithies, D. (2012) "A Simple Theory of Introspection," in D. Smithies and D. Stoljar (eds), *Introspection and Consciousness*. Oxford: Oxford University Press, pp. 3–26.

— (2014) "Can Foundationalism Solve the Regress Problem?" in R. Neta (ed.), *Current Controversies in Epistemology*. New York: Routledge, pp. 73–94.

Sosa, E. (1999) "How to Defeat Opposition to Moore," *Noûs*, 33(s13), 141–53.

Stalker, D. F. (1994) *Grue!: The New Riddle of Induction*. Chicago: Open Court Publishing Company.

Stanley, J. (2005) *Knowledge and Practical Interests*. Oxford: Oxford University Press.

Steinberger, F. (ms) "Explosion and the Normativity of Logic."

Stove, D. C. (1986) *The Rationality of Induction*. Oxford: Clarendon Press.

Strawson, P. F. (1952) *Introduction to Logical Theory*. London: Methuen (1952).

Strevens, M. (1999) "Objective Probability as a Guide to the World," *Philosophical Studies*, 95, 243–75.

— (ms) *Notes on Bayesian Confirmation Theory*, http://www.nyu.edu/classes/strevens/BCT/BCT.pdf

Swinburne, R. (1971) "The Paradoxes of Confirmation—A Survey," *American Philosophical Quarterly*, 8, 318–30.

Talbott, W. (1991) "Two Principles of Bayesian Epistemology," *Philosophical Studies*, 62, 135–50.

Teller, P. (1973) "Conditionalization and Observation," *Synthese*, 26(2), 218–58.

Titelbaum, M. (forthcoming) "Self-Locating Credences," in A. Hájek and C. R. Hitchcock (eds), *The Oxford Handbook of Probability and Philosophy*. Oxford: Oxford University Press.

Tversky, A. and Kahneman, D. (1983) "Extensional versus Intuitive Reasoning: The Conjunction Fallacy in Probability Judgment," *Psychological Review*, 90(4), 293.

Unger, P. (1971) "A Defense of Skepticism," *Philosophical Review*, 80(2), 198–219.

— (1975) *Ignorance: The Case for Scepticism*. Oxford: Oxford University Press.

van Cleve, J. (1979) "Foundationalism, Epistemic Principles, and the Cartesian Circle," *Philosophical Review*, 88, 55–91.

— (1984) "Reliability, Justification, and the Problem of Induction," *Midwest Studies in Philosophy*, 9(1), 555–67.

van Fraassen, B. C. (1980) *The Scientific Image*. Oxford: Oxford University Press.

— (1984) "Belief and the Will," *Journal of Philosophy*, 81(5), 235–56.

— (1988) "The Problem of Old Evidence," in David F. Austin (ed.), *Philosophical Analysis*. Netherlands: Springer, pp. 153–65.

— (2010) "Indifference: The Symmetries of Probability," in A. Eagle (ed.), *Philosophy of Probability: Contemporary Readings*. Chicago: Routledge, pp. 296–316.

Vickers, J. "The Problem of Induction," in E. N. Zalta (ed.), *The Stanford Encyclopedia of Philosophy* (Fall 2014 Edition), http://plato.stanford.edu/archives/fall2014/entries/induction-problem/

Vineberg, S. (2011) "Dutch Book Arguments," in E. N. Zalta (ed.), *The Stanford Encyclopedia of Philosophy* (Summer 2011 Edition), http://plato.stanford.edu/archives/sum2011/entries/dutch-book/

Vogel, J. (2000) "Reliabilism Levelled," *The Journal of Philosophy*, 97(11), 602–23.

Von Neumann, J. and Morgenstern, O. (1944) *The Theory of Games and Economic Behavior*. Princeton, NJ: Princeton University Press.

Weisberg, J. (2007) "Conditionalization, Reflection, and Self-Knowledge," *Philosophical Studies*, 135, 179–97.

White, R. (2005) "Epistemic Permissiveness," *Philosophical Perspectives*, 19, 445–59.

— (2006) "Problems for Dogmatism," *Philosophical Studies*, 131, 525–57.

Williamson, T. (2000) *Knowledge and Its Limits*. Oxford: Oxford University Press.

Wittgenstein, L. (1969) *On Certainty*, D. Paul and G. E. M. Anscombe (trans), G. E. M. Anscombe and G. H. von Wright (eds). Oxford: Basil Blackwell.

Index

Made in the USA
Lexington, KY
10 September 2018